DESPERATELY SEEKING
MADONNA

In Search of the Meaning
of the World's Most
Famous Woman

DESPERATELY SEEKING MADONNA

Edited By **Adam Sexton**

Delta

Pepsi Commercial

(good) rep of music reviews lacking in our book Kaplan + diegetic worst ex of academic reading no credit to loos or even M Monroe

some dreadful reviews (NY Times) NYorker cartoons Top Ten list he see the point but give book desperate, depressing feel of manic compilation — DAVE MARSH —

hateful content of 9 groups / singers to trace detriment

better at femg t by Ty Milman

Fiske — good fan work but bad new crit analysis etc fk u ✓

Baker on Updike: Why? *Haw on Pop : why? icus*

Canby: review Who's That Girl? yawn *Bernhardt ?*

A Delta Book
Published by
Dell Publishing
a division of
Bantam Doubleday Dell Publishing Group, Inc.
666 Fifth Avenue
New York, New York 10103

Library of Congress Cataloging-in-Publication Data

Desperately seeking Madonna : in search of the meaning of the world's
    most famous woman / edited by Adam Sexton.
        p.   cm.
    ISBN 0-385-30688-1
    1. Madonna, 1958–   . I. Sexton, Adam.
ML420.M1387D47   1993
782.42166'092—dc20   92-394
                                                          CIP
                                                          MN

Manufactured in the United States of America
Published simultaneously in Canada
Book design by Nancy Field

January 1993

10 9 8 7 6 5 4 3 2 1
RRH

Liz Smith
On Madonna Books (from *Newsday*, July 1, 1991 and October 11, 1991).
Used by permission of the author.

"Madonna Tongue n' Chic' " Sandwich
(from the Stage Deli).

Elizabeth Tippens
"Madonna and Me" (1992).
Used by permission of the author.

Madonna postage stamps from the island of St. Vincent (1991).

"Madonna Interview" (from *Nightline*, December 3, 1991). Used by Permission of *ABC News*.

To Paul Chrystie,
True Blue Madonna fan
—and the friend

This is a great and beautiful artist. She is superb.
—Jacques Chirac,
former Prime Minister of France

She gives us ideas. It's really women's lib, not being afraid of what guys think.
—seventeen-year-old fan

WHAT A TRAMP!
—*New York Post* headline

"I *like* your hair the new way."
—John Updike
"The Alligators"

Contents

Acknowledgments

Thanks first of all to Dave Marsh; to Sandra Choron, Dave's agent and now mine, too; and to Betsy Bundschuh and Dan Levy at Dell.

Thanks also to the creators of the works that follow, especially those who provided previously unpublished material for use here.

Thanks to those who opened their Madonna files to me or tipped me off regarding obscure material, most of which ended up included within: Gina Arnold, Manuel Barrientos, Robert Christgau, Paul Chrystie, Claire Connors at *Seventeen*, Denis Ferrara in Liz Smith's office, *Late Night*'s Barbara Gaines, E. Ann Kaplan of SUNY Stony Brook, Lisa Jones, Jenny Kalina, Brian Lipman, Greil Marcus, Jennifer Martinez, Genevieve Nelson at *Sassy*, Anne O'Sullivan, Maureen Ryan, Jeff Salamon, Reed Sparling at the *Star*, Sam Turner, and Sarah Williams.

Thanks to the New York Public Library and to the libraries at Columbia University, Yale University, and the State University of New York at Binghamton.

Thanks especially to the following for Madonna talk, which influenced the thoughts expressed in my Introduction: bell hooks of Oberlin, Harvard's Lynne Layton, Aari Ludvigsen, Merrill Markoe, Patrick O'Sullivan, Elizabeth Tippens, Mim Udovitch, Nancy Vickers at Penn and USC, and Tom Ward.

Thanks to Jean Heinemann for teaching me the lyrics to "Vogue."

And thank you for general support and interest while I was assembling this book: Janet Capron, Suzanne Osmun, Marguerite Rigoglioso, James Sexton, Mark McCarthy Sexton, and Sarah Wolf.

Most of all, thanks to my parents, for never preaching.

DESPERATELY SEEKING
MADONNA

prolix intro i odd confessions + dubious (confession) sec: in 8: I'm not a M. fan

Introduction: Justifying My Love

attempts to summarise multi facet Maddie corporate, artist performer actor radical pepsi politico sponsor author autobiographer

by Adam Sexton

by presenting carefully collected scores of her — penses overview of phases of career

What is there to say about Madonna that her clothes, accessories, hairstyle, and historical references don't already explain?

—J. Hoberman

Essence of book in R Stone lists — she is worst and best dressed — she is a contradiction! YAWN

▶ 1. Express Yourself

In the winter of 1987 I wrote my last published piece of rock and roll criticism, a Jonathan Richman review for a weekly newspaper located in Texas. When friends asked me how I could willingly forsake the free albums, the promo goodies, the press box perspectives and plus-ones that went with the gig, I told them it was simple: I'd run out of adjectives.

That wasn't much of an exaggeration. I was plain tired of having an opinion on everything, especially the vast, decidedly second-rate bulk of mid-eighties major-label record releases (remember records?)—on which, frankly, I had no real opinion at all. Worse, the process of fabricating passion in situations where none existed had made me cynical about popular music in general, the very pop that once had sent me into raptures regarding its ability to surprise, its capacity to satisfy, and, ultimately, its (I believed) essential importance.

At the time, I was living in Hoboken, New Jersey, Frank Sinatra's hometown and the world capital of jangly guitar bands, with my girlfriend, an architect. My girlfriend *made* things, and suddenly I wanted to make things too—instead of just passing judgment on the things others had made. I thought that doing so might, at the very least, serve as a kind of physical therapy for my rock-crit malaise. And so I decided to sum up my abortive career with a few concrete gestures, and thereby either find a way back in, renewed, or let go for good. I began planning my projects.

For starters, I figured I'd unwind an entire roll of Bounty, print a single modifier culled from an actual review of mine on each sheet, one of the very adjectives I'd used up—you know those rock reviewer adjectives: *stunning*, *quirky*, *plodding*, and the like—and roll it all up again. Then proudly, ironically, I'd hang the results over my desk.

What else? Well, rock and roll was about hero worship, so I'd build an altar to Bruce Springsteen in a corner of the living room. That's more or less what I'd been doing in print anyway.

Finally, I was going to buy the latest issue of a mainstream skin magazine, *Playboy* or *Penthouse*, and then paste, over the models' faces but making sure to leave the rest exposed, photos I'd clipped from *Rolling Stone*, *Spin*, and *People*.

Photos of Madonna.

▶ 2. You Tried to Criticize My Drive

Rock and roll has always been about sex—"rock and roll" *means* sex, for God's sake—but especially after the advent in 1981 of MTV, much of rock and roll began to seem, to me at least, like pornography. Not *community*; not a voice for those who otherwise would have none (my ideals regarding the aforementioned significance of the form)—just an aggregate of two-dimensional images representing male fantasies of carnal and material desires satisfied: porn. And although she was far from the only practitioner of the burgeoning MTV ethic, Madonna seemed the most egregious at the time. Already there were stirrings to the effect that Madonna meant more than she appeared to, but I gave it a few seconds' thought and decided that my interest in her, and probably most people's, was primarily prurient.

I wasn't alone in my essential disrespect for Madonna, either. The so-called Virgin Tour (Madonna's first, logically) had been launched nearly two years earlier, in the spring of 1985. Apparently the show pleased Madonna's fans, but it was received by at least one critic less than warmly. "The fact of the matter was," wrote Robert Palmer, that Madonna—backed by a competent but rather ordinary touring band—simply didn't sing very well. Her intonation was atrocious; she sang sharp and she sang flat, and the combination of her unsure pitch and thin, quavery vocal timbre made the held notes at the end of her phrases sound like they were crawling off somewhere to die. In her higher range, she had a more attractive sound, with just a smattering of street-corner edginess to it. But this woman needs to see a good vocal coach before she attempts another tour.

Indeed, the nay-sayers were all but ubiquitous. Paul Grein of *Billboard* sniffed, "Cyndi Lauper will be around for a long time. Madonna will be out of business in six months. Her image has completely overshadowed her music."

Greil Marcus was less censorious but still (so far) wide of the mark: "I don't think Madonna, whom I like, has any particular interest in music," he said in 1985. "She's going to end up a big movie star. There's nothing wrong with that." Cult icon Morrissey, of Britain's The Smiths, asserted that "Madonna is closer to organized prostitution than anything else."

And to Mick Jagger, last seen in an Emilio Estevez vehicle entitled *Freejack* (available for rental at a video emporium near you), her records were characterized by "a central dumbness." Barry Walters summed up the prevailing attitude (the epitome of which was Christopher Connelly's *Rolling Stone* hatchet-job cover story) in the parodic opening paragraph of his own astute and complimentary *Like a Virgin*/Virgin Tour review: "MADONNA is a slut. Madonna IS a slut. Madonna is A slut. Madonna is a SLUT."

Madonna's fans, most of them teenage girls, didn't care. At Radio City Music Hall, all 17,622 Virgin Tour tickets sold out in thirty-four minutes, a house record. And on May 27, 1985, Madonna, a virtual unknown two years before and still unheard of by many (see Russell Baker's column reprinted herein), appeared on the cover of *Time*.

The profile inside was written with the glibness characteristic of the magazine, but it was surprisingly sympathetic (if a little patronizing) to Madonna, and almost before it began it had introduced a new term to the language:

Now then, parents, the important thing is to stay calm. You've seen Madonna wiggling on TV—right, she's the pop-tart singer with the trashy outfits and the hi-there bellybutton. What is worse, your children have seen her. . . . The bright side of this phenomenon is that these Wanna Be's (as in "We wanna be like Madonna!") could be out somewhere stealing hubcaps. Instead, all of them . . . are saving up their babysitting money.

Having dubbed them Wanna Be's, *Time* proceeded to interview a few. The responses—some of which are quoted in the John Fiske piece that follows—remain significant.

Madonna was most often compared in those days to fifties blond bombshells like Jayne Mansfield, Mamie Van Doren, and—ad nauseam—Marilyn Monroe. To photographer Francesco Scavullo, she was "Little Dietrich"! And *Time*, groping for a rationale for her youth appeal, proposed that

the neoconservative mood of the kid culture seems to be just right for an entertainer whose personality is an outrageous blend of Little Orphan Annie, Margaret Thatcher and Mae West.

A year later, after the first of dozens, it now seems, of startling shifts in appearance, Madonna would be matched with the gamines of 1950s and 1960s movies: Audrey Hepburn, Leslie Caron, and Jean Seberg—polar opposites of the era's sex goddesses that Madonna had seemed to emulate at first. And since then the list has expanded to encompass Jean Harlow and Judy Holliday, Rita Hayworth in *The Lady from Shanghai*, and Elvis Presley (in Jim Jarmusch's *Mystery Train*).

What's most interesting about these analogies, I think, is not which actress, singer, despot, or cartoon character Madonna is being likened to but rather the theme of comparison itself. Is it merely a sign of our current, postmodern condition that Madonna hasn't (until recently) been taken on her own terms?

Or does our culture need to pigeonhole women in order to (pretend to) understand them? Certainly American literature has featured a few heroines who ultimately are destroyed by the tragic inability of the men in their lives to classify them as something besides . . . well, virgins or whores: Temple Drake in Faulkner's *Sanctuary*, for example, and Henry James's Daisy Miller. (Interestingly, Madonna revealed in a recent interview that "Daisy" is tattooed on her ex-husband Sean Penn's toe. She says it was Penn's nickname for her—after Daisy Miller.) Inasmuch as Madonna messed, from the start, with our apparent need for such a dichotomy (being a woman named after the Virgin Mary who sang primarily about sex), maybe the best observers could do, in their frustration, was reach for, say, Monroe—a rather forced simile, after all. I mean, besides blond hair, a big chest, and the "Diamonds Are a Girl's Best Friend" number that Madonna appropriated for her "Material Girl" video, what do the two have in common? (See Liz Smith herein.)

▶ 3. Music Can Be Such a Revelation

In his excellent *New Republic* essay included in *Desperately Seeking Madonna*, Luc Sante insists that Madonna is

> a bad actress, a barely adequate singer, a graceless dancer, a boring interview subject, a workmanlike but uninspired (co-)songwriter, and a dynamo of hard work and ferocious ambition.

I would argue that "a dynamo of hard work and ferocious ambition" is hardly the burning indictment it seems meant to be. Madonna's supporters would argue (and Madonna herself has done so, in *Truth or Dare*) that musicianship is beside the point anyhow.

And yet, Madonna's *oeuvre* is characterized by some of the most sheerly satisfying popular music made during the past decade. Is "Borderline" not the sweetest song ever recorded about an orgasm? ("Into the Groove" is certainly the best song ever recorded about a vagina—and arguably Madonna's best song ever, especially in its Shep Pettibone–remixed incarnation on the *You Can Dance* collection.) Or consider most of the *Like a Virgin* album, produced with an astonishing—and still underrated—combination of muscle and sweetness by Nile Rodgers.

How about "Papa Don't Preach," "Live to Tell," and especially "Open Your Heart," from *True Blue*? Not to mention *Like a Prayer* from start to finish. Its high points: the monumental mélange "Like a Prayer"; "Love Song," a duet with Prince that is nothing if not existentially funky; and "Cherish," especially notable for its compulsive allusiveness (thanks to James Hunter for this observation), its sophisticated use of enjambment and internal rhyme, and its equally sophisticated, though *faux*-naive, lyrics—lines like "Romeo and Juliet, / They never felt this way, I bet" are worthy of Cole Porter.

The rock writers who have unabashedly celebrated Madonna's music per se are few and far between but one such is collected here: Robert Christgau writes of Madonna that "[c]elebrity is her true art" (more on that later), but he suggests that her music will last "long after her celebrity has become a bore, escaped her control, or both."

And speaking of Madonna's music, "Living to Tell: Madonna's Resurrection of the Fleshly," by Susan McClary, is probably the most radical piece in this anthology, suggesting that at least a couple of Madonna's tunes are more than just catchy; indeed, McClary writes that they serve as models for a new kind of song altogether, free from the patriarchal elements that she says characterize nearly all Western music. "By thus creating songs that refuse to choose between identity and Other—that invoke and then reject this very schema of narrative organization—Madonna is engaged in rewriting some very fundamental levels of Western thought," McClary claims—and quite convincingly so.

(Well, come to think of it, Mark Rowland's "Musician of the Decade" is even more radical than that. After all, *Musician* magazine, where the piece first appeared, is the very Bible of male, adolescent, fusion-crazed MIDIheads and whammy-bar freaks.)

Significantly, co-writer/producer Patrick Leonard has credited the sound of her records, if not the substance, to Madonna herself—and not to her collaborators, whom many have presumed to be responsible.

> [I]f you listen to what she says, it instantly becomes a "Madonna" record . . . no matter what producer she's working with. She likes bells, and that's a good call, because that kind of high-end information's very important to the ear. . . . And she's adamant about bass parts—that's her key to the song. So put those two elements together with the voice in the middle, and you've got the spectrum covered.

Most critics continued to resist, at least until the release of *Like a Prayer*. Stephen Holden's assessment (in response to *True Blue*) that "obviously, Madonna is still much more significant as a pop culture symbol than as a songwriter or singer" was typical. Yet on her Who's That Girl Tour, which packed soccer stadia worldwide during 1987 while the eponymous Major Motion Picture was flopping in mall multi-plexes across the land, Madonna proved herself not just an all-around buoyant presence but a tireless dancer and a completely competent singer—in short, the quintessential trouper. Perhaps a headline from that period best demonstrates her growing (albeit a little incredulous) respect among critics—"It's True: Madonna Is Really Good."

▶ 4. Step into the Spotlight

Shortly after the release of *Desperately Seeking Susan*, director Susan Seidelman told me, "It was easy working with her. She's got a natural something-or-other. The camera likes her." To Pauline Kael of *The New Yorker*, Madonna had "dumbfounding aplomb." And David Edelstein, in *The Village Voice*, agreed:

> Madonna has enormous authority. With her meaty little body, flared nostrils, and lewdly puckered lips, she's imperiously trampy—just walking down the street she seems X-rated.

The movie in general and especially Madonna got (well-deserved) glowing reviews, which neither Madonna the actress nor Seidelman has equaled since. Not so Madonna's sophomore effort (sophomore, that is, if you discount—and you should—the no-budget *A Certain Sacrifice*, shot in New York City prior to Madonna's first record deal).

"The nicest thing about *Shanghai Surprise*," wrote Janet Maslin of the film starring Madonna and husband Sean Penn, ". . . is that you can watch it in near-total privacy." Maslin summed up the feelings of the handful who attended by pointing out that

> just because something takes up two hours' worth of screen time and offers well-known people the chance to dress cleverly and talk about stolen opium and jewels and secrets of the Orient, it isn't necessarily a movie. We'd all be better off if that were more widely known.

Yet Barry Diller, chairman and CEO of Fox, has said that

> Madonna is a movie star without a movie. She's such a movie star, in fact, that I'd say she's got a good ten years to find the right movie to

prove it. You want to know why she's such a movie star? Because she's incapable of doing anything that's not interesting. If she's in a photograph, it's interesting. If she sings a song, it's interesting. Her videos—all interesting . . . .

She's smart, too.

Although Madonna was admittedly "interesting" in *Dick Tracy* (her casting in which became a delightful joke just before the final credits rolled), it is only *Truth or Dare*, a kind of nineties *Don't Look Back*, that fully exploits her talents on the big screen. As a result, Vincent Canby's tribute reprinted in this book is the only full-length appreciation of her acting abilities I was able to locate (and even it neglects to mention Madonna's finest screen turn to date, in the video for "Papa Don't Preach").

However, Madonna's reviews for David Mamet's *Speed-the-Plow*, in which she appeared during its 1988 Broadway run, ranged, for the most part, from positive to positively adulatory. John Simon was wrong when he objected that Madonna had merely been "cast for the hype and fans she attracts"; Mamet seemed almost to have written the part of Karen with her—or her reputation, at least—in mind:

> **Fox:** "We"? "We" . . . ? I know who *he* is, who are *you?* some broad from the Temporary Pool. A Tight Pussy wrapped around Ambition. That's who *you* are, Pal.

Clive Barnes had reservations—

> As for the cast of three, it is two-thirds perfect and one-third hopeful. Madonna tries hard in the Judy Holliday role, but sounds more as if she were auditioning than acting, and the audition is scarcely for the big-time. There is a genuine, reticent charm here, but it is not ready to light the lamps on Broadway

—but not so Frank Rich, the dread "Butcher of Broadway":

> Although her role is the smallest, Madonna is the axis on which the play turns—an enigma within an enigma. . . . It's a relief to report that this rock star's performance is safely removed from her own Hollywood persona. Madonna serves Mr. Mamet's play much as she did in . . . *Desperately Seeking Susan*, with intelligent, scrupulously disciplined comic acting. She delivers the shocking transitions essen-

tial to the action and needs only more confidence to relax a bit and fully command her speaking voice.

"In a sense, Madonna has been a character actress all along," David Ansen has suggested, "but instead of slipping in and out of movie roles, she has used music videos continually to reinvent her persona." And who would dispute that the most *influential* moments, certainly, of Madonna's career have been those recorded on videotape? In fact, E. Ann Kaplan writes in a piece reprinted here from her book *Rocking Around the Clock* that the aforementioned Mary Lambert–directed "Material Girl" video's very structure contains contradiction, encourages confusion, and rejects Hollywood's classical construction of female "subjects" as no more than objects of a male gaze. (It thus serves as the ideal companion piece to the McClary article.)

▶ 5. Experience Has Made Me Rich

Andy Warhol (who, incidentally, attended Madonna's wedding) wrote that "Business Art is the step that comes after Art." In "McRock: Pop As Commodity," Mary Harron uses Bruce Springsteen as a foil in her discussion of Madonna's image and how it is sold, an engaging example of the peculiarly British notions of "rock" and "pop" and how the two differ. But I wonder if she misses the point—the point being, perhaps (as illustrated herein by Matthew Schifrin and Peter Newcomb), that Madonna is very much in control of her own destiny in this realm and always has been. (A truism at this late date? Maybe. Still, I'm astonished at how many people have asked me, since I began compiling this collection, if her success wasn't actually engineered by some man.) And in a move that was justified even as it was deeply cynical, *Forbes* featured her on its cover late in 1990, posing in a maribou-trimmed pink corset as "America's Smartest Business Woman?" Madonna was ranked eighth by the magazine among top-earning entertainers (behind Cosby, Michael Jackson, the Rolling Stones, Spielberg, New Kids on the Block, Oprah Winfrey, and Stallone—and ahead of, among others, Schwarzenegger, Eddie Murphy, Jack Nicholson, and Stephen King), with an estimated two-year (1989–90) income of $62 million.

Despite her omnipresence on the nation's newsstands, Madonna's appearance on the front of *Forbes* (though she had denied the magazine not only an interview but access to any member of her retinue as well) seemed a kind of watershed. And at this point, what periodical has her face *not* graced? *The National Review*? *MAD*? (Sorry—both succumbed post–*Truth or Dare*.) Okay: *Sports Illustrated*. But surely things are getting out of hand; an author can't even write a book-length essay on the writer he's obsessed by without mentioning Madonna's name and his hero's reaction to her music! (See Nicholson Baker's contribution to *Desperately Seeking Madonna*.) Well, in the words of co-writer/producer Stephen Bray, "she was always like this. She wanted attention—now it's her job."

▶ 6. It Makes No Difference If You're Black or White, If You're a Boy or a Girl

To Boston University president John Silber, Madonna "has no more right to set [an example] for our kids than Adolf Hitler did or than Saddam Hussein does." Performance artist Karen Finley, on the other hand, has averred that "all women should be as Madonna as possible."

If Madonna's multipronged assault on our culture can be characterized as being "about" a single issue, that issue (as put forth so convincingly here by Lynne Layton, clinical psychologist and lecturer in the women's studies department at Harvard) is identity. Madonna's motto might be Norman Mailer's assertion that "Any lady who chooses to become a blonde is truly blonde." More important, it is the motto of many of her followers.

Thus, in "Primadonna," Joyce Millman places Madonna within the tradition of sixties girl groups, who spoke not just to but for their teenage female fans. John Fiske, writing from the point of view of British cultural studies (that's ethnography plus semiotics), goes even further, positing Madonna as a bona-fide empoweress of her constituents. "In fact," Nell Bernstein has agreed,

> Madonnaism is ultimately less about the star than about the fan. The idea is not simply to look at Madonna, but also to look at yourself looking at Madonna.

For a look at a fan looking at herself, etc., *vide* "Madonna and Me" by fiction writer/personal essayist Elizabeth Tippens.

By contrast, John Simon's *Truth or Dare* review *starts* with an assault on Madonna's looks ("natural endowments had little to do with any of [her success]") and moves on to what is perhaps an unwitting admission, ostensibly regarding Madonna's papa: "The old-style patriarch is putty in the hands of the revisionist goddess." For Simon's colleague Joseph Sobran, "Madonna offers something new under the sun: vicarious self-absorption." He's got a point. *Truth or Dare* struck many viewers, including this one, as some kind of bleating black (-and-white) hole, sucking nearly everything into it and giving back only a blinding headache. (And for once, Madonna's patented Best Defense Is a Good Offense strategy wasn't sufficient to preempt effective attack; I especially recommend Julie Brown's delicious, vicious Showtime special, *Medusa: Dare to Be Different*.) "Real love," Sobran writes, "is like art: it demands the subordination of the ego." Ultimately his essay becomes a critique of masturbation, which Sobran warns leads to "moral blindness." Hm.

Yet, as J. Hoberman has pointed out, "To criticize Madonna for her narcissism is to complain that water is wet." Freud wrote in "On Narcissism" that

> One person's narcissism has the greatest attraction for those others who have renounced part of their own narcissism and are seeking after object-love; the charm of a child lies in his narcissism . . . as does the charm of certain animals . . . such as cats. . . . It is as if we envied their power of retaining a blissful state of mind.

It is just this dynamic that many of Madonna's followers seem to crave—and that her detractors so vigorously resist. Indeed, only a process so primal could yield the passions for and against her that Madonna has always aroused. Contributor Tom Ward, for example, discovered "perfectly whorish sentiments" on *Like a Virgin* (and as a result, much of his newspaper's staff signed a letter protesting his review).

Dave Marsh highlights here what he sees as the sexism implicit in much early Madonna criticism (Ward's, for example, to which he alludes). And it is true that a new kind of feminist (and *Sexual Personae* author Camille Paglia, a new kind of new kind of feminist) has embraced Madonna, mole and all.

But *The Progressive*'s Ruth Conniff begs to differ: "Surely, even in our 'post-feminist age,' we can do better than this," she laments in "Politics in a Post-Feminist Age." "We need a better role model than Madonna. We need a sense that we can do something more productive for society than getting and spending." Kathleen Talvacchia of *Christianity and Crisis* acknowledges Madonna's status as icon to the disenfranchised but points out that "wealth, fame, heterosexuality and whiteness shield Madonna from the threats marginalization brings"—a theme that bell hooks, author of *Yearning: Race, Gender, and Cultural Politics*, treats at length in her article, "madonna: plantation mistress or soul sister?" original to this book.

Ellen Goodman seems most disturbed, in her *Nightline*-inspired column reproduced here, by the swirling mess of contradictions that is Madonna, but Don Shewey has offered an explanation:

> Madonna's attention span and her ability to withstand barrages of computer-age information make her uniquely unafraid of contradiction. In fact, in true postmodern fashion, she is drawn to complexity, contradiction, and ambiguity over harmony, clarity, and simplicity. And she embraces a fragmented wardrobe of personas (Bitch, Little Girl, Vulnerable Love-Seeker) rather than a false, integrated personality.

Madonna *does* embrace such a wardrobe. Why then, do so many continue to insist upon seeing her in but a single costume? James Russell Lowell wrote, "The idol is the measure of the worshipper," and clearly, what each of us thinks of Madonna says as much about us as about her.

In Lucy Hughes-Hallett's *Cleopatra: Histories, Dreams and Distortions*, the author writes that even while she lived, Cleopatra was obscured by what we might now call point-of-view. To her enemies, the Romans, she was a paragon of depravity, the embodiment of Otherness. To her Egyptian subjects, at the mercy of her sophisticated PR machine, Cleopatra was very literally a goddess and also a national liberator. And since her death, Hughes-Hallett writes, each successive era has "imagined" Cleopatra to be something different. (To Chaucer, for instance, she was "Cleopatra the Martyr," a model of female virtue.)

Were the ancients less threatened than contemporary Americans by apparent contradiction? Cleopatra was iconographically associated with the goddess Isis, and Isis in turn was associated with Aphrodite, who personified sexual love. According to Hughes-Hallet, the Roman writer Juvenal called Isis "a bawd," and, in fact, the shrine of Isis in Pompeii is located adjacent to a whorehouse. An early Christian writer claimed that Isis herself had worked for ten years as a prostitute in the city of Tyre.

But Isis was also addressed as "the Great Virgin"; indeed, Hughes-Hallet argues that Isis served as the model for the Virgin Mary, inasmuch as she conceived her son Horus immaculately and was often depicted feeding the infant with the milk of life. Perhaps it was this head-spinning hodgepodge of identities that yielded the vast popularity of the cult of Isis in Rome at about the time of Julius Caesar. Interestingly, the core of the goddess's followers consisted of the disenfranchised: slaves, immigrants from the East—and upper-class Roman women. Propertius wrote of being ejected from his lover's bed for ten nights while she kept a vigil on behalf of Isis. And the ever-satirical Juvenal wrote of the average Roman matron,

> If some Egyptian goddess instructs her to make a pilgrimage to the Nile, she'll leave at once, follow the river to its source, and return with a phial of sacred water to sprinkle on the temple. She actually believes that Isis speaks to her!

No, I'm not saying Madonna is a full-blown avatar of an ancient Egyptian goddess. Just that the two might speak to the same needs—answer, in a sense, the same prayers.

▶ 7. I Know Where Beauty Lives

Talvacchia writes that Madonna has made "being able to shock, tease, and fascinate [her] fans with a constant stream of acts designed to keep [her] in the public eye" into "her art form." On this matter, Sante appears to agree: "while she had a small talent as a pop singer, as an image strategist she possessed something approaching genius." And musicologist McClary suggests,

> It may be that Madonna is best understood as head of a corporation that produces images of her self-representation, rather than as the spontaneous, "authentic" artist of rock mythology.

"[H]ead of a corporation that produces images . . . rather than . . . the spontaneous 'authentic' artist": more than Marilyn Monroe, more than Elvis or the Beatles or Michael Jackson, Madonna resembles Andy Warhol. For Madonna is, most of all, a canny manipulator of images and of public opinion—just like Warhol. They say she can't sing, act; they said he couldn't draw. She is "accused," essentially, of collaborating in the creation of her work, and so was he. Both represent an embodiment of the Puritan-American work ethic so complete that it seems a perversion. ("Business Art is the step that comes after Art.")

Madonna may be, in fact, the ultimate conceptual artist. And like a kind of Chris Burden for the masses, Madonna defaces her own work on an almost daily basis. I'm not talking about just The Hair, either. Much was made of the sheer ugliness of the Blond Ambition costumes, makeup, and yes, that 'do. I'm convinced that that ugliness was intentional. For this is a performer who in 1987, back when she was still playing the consummate trouper, trashed her own hits, her *greatest* hits, onstage before thousands: examine the *Ciao, Italia* video if you want to see Madonna, in cat glasses and Carmen Miranda–tribute headgear (and Cyndi Lauper's voice), massacre "Dress You Up," "Material Girl," and "Like a Virgin" all in a row, coming out the other side (and out of her dopey getup) just in time to save The Four Tops' "I Can't Help Myself."

It doesn't get much more conceptual than that.

▶ 8. Causing a Commotion

I'm not a Madonna fan, not the way I'm a Prince fan, a Bruce Springsteen fan—or a Frederick Barthelme or Jonathan Demme fan, for that matter. By that I mean that, although I'm generally interested in what she does, I don't wait breathlessly for her to do it. Anyway, I agree with Merrill Markoe, who writes, "I keep trying to like her, but she keeps pissing me off."

Madonna has been pissing people off since she entered the public eye (maybe even longer). During the summer of 1985, nude photos taken by three photographers shortly after her arrival in New York City appeared in *Penthouse* and *Playboy*, prompting the classic *New York Post* headline MADONNA: I'M NOT ASHAMED—and prompting *Penthouse* publisher Bob Guccione's curious criticism, "She wasn't well-groomed, there was lots of hair on her arms and hair sticking out of her armpits."

This incident was followed about a year later by what remains the quintessential Madonna scandal (at least to date). "Papa Don't Preach," written by Brian Elliot and sent to Madonna (who "contributed a couple of minor lyrical revisions") by Michael Ostin, the Warner Bros. executive who had unearthed "Like a Virgin," was released as a single in mid-1986, and the song was promoted by a melodramatic yet affecting video in which Madonna shakes her stuff like a Jell-O mold but also does some fine acting on an admittedly small scale.

The "Papa Don't Preach" debate, occasioned by an achingly, breathtakingly defiant reading of the line "I've made up my mind: I'm keeping my baby," made for strange bedfellows. Alfred Moran, executive director of Planned Parenthood of New York City, was outraged:

the message is that getting pregnant is cool and having the baby is the right thing and a good thing and don't listen to your parents, the school, anybody who tells you otherwise—don't preach to me, papa. The reality is that what Madonna is suggesting to teenagers is a path to permanent poverty.

Moran told *The New York Times* that his agency's clinics had been filled for a year with Wanna Bes, and he feared her influence over teenage girls:

Everybody I've talked to believes she has more impact on teenagers than any other entertainer since the Beatles. That's what makes this particular song so destructive.

The New York chapter sent what it called a "critical memo" to radio and TV stations advising them to "think carefully about playing this song to young audiences." Planned Parenthood also asked Warner Bros. to donate twenty-five percent of the song's earnings to programs promoting responsible sexual behavior.

Ironically, the same Tipper Gore who only a year before had placed Madonna's "Dress You Up" on her top ten list of dangerous pop songs (more because of its anticapitalist bias than anything else, I would suggest) came out with this statement:

To me, the song speaks to a serious subject with a sense of urgency and sensitivity in both the lyrics and Madonna's rendition. It also speaks to the fact that there's got to be more support and more communication in families about this problem, and anything that fosters that I applaud.

As for the performer herself, Madonna refused to comment on the song's use as an antiabortion anthem. Liz Rosenberg, her publicist, passed along the following noninformation: "She's singing a song, not taking a stand. Her philosophy is 'People can think what they want to think.'"

Perhaps this was what Greil Marcus had in mind when he said recently that

> Madonna is one popular artist who clearly believes she's subversive and means to be subversive and is constantly trying to find new ways to be more subversive. Her goal, I would think, is to do things that will sooner or later make you very uncomfortable and me very uncomfortable, even though as we sit here today we could both agree that we are the two biggest Madonna fans in the world. . . . She wants to come up with something that is going to challenge everybody's view of the way things ought to be—and she's pretty good at it.

J. Hoberman agrees: "Part of her role is to test the limits of permissible representation," he has written of Madonna, and she certainly played that role to the hilt during the spring of 1989 in her dealings with Pepsi-Cola. (See Richard Morgan's *ADWEEK* response herein.) The controversy was inspired by a "Like a Prayer" video that was probably the most brazen melding of the sacred and the sexual since John Donne's "Holy Sonnet 14," but that didn't make the clip less than legitimate to *Desperately Seeking Madonna* contributor Andrew Greeley: "This is blasphemy? Only for the prurient and the sick who come to the video determined to read their own twisted sexual hangups into it." Amen.

The Pepsi brouhaha had been preceded by the Sandra Bernhard "scandal" (see *Gay Community News* reporter Deb Schwartz's piece on this) and the stir over Sean Penn; it was followed by Nike-gate—and by more video mischief. The "Like a Prayer" clip was succeeded by the release of the lyrically muddled but nonetheless irresistible disco anthem "Express Yourself" and its accompanying video, a big-budget, *Metropolis* (and perhaps *5000 Fingers of Dr. T*)–inspired affair directed by David Fincher (responsible for Paula Abdul's awesome "Straight Up" spot) and choreographed by avant-garde dancer Karole Armitage. Not surprisingly, Madonna's rubbery dress, the heavy-gauge chain around her neck, and her appropriation of Michael Jackson's stylized crotch-grab (Marjorie Garber's *Vested Interests: Cross-Dressing and Cultural Anxiety* has much to say on this topic) were more commented upon than the clip's pronounced Marxist sensibility or even its blatant homoeroticism.

"Express Yourself" wasn't the last Madonna clip to cause a commotion, either; Herb Ritts's "Cherish" was a riot of taboo-toppling and genuine kink (if you wanted it to be—*vide* Schwartz again), and Fincher's "Oh Father" dared to quote, and quote, and quote some more from *Citizen Kane*. And speaking of appropriation, "Vogue" (again directed by Fincher) was criticized not because it resurrected a played-out gay fad without acknowledging voguing's source, but because the video's images themselves were ripoffs. Photographer Horst P. Horst, eighty-three at the time, was furious that the song's promo clip utilized ten of his signature images (including the classic 1939 "Mainbocher Corset"), saying he had never given Madonna permission for their use and complaining that he received no credit for inspiring the video's look. Richard Tardiff, Horst's manager, admitted of Madonna that

> You can't fault her taste. But the video should have been called "*Hommage* to Horst." We just wish we could have worked something out beforehand—like doing an original photograph of her in the nude.

Madonna's spokeswoman was uncharacteristically apologetic: "She's a great admirer of Horst. We didn't mean to upset him." Silky black and white, "Vogue" was choreographed by Armitage, and it featured a shot in which Madonna's breasts were plainly visible through a black net top. The video immediately became an MTV staple.

In a by-then predictably sly career move, Madonna next created a Public Service Announcement for television—a sixty-second message in which two flag-waving chorus boys in tight shorts and army boots pretended to spank her. (Ostensibly, they were illustrating the spot's tag line: "And if you don't vote, you're going to get a spankie.")

The commercial, shot just prior to Election Day 1990, was part of the so-called "Rock the Vote" campaign by the recording industry to inspire eighteen-to-twenty-four-year-olds to vote and to oppose obscenity prosecutions directed at record companies. And Madonna's PSA was a stroke of genius: it further flogged "Vogue," the ad's backing track; it attempted to resuscitate interest in "Hanky Panky," a song about sexual spanking off the essentially unlistenable *I'm Breathless* album; it strengthened Madonna's ties to the increasingly hip anticensorship crusade; and, of course, it put her at the center of another minicontroversy.

Some viewers objected to Madonna's use, in the video, of the American flag as a poncho. Steve Vanbuskirt, a Veterans of Foreign Wars spokesman, summed things up on behalf of the group, saying, "We have a strong stand against the desecration of the flag. This borders on desecration."

Liz Rosenberg replied,

That was certainly not Madonna's intention at all. My sense is that wrapping the American flag around her is not insulting. It is essential that people should vote. She's trying to get that message across in a humorous, dramatic way. But she's very serious about the issue.

So serious, in fact, that Madonna rapped the following lines while wrapped in Old Glory:

> Abe Lincoln, Jefferson Tom,
> They didn't need the atomic bomb.
> We need beauty, we need art,
> We need a government with heart.
> Don't give up your freedom of speech,
> Power to the people is in our reach . . . .
> Dr. King, Malcolm X,
> Freedom of speech is as good as sex.

Next came the notorious "Justify My Love" video. This one ripped off Liliana Cavani's *The Night Porter* and depicted nudity, homosexuality, group sex, transvestitism, voyeurism—pretty much all the isms, in fact. The appearance of the MTV-banned clip and a Madonna interview on ABC's *Nightline* (the text of which appears in this book) yielded that program's second-highest ratings, inferior only to those garnered by Tammy Faye Bakker's appearance on the show. The following spring, *Truth or Dare* hit the fans.

Oh, and some guy complained that her hedges were too high.

There are those who argue that what Madonna is doing, though it may be controversial, is hardly radical. Jon Pareles wrote of the Blond Ambition Tour, for example, that "If Blond Ambition were a TV variety show, Madonna might be testing taboos, but she is hardly breaking new ground in rock theatrics." Too, her "legitimacy" continues to burgeon (with the likes of an *Architectural Digest* cover story becoming ever more common), although this hasn't done much to stem the tide of tab headlines like "Gutsy Madonna: 'I'll sleep with Saddam to save our hostages'." Perhaps the point is that, unlike Madonna, those who are most boldly testing the limits remain unknown—unheard of, for the most part, with the exception of the occasional Robert Mapplethorpe or Salman Rushdie—by the great majority of our society.

▶ 9. Open Your Heart

Being a freelance explorer of spiritual dangers, the artist gains a certain license to behave differently from other people; matching the singularity of his vocation, he may be decked out with a suitably eccentric lifestyle, or he may not. His job is inventing trophies of his experiences—objects and gestures that fascinate and enthrall, not merely (as prescribed by older notions of the artist) edify or entertain. His principal means of fascinating is to advance one step further in the dialectic of outrage. He seeks to make his work repulsive, obscure, inaccessible; in short, to give what is, or seems to be, *not* wanted. But however fierce may be the outrages the artist perpetrates upon his audience, his credentials and spiritual authority depend on the audience's sense (whether something known or inferred) of the outrages he commits upon himself.

—Susan Sontag

Sound familiar? Well, maybe not the "obscure" and "inaccessible" part. And that is what might make Madonna, if not plainly better, at least more significant than, for example, Warhol. She's arguably the most famous woman on the planet—and certainly the most famous living artist, if you'll grant her that.

Of course, there are so many who just won't. Mass culture still gets short shrift in our society—especially when that mass culture started out as Disco, more or less. (An aside: Someone pointed out to me recently that a collection like this, with about fifty voices clamoring over the same pop star, demonstrates something not only about that pop star, but about the multitude of uses to which mass culture can often be put.)

Still, you'd think doubters would admit by now that she's—well, important, at least. I've collected scores of responses to Madonna for inclusion here, yet no two express precisely the same point of view. Meanwhile, this woman is still in her mid-thirties; who knows what outrages, and what reactions to them, lie over the horizon? The J. Hoberman epigraph at the start of this chapter notwithstanding, it seems there will always be more to say about Madonna, and in this sense she is indeed like Marilyn—or, better yet, the JFK assassination. (Don't get any ideas, Oliver Stone.)

And still I keep hearing from People You'd Think Would Know Better that: "She's utterly without talent, and not only that she's not even pretty in my opinion." Or, after all these years, "She's a *slut*."

Well, if it's just about sex, as I too once believed, then why do Madonna's core constituencies comprise adolescent girls and gay men—precisely the groups you'd assume to be most immune to her sexual allure? (In fact, at least one observer has noted that *Truth or Dare*'s publicity was specially encoded to target a gay audience.) And why isn't a more obvious hetero object—Paula Abdul, or Vanessa Williams, or even LaToya Jackson—ruling the world? Maybe Nell Bernstein put it best in writing that "she has established herself as a sexual subject, not a sex object, and that, her admirers say, makes all the difference." Gina Arnold perhaps went overboard when she stated that "if you're a really smart guy you shouldn't like Madonna much more than smart women like Andrew Dice Clay," but her point is well taken. Anecdotally speaking, at least, I don't know a whole lot of straight, male Madonnaphiles. "[W]hen it comes to the process of deliberately titillating men," Arnold continued in her review of the Blond Ambition Tour,

she might as well have just put her thumbs in her ears, flapped her fingers and yelled "neener neener neener" at every single person who went to the show with the idea, however subconscious, of ogling her bod.

▶ 10. Who's That Girl

By the time I left Hoboken in the autumn of 1987, I wasn't so sure anymore that Madonna was porn. I had seen her perform live at Veterans Stadium in Philadelphia and come away impressed. I'd watched *Who's That Girl*, the movie, and *enjoyed* it.

Not to mention that Madonna already had inspired an entire radio format in her own image, as noted at the time by Jon Pareles. It was called "Hot" radio in New York City, where it appeared as WQHT 103.5 FM, and "Hot" or "Power" radio elsewhere, and the format was characterized by electronic drums and keyboards, ersatz Latin percussion, and girlish vocals by the likes of Jody Watley, Stacy Q, Lisa Lisa, the Cover Girls, Miami Sound Machine, and others. Between September and December 1986, 'QHT ranked as high as number two in New York during the day among twelve- to seventeen-year-olds. A "Hot" chart was duly added to the pages of *Billboard* magazine.

That final Hoboken summer, I'd walk down the street on my way to the PATH train, or to the neighborhood *pouleria* for eggs, and I'd hear Madonna singing the film's theme song from some Latina girl's bedroom boom-box: a few words in Spanish, then the phrase *"Who's That Girl."* Then more Spanish, and again *"Who's That Girl."*

Controversial. Canny. Contradictory. Chameleonlike. . . .

Maybe I didn't run out of adjectives after all.

▶ Notes

P. 1 "What is there to say" J. Hoberman, "Blond on Blond," *The Village Voice*, May 14, 1991, p. 56.

P. 2 "The fact of the matter" Robert Palmer, "Pop: Madonna Sings at Radio City," *The New York Times*, June 7, 1985, p. C4.

P. 3 "Cyndi Lauper will be" "I don't think" Jay Cocks, "These Big Girls Don't Cry," *Time*, March 4, 1985, pp. 74–75.

P. 3 "Madonna is closer" Mick St. Michael, *Madonna in Her Own Words* (London: Omnibus Press, 1990).

P. 3 "a central dumbness," John Skow, "Madonna Rocks the Land," *Time*, May 27, 1985, pp. 74–75.

P. 3 "MADONNA is a slut." Barry Walters, "The Virgin and the Dynamo," *The Village Voice*, June 18, 1985, p. 69.

P. 3 Radio City statistics and "Now then, parents" John Skow, "Madonna Rocks the Land," *Time*, May 27, 1985, pp. 74.

P. 4 "Little Dietrich!" "The neoconservative mood" Jay Cocks, "These Big Girls Don't Cry," *Time*, March 4, 1985, pp. 74–75.

P. 5 She says it was Penn's nickname. Carrie Fisher, "True Confessions: The *Rolling Stone* Interview with Madonna," Part I, *Rolling Stone*, June 13, 1991, pp. 35–36, 39–40, 120.

P. 6 "If you listen" Fred Schruers, "Can't Stop The Girl," *Rolling Stone*, June 5, 1986, p. 60.

P. 6 "Obviously Madonna is still" Stephen Holden, "Madonna Goes Heavy on Heart," *The New York Times*, June 29, 1986, sec. 2, p. 22.

P. 7 "It's True" Robert Hillburn, "It's True: Madonna Is Really Good," *Los Angeles Times*, June 29, 1987, pp. 1, 6.

P. 7 "dumbfounding aplomb" Pauline Kael, "Passion," in *State of the Art* (New York: E.P. Dutton, 1985).

P. 7 "Madonna has enormous" David Edelstein, "Seek and Ye Shall Founder," *The Village Voice*, April 2, 1985, p. 56.

P. 7 "The nicest thing" Janet Maslin, "Film: *Shanghai Surprise*," *The New York Times*, September 21, 1986, p. 67.

P. 7 "Madonna is a movie star" Kevin Sessums, "White Heat," *Vanity Fair*, April 1990, pp. 140–149, 208, 210, 212, 214.

P. 8 "cast for the hype" John Simon, "Word Power," *New York*, May 16, 1988, p. 106.

P. 8 FOX: "We"? David Mamet, *Speed-the-Plow* (New York: Grove Press, 1987).

P. 8 "As for the cast of three" Clive Barnes, "A Harvest of Riches," *New York Post*, May 4, 1988, pp. 29, 37.

P. 8 "Although her role" Frank Rich, "Mamet's Dark View of Hollywood as a Heaven for the Virtueless," *The New York Times*, May 4, 1988, p. C17.

P. 9 "In a sense" David Ansen, "Madonna: Magnificent Maverick," *Cosmopolitan*, May 1990, pp. 308–311.

P. 9 "Business Art" Andrew Ross, *No Respect: Intellectual and Popular Culture* (New York: Routledge, 1989).

P. 9 Madonna was ranked eighth. Peter Newcomb with Matthew Schifrin, "Golden Boys and Girls," *Forbes*, October 1, 1990, pp. 139–160.

P. 10 "She was always like this" Steve Dougherty et al., "Madonna and Michael," *People*, April 15, 1991, pp. 64–68.

P. 10 "has no more right" R.J. Lambrose, "Like a Metaphor," *Lingua Franca*, June 1991, p. 8.

P. 10 "All women should" Don Shewey, "The Saint, the Slut, the Sensation . . . Madonna," *The Advocate*, May 7, 1991, pp. 42–51.

P. 10 "Any lady" Norman Mailer, *Tough Guys Don't Dance* (New York: Random House, 1989).

P. 10 "In fact, Madonnaism" Nell Bernstein, "Post-Madonnaism: An Exploration of Boy Toy as Feminist Icon," *San Francisco Examiner-Chronicle Image*, October 28, 1990, pp. 6–8.

P. 11 "Showtime special" Julie Brown and Charlie Coffey, *Medusa: Dare to Be Different*. Showtime special, December 1991.

P. 11 "To criticize" J. Hoberman, "Blond on Blond," *The Village Voice*, May 14, 1991, pp. 51, 56.

P. 11 "One person's narcissism" Sigmund Freud, "On Narcissism: An Introduction," in *Collected Papers*, vol. 4 (London: Hogarth Press, 1950).

P. 12 "Madonna's attention span" Don Shewey, "The Saint, the Slut, the Sensation . . . Madonna," *The Advocate*, May 7, 1991, pp. 42–51.

P. 12 Lucy Hughes-Hallett, *Cleopatra: Histories, Dreams and Distortions* (New York: HarperPerennial, 1991).

P. 15 "She wasn't well-groomed" Lee Friedlander, *Nudes* (New York: Pantheon, 1991).

P. 15 "The message is" "To me" "she's singing a song" Georgia Dullea, "Madonna's New Beat Is a Hit, but Song's Message Rankles," *The New York Times*, September 18, 1986, pp. 131, 139.

P. 16 "Madonna is one popular artist" "A Hunka' Hunka' Burnin' Text: Greil Marcus on Dead Elvis and Other Pop Icons," *Lingua Franca*, August 1991, pp. 28–31, 42.

P. 16 "Part of her role" J. Hoberman, "Blond on Blond," *The Village Voice*, May 14, 1991, pp. 51, 56.

P. 17 choreographed by avante-garde. Ron Givens, "Madonnarama," *Entertainment Weekly*, May 11, 1990, pp. 34–40, 42–43.

P. 17 Marjorie Garber, *Vested Interests: Cross-Dressing and Cultural Anxiety* (New York: Routledge, 1991).

P. 17 "You can't fault her taste." Jeannette Walls, "Voguing Madonna Hoists Horst's Images," *New York*, May 14, 1990, p. 22.

P. 17 "She's a great admirer" Jeannette Walls, "Voguing Madonna Hoists Horst's Images," *New York*, May 14, 1990, p. 22.

P. 17 "Vogue" was choreographed. Jennifer Dunning, "Ballet, Boogie, Rap, Tap and Roll," *The New York Times*, August 26, 1990, Section 2, pp. 1, 19.

P. 18 shot just prior. "We have a strong" "That was certainly" Robert D. McFadden, "Wrapped in U.S. Flag, Madonna Raps for Vote," *The New York Times*, October 20, 1990, p. 7.

P. 19 and some guy complained. Jay Cocks, "Madonna Draws a Line," *Time*, December 17, 1990, pp. 74–75.

P. 19 "If Blond Ambition" Jon Pareles, "In Kitsch and Patter, Iron-Willed Madonna Flouts the Taboos," *The New York Times*, June 13, 1990, p. C11.

P. 19 Deborah Gimelson, *"Architectural Digest* Visits: Madonna," *Architectural Digest*, November 1991, pp. 198–209.

P. 19 Jasmine Lafleur, "Gutsy Madonna: 'I'll Sleep with Saddam to Save Our Hostages,'" *News Extra*, December 11, 1990, p. 1, 28.

P. 19 "Being a freelance explorer" Susan Sontag, "The Pornographic Imagination," in *A Susan Sontag Reader* (New York: Vintage Books, 1983), pp. 212–13.

P. 20 "She has established" Nell Bernstein, "Post-Madonnaism: An Exploration of Boy Toy as Feminist Icon," San Francisco *Examiner-Chronicle Image*, October 28, 1990, pp. 6–8.

P. 20 Gina Arnold, "Hail Madonna, Full of Face," *Express*, May 25, 1990, pp. 34–35.

P. 21 Madonna already. Jon Pareles, "Clones of Madonna," *The New York Times*, April 9, 1987, p. C25.

(from *The Village Voice*)

Madonnarama

by Eric Schmuckler

Madonna materialized on black radio a year ago with "Everybody," an astonishing twelve-inch that practically floated off the radio with its spacey mix and pip-pip-pipping synthesizers yet remained anchored to the dance floor by a bass riff plunking as priapically as Prince's on "Do Me, Baby." The extended dub version put this bass center stage and came off even funkier. Her next single was a double A-side, "Burning Up" and the grinding "Physical Attraction," with a beat sinuous enough to make the title a self-fulfilling prophecy. But when early last fall Madonna released an eponymous LP, it didn't cause much of a stir at first. Her idiosyncratic take on black music sounded delicate, if not disposable.

Then Madonna broke pop with "Holiday," a loping disco ditty whose ineffable charm hits me as an infectious syncopation of banjo-tinted guitar, drums that sound happy to be slapped, and Madonna's funky "cowbelle" (sic). "Holiday" 's crossover greased the way for "Borderline," now winging its way up the charts. At worst, "Borderline" is inoffensive Adult Contemp fodder and as such could introduce Madonna to a wide (read: white) audience. Though she's apparently more commercial than such skilled artists as Teena Marie or Nona Hendryx, whether Madonna can ascend to the level of a Debbie Harry or Donna Summer is another story. But she's clearly poised to make her superstar move. She's already parlayed her blowzy alabaster looks and junkheap fashion into quasicenterfold status; feel free to drool over the glitzy glamour shots on the "Borderline" seven-inch's deluxe foldout or the arty spreads that have splashed across the pages of *Mademoiselle* and *Interview*. Another magazine went so far as to proclaim, "Madonna is, in some sense, still a virgin." What sense might that be? It wouldn't surprise me if Madonna were a natural blonde who dyes her roots black.

Dark roots are very much part of Madonna's tarnished-angel come-on, but the iconography is skin deep. Donna Summer celebrated prostitution only to reenact her salvation; Madonna's comment on religion ends with the crucifix earrings. The real trick for female rockers cultivating a sexually assertive image—besides making a pile of money—is informing healthy sexuality with self-respect, i.e. not pandering to adolescent jack-off fantasies. By this standard Madonna has a lot to learn before making a record as tough as "She Works Hard for the Money." Instead, Madonna taunts, "Do you wanna see me down on my knees / Or bending over backwards now would you be pleased?"—just one sample of the degradation Madonna heaps upon herself when she's not partying heartily. She usually saves a psychological comeuppance for the final verse, but "I'm not going to cry for you / Cause that's what you want me to do" is pretty mild revenge. For Madonna the bullshit of relationships only gets in the way of true lust, signified by the leash of chains Madonna holds around her neck on the album's back. Then again, you could just say she's all wrapped up in herself.

Not surprisingly, though, Madonna's musical strengths redeem songs with retro-lyrics like the guitar-driven "Burning Up" and the girl-group-styled "I Know It." Even "Borderline," which on first listen seems just that, turns out to be a sturdy piece of fluff propelled in the single remix by the sprightly signature drum sound of producer John "Jellybean" Benitez, her own Giorgio Moroder. When Madonna gets the right kind of help, she can lay down a groove in any tempo from slow burn to white heat. She even makes her let's-go-party lyrics stick, not as words but as sheer sound. Madonna's lead vocals tend to stay safely put in the middle register, her clear tones fleshing out some rather thin synthesized instrumentation. Live, Madonna sings to recorded tracks (which won't fill up arenas) and dances up a storm (which might). Her background with Alvin Ailey suggests Madonna's ultimate function: what her ultimate purpose might be is anybody's guess.

▶ From *Rolling Stone* Polls, 1984

BEST NEW ARTIST

1. Cyndi Lauper
2. *Madonna*

BEST FEMALE VOCALIST

1. Tina Turner
2. Cyndi Lauper
3. *Madonna*

BEST FEMALE VOCALIST

1. Tina Turner
2. Cyndi Lauper
3. Christine Kerr (Hynde)
4. *Madonna*

(from *The Village Voice*)

Opaque Object of Desire

by Tom Ward

Ah, rock and roll, "a cruel hoax perpetrated by good-looking boys and girls who don't want to do honest work." Thus spake Devo, and the meteoric ascension of Madonna Louise Ciccone has hardly refuted the old spuds. Now let it be clear that I have *nothing against* either beautiful women or the refusal of work—indeed, *everything for* would more nearly approximate my position on both. Yet I maintain that pop stars are best judged by the signal they transmit toward those still trapped in the Piss Factory; that is, those who derive little or no creative satisfaction from their own jobs, for whom life isn't glamorous or fun. In a word, proles. Recently I heard Annie Lennox explain, ever so blithely, her music's message: people should be contented in their lowly slots, just as she is in Her Exalted One. At which point I began to plot the imminent liquidation of Annie Lennox. (Recent stints as a furniture mover, temp office drudge, etc.—plus my family's four generations of sheet-metal work—have rendered me snarlingly militant on this score.) Happily, my overall view of rock's role among proles is neither so dour nor so dire. While too few pledge the solid populist allegiance of Springsteen/Weller/Davies/Mellencamp, much less posit the determinate negation of work McLaren once tried to propagate, I find the usual escapist function, on the whole, benign. Like any other party animal, I wish only that my escapism be pure—that is, not laced with pretty poison.

And speaking of Madonna, have you checked out the lyrics on her new *Like a Virgin* LP? When they're not meaningless (which, perhaps fortunately, is most of the time) they're pernicious enough to ruin the music (which, perhaps deservedly, isn't nearly as entrancing as it was on her eponymous debut album). It starts with "Material Girl," wherein such perfectly whorish sentiments as "the boy with the cold hard cash / Is always Mister Right" or "Only boys who save their pennies make my rainy day" are given her cutest "Boy Toy" treatment. Harrumph. Not to quote Marx on anybody, but a world where "because I have money I can surround myself with beautiful women" is still an *ugly* one. Furthermore, if we were truly "living in a material world," we would no longer allow materials to be produced and distributed in such a way that millions of "boys who save their pennies" find their real wages steadily eroded and, periodically, their very livelihoods pulled out from under them. (Sorry, but now and then me old pamphleteering self takes charge.)

But to turn down the political heat for a cooler aesthetic assessment, what's flawed about this package? First (and in her defense), it's much less Madonna's own than was the first LP; hence, it feels too *groomed*, by too many Svengalis. The result is a sense of multiple hedging, not to be confused with having it both ways, as Sheena Easton does on "Strut," or better, Sheila E. on *The Glamorous Life* (which gets my vote for self-deconstructing, inside/outside album of the year). For instance, while Madonna toys with a softcore porn look, she contrives to innocentize it with Lower Manhattan punkette artiness (wouldn't wanna smudge that mascara, fellas). Net effect: Apollonia 6 does better, and more honest, porn—a male-defined catering service, if you like, but such great cakes! Moreover, Madonna hasn't the courage of her rancidly Reaganite convictions: she hedges on the stark brutalism of "Material Girl" and the ruthless careerism of "Over and Over" when she tries to come on all vulnerable and abandoned for "Pretender" or Streisand's old hit, "Love Don't Live Here Anymore." This latter stance is particularly grating in the light of Christopher Connelly's recent *Rolling Stone* profile, which makes amply clear who's always done the abandoning in her case, ruthless ambition being her sole autobiographical truth. (In fact, if she'd do something thematically consistent along the lines of: "I'm a vile, heartless capitalist slut, and guys who fall for me are chumps," I'd respond: Bravo, wotta concept, Brecht lives!) Similarly noxious, both on "Over and Over" and in her *Rolling Stone* remarks, is her est-ian, *Fame*-derived horseshit about "having the drive"—which, of course, invariably takes the narrowest bourgeois direction. You know, I'm getting-my-act-together-because-*bellum-omnia-contra-omnes*-is-the-only-game-in-town-or-at-any-rate-the-only-one-my-polluted-imagination-can-envisage. In this view, as you may be aware, everyone else simply doesn't "have the drive." But what if some of us would rather drive somewhere else? Such as those inexorably advancing toward the main arteries around San Salvador? *No pasarán!* And just think: while many of us, driveless fools, were squandering valuable, or valorizable, time on negotiating a delicate give-and-take with our lovers, seeking to better the world, or simply enjoying our friends, this young perox calculator was singlemindedly scratching her way up the careerist ladder. Let us, therefore, learn from her example.

Nonetheless, or allthemore, *Like a Virgin* is presently bulleting the charts, largely because it's the long-awaited sequel to a remarkably strong, durable, and singles-rich predecessor. But unless there's even less justice in the world than Union Carbide is counting on, this one should peak soon and fade fast (then again, maybe she'll do something *really* lascivious in a video). Given what Madonna herself once put together on a four-track for the original version of "Everybody," I'm amazed at how unfunky and thinly textured the whole thing is. Even the most enjoyable cuts here—innocuous, well-crafted fluff like "Angel," "Dress You Up," or "Shoo-Bee-Doo"—while continuing the girlish exuberance, lack the bottomy presence that Reggie Lucas achieved on *Madonna*. For once, Nile Rodgers's production is oddly disappointing. The rhythmically retro title track, for instance, exposes the not-necessarily-endearing frailty of her voice. But it's Number One, right? Just goes to show you how little musical merit can matter. Since Sheila E. and Teena Marie both have a dozen times the chops . . . Oh, never mind. Jack Nicholson gave the answer in *Carnal Knowledge*: "Believe me, looks are *everything*."

(from *The First Rock & Roll Confidential Report*)

Girls Can't Do What the Guys Do: Madonna's Physical Attraction

by Dave Marsh

Just take this advice I give you, just like a mother . . .
Don't try to do what the guys do.
'Cause girls, you can't do what the guys do—and still
be a lady.

—Betty Wright

In a sense, rock has attempted to refute Betty Wright's teen-aged vision of the way its world works ever since she made her 1968 hit. For years, the situation seemed all but hopeless, unless you imagined that a choice between a brassy alcoholic mama like Janis Joplin or a woozy alcoholic harridan like Grace Slick was worth getting excited about.

For white rock singers at the time Wright (fourteen, black, and knowing) sang, Joplin and Slick were the only models offered. As a result, rock's sexual dialogue became stunted. In soul, Otis Redding had to answer to Carla Thomas; in country, Conway Twitty's roving eye was matched by Loretta Lynn's sass and suss. But in rock, from its infancy through the mid-seventies, sexual expression is characterized by a startling, matter-of-fact adolescent chauvinism. Even during the soft-rock, singer/songwriter period of the early seventies, when more white female voices returned to the radio, such stereotypes remained inviolate. Through Joni Mitchell and Carly Simon, rock reabsorbed the guitar-strumming long-haired folk "chick"; through Linda Ronstadt, it recycled its earth mother fetish. That wasn't progress. And the few women who stood outside of or transcended their assigned roles (Mitchell, Carole King, Sandy Denny) were isolated in every sense. Think of great black pop or country artists, and you're at least as likely to think of women as men: Diana Ross, Aretha Franklin, Tina Turner, Loretta Lynn, Dolly Parton, Tammy Wynette. Yet, from rock's beginning to the mid-seventies of the Eagles and Led Zeppelin, women figure in rock mostly as objects of defamation and desire.

The boys' club atmosphere began to give way by the end of the seventies, when rock was again integrated with black-based styles in disco's aftermath. Around the same time, the rise of the punk esthetic (marketed in its own aftermath as "new wave") allowed a few women to begin asserting some of the cherished prerogatives of male stars: to appear loud, vulgar, arrogant, self-indulgent, angry, hotheaded, wearing leather and studs, snarling and swearing, coming on to the crowd. Patti Smith, Donna Summer, Chrissie Hynde, Ann Wilson, Nona Hendryx, and Joan Jett spearheaded an assault on musical and visual stereotypes. Their effect can best be measured by comparing any of them to Stevie Nicks and Christine McVie, the women at the center of Fleetwood Mac and just about the only women in any of the top rank of popular late-seventies acts.

This trend toward more independent, harder-rocking female performers came to a head in 1984. Tina Turner, Madonna, Cyndi Lauper, Jett, the Bangles, Sheila E., Chaka Khan, the Pointer Sisters, and a whole bunch of sexually integrated groups took part in it. Eurythmics' Annie Lennox epitomized what was happening by appearing in her videos in perfect, pin-stripe tailored male drag. This was both a way of highlighting the independence available to Lennox, as a star regardless of gender, and of emphasizing that the basic rock roles remain male-defined.

Part of Lennox's point was that rock was a long way from resolving its sexual dilemmas, but her performance also established that it had at least begun to confront them. The termite feminism of Cyndi Lauper's giddy Day-Glo Gracie Allen act, the strut-your-stuff heavy metallisms of Wilson and Jett, even the one-of-the-guys rock band metaphors used by the Go-Gos and the Bangles, challenge unconscious assumptions about how rock is made and heard. Tina Turner has seized on this intelligently, and her maturity, raging emotionalism, and self-sufficiency perfectly offset her onstage sultriness; she's a lot more interesting and attractive now than when she was Ike's pet microphone fellatrist.

Madonna, on the other hand, asks much more from this confrontation. Alone among her generation of female rock stars, she seems, superficially, a hidebound throwback to all that was meretricious and maybe even outright evil about the roles into which women were earlier forced. And to compound the problem, she seems to have adopted those roles and stratagems eagerly. As a result she has been called a slut by at least one *Rolling Stone* editor and an enemy by *The Village Voice. Boston Phoenix* music editor Milo Miles has described Madonna as "the kind of woman who comes into your room at three A.M. and sucks your life out."

There isn't much in Madonna's music—songs like "Lucky Star," "Physical Attraction," "Like a Virgin," "Material Girl," "Borderline," and "Holiday"—to inspire such critical and reportorial venom. True, Madonna's voice, for all its huskiness, is thin and not a little reedy. Goodness knows, her style is not only unoriginal; the disco divas and show-tune belters on whom she's based it are among the most overwrought and overenunciated in pop. A white Deniece Williams we don't need.

On the other hand, *Madonna*, her first album, released in late 1983 but containing material made as early as 1982, is impeccably produced, the songs are consistently interesting, and Madonna sings them freely. Mostly produced by Reggie Lucas (two ex-boyfriends produced a track each), the music is simple, with a light touch and a mobile groove. If you listened to the radio much in 1983 and 1984, Madonna almost certainly captured your ear—willingly or unwillingly—at some point with one of these tracks.

Her second album, *Like a Virgin*, was considerably weaker, but by the time it was released, the critics and journalists had already made up their minds (and they'd been doing precious little thinking about the music anyway). They're more upset by her lyrics and her persona as expressed in her videos and on her album covers. There Madonna comes on not just sensuous but positively horny. She describes her persona as "flirty," but too many of her listeners and viewers see it as something much worse. To them, she's a cocktease, a slut, a sleaze, a shameless wanton. Madonna, after all, wears lace and lingerie as outerwear; she exposes her midriff and wears a belt buckle reading "Boy Toy." She flaunts her clothes, jewelry, and hairstyle as brazenly as any tart.

Rolling Stone's Madonna cover story, the nastiest such hatchet job the magazine has run in many years, rested its indictment on the idea that her private life is consistent with her public image. According to writer Christopher Connelly, Madonna used a series of boyfriends to advance her career, teach her about music and the music industry, provide connections—and then each boyfriend was dumped and Madonna was on to someone else with more pull or expertise. Connelly, not alone among Madonna-watchers, seemed to take this abandonment personally.

Madonna denies none of the facts. But, she told Laura Fissinger, "If anybody wants to know, I never fucked anyone to get anywhere. Never. . . . Yes, all my boyfriends turned out to be very helpful to my career, but that's not the only reason I stayed with them. I loved them very much."

Unfortunately that's not the issue, either. Connelly's criticisms really stem from a more sexist assumption—that Madonna should have stayed with her boyfriends *no matter what*, that she had no business indulging in summary serial romances. This is pretty funny coming from a magazine—and a reporter—in the habit of canonizing the sluttish behavior of the likes of Mick Jagger. By the time he was Madonna's age (twenty-six), Jagger had been through a hell of a lot more lovers than the four or five anybody has pinned on Madonna—and a lot of his lovers were equally useful to his career. Nobody ever called Mick Jagger a strumpet. Nor should they have.

Instead of dealing with this forthrightly, as a syndrome in pop culture, reporters (Connelly is only the most juvenile) have mostly written in tones of titillated innuendo combined with creepy moralism. Reading articles about Madonna, you could get the idea that it was the habit of pop journalists to marry the first person they slept with. Or you could start to feel that you were overhearing some particularly ugly eighth-grade locker-room gossip about a girl with a "bad reputation." Maybe this just shows how much feminism hasn't changed the world. But judging from the outraged reaction received when *RRC* published a few kind words for Madonna's hits, such writing speaks also for a large part of the rock listenership that considers itself on the side of the feminist angels.

So if Madonna's hits were less enjoyable, she'd still be intriguing, because she flies in the face of the orthodox postfeminist idea of how a young woman ought to present herself. The point of Betty Wright's hit is in its final words: "*. . . and still be a lady.*" Uniquely among pop singers, Madonna doesn't want to do what the guys do—but she would like to remain "a lady," that is, someone comfortable within a relatively conventional role as a woman.

Most female rock stars have dealt with the truth Wright expresses by abandoning femininity, adopting poses that deny, disfigure, or distance them from the fundamentally feminine aspects of their sexuality. Thus, we get the more-macho-than-thou stance of Hynde, Cyndi Lauper's subordination of sexuality to weirdness, Lennox's "androgyny" (a denial of gender itself). Or else the forbidding expressionism of post-punk singers like Lora Logic and Lydia Lunch, the disembodied vocalisms of Laurie Anderson, the didacticism of the Raincoats and Au Pairs. Cyndi Lauper sings that girls just want to have fun, but very few women in pop seem to be having a good time without forcing the issue (the Go-Gos must have had their smiles painted on). Of them all, only Madonna sings like the girl who is willing to live up to the scariest implication of Lauper's hit: She is a girl having fun and *fuck the consequences.*

Cyndi Lauper stumbled into her feminist role without intending to do so. Madonna will never face that option—or that problem. But Lauper is mostly talk: Madonna's all action. She's the girl who has stopped wanting and started having and suddenly realizes fun in all its dimensions, including the hurt when the fun starts to stop. Because Madonna has no better solution to this pain than to party some more, she may seem the enemy of those who wish the world was a better place, I guess. But isn't it interesting that men who say the same thing—Jagger and David Bowie leap to mind—are almost never criticized for *their* indulgence and hedonism? Madonna's supposed to be the slut but, unlike Jagger or Sheila E., she has *never* feigned giving anyone an onstage blowjob.

Madonna's songs consistently speak from a woman's perspective. Even putting the words in Cyndi Lauper's mouth, Tom Gray's "Money Changes Everything" is a song that outlines a male point of view. By the same token, even though "Material Girl" was also written by males, only a woman could make it make sense. In "Material Girl," Madonna speaks for the otherwise unheard girl in "Money Changes Everything."

A lot of what she says is steeped in lame self-justification ("Experience has made me rich"; "If they don't give me proper credit / I just walk away"). But Madonna properly rejects the misconceptions that the person who ends a relationship is usually wrong and that affairs ought to end as the result of purely emotional problems, never because of material ones. "Material Girl" is the closest rock comes to showing us how such a person might think and feel as she's walking out the door. In the end, she even hits on a rationalization that makes sense:

> 'Cause *everybody's* living in a material world
> And I am a material girl

That doesn't sound like anyone who would suck your breath away in your sleep. It sounds like a person who knows what she wants, has a pretty good idea why, and isn't afraid to slam it right in your face if you think she should give it up for something as ephemeral as rock 'n' romance. (In that sense, "Material Girl" even doubles back and functions as a waspish commentary on Madonna's own gushing love fantasies.)

"Material Girl" is a perfect expression of the rock and roll dance club world with its wealthy, hyped-up clientele rubbing elbows with lowlifes and street flotsam, everybody drifting, desperate to connect. Madonna probably speaks more clearly about the twisted values of this scene, which produces much of the best and worst in contemporary pop, than anyone before her. And she does this less out of arrogance than out of defensiveness.

"There was this one review that said things about me that boys said to me in the seventh grade . . . for instance—'slut,' " Madonna told Fissinger. "Yep, they called me that in this review. And 'cheap coquette,' a girl who made her way into lots of back seats in the drive-in theater, the kind of girl that made your father slip you a Trojan and pat you on the back and say, 'Have a good time, don't stay out too late.' I remember guys saying that sort of stuff to me when I was really young. I thought suddenly that the whole experience was repeating itself all over again. Those boys didn't understand me, and they didn't like me because I wasn't stupid and I *was* blunt and opinionated, but I was a flirt at the same time. They took my aggressiveness as a come-on. They didn't get it. And they didn't *get it*, if you know what I mean, so I guess they had to say things because they knew that was the only way they could hurt me. That review felt like junior high all over again."

In many ways, Madonna sounds like junior high all over again—the same confusion and anger, the same insensitivity on everybody's part, the same inability to reckon with the consequences of appearance and image. In many ways, she is the stellar product of the environment that produced her—which means contemporary pop culture itself, with all its male domination, juvenilia, and lust to consume before being consumed.

But compensation for Madonna shouldn't be extended to an endorsement of her lifestyle of absolute hedonism, her damn-the-side-effects outlook—although the fact that even such an attractive "have" can feel like an abused outsider ought to inspire some reaction more complicated than cries of envy and enmity, some words more compassionate than slurs like "slut."

There's something horrifying taking place in "Holiday," the first club hit Madonna had (and the only one produced by a boyfriend). "You can turn this world around / And bring back all of those happy days," she sings. It would be hard to conceive of another pop song that so closely resembles that false optimism of the fake economic recovery of the eighties. "It's time for the good time / Forget about the bad times"—it could be a campaign slogan.

That's where Madonna started out. And such sentiments walk hand in hand with the mindset that produced "Physical Attraction": "You say you wanna stay the night / But you'll leave me tomorrow—I don't care / All of your moves are right." If we can't be real, if we can't touch below the surface of our lives, let's at least be *cool*.

Compare those lines to the Shirelles' "Will You Still Love Me Tomorrow," one of the few girl group songs that actually articulates a girl's feelings (as opposed to a male fantasy of those feelings), and you've traveled about as far as rock can currently reach. "Will You Still Love Me Tomorrow" is transported to greatness by its innocence, but that innocence is feigned: If you have to ask the question, you already know the answer.

There are plenty of forces on the sexual battleground insisting that we replay some version of this fake struggle. Or else, demanding that we bottle up our sexual energies in some other way. Ultimately, that means denying not only sexual desires, but all material aspirations. The goal is to get us to settle for what we already have. Madonna is, in her way, more radical than Cyndi Lauper. She argues not only that girls want to have fun but that girls—like everybody else—want to *have*. This is the side of what she is saying and doing that brings puritanism out of its ugly closet, in one last attempt to put material desire in a defensive shell.

The demand is unrealistic and oppressive. *People* want to have, and insisting that those wants be perpetually delayed or that they're just "bad" flies in the face of human nature and human needs. Such demands inevitably beget an extremely unrealistic agenda of the opposite stripe. Understood that way, Madonna becomes the incarnation of a dialectical process—she really is a material girl. In that sense, her fame is not the product of an extremely shrewd individual calculation (which is what she seems to believe) but the consequence of historic necessity.

Such necessities have an odd way of throwing up exactly the kind of personifications who not only symbolize the contradiction but push it toward a resolution. "Holiday" was Madonna's first hit. "Material Girl" is her most recent. That sounds like progress to me.

(from *The New Yorker*)

by Modell

"Since when was Madonna your cup of tea?"

(from *Rocking Around the Clock*)

On the "Material Girl" Video

by E. Ann Kaplan

Let me begin with a video, "Material Girl," featuring Madonna, the female star who perhaps more than any other embodies the new postmodern feminist heroine in her odd combination of seductiveness and a gutsy sort of independence.

"Material Girl" is particularly useful for discussion because it exemplifies a common rock-video phenomenon, namely that of establishing a unique kind of intertextual relationship with a specific Hollywood movie. Because of this, as well as the difficulty of ensuring the text's stance toward what it shows and the blurring of many conventional boundaries, I would put the video in the "postmodern" category, despite its containing more narrative than is usual for the type.

As is well known, "Material Girl" takes off from the famous Marilyn Monroe dance/song sequence in *Gentlemen Prefer Blondes*, namely "Diamonds Are a Girl's Best Friend." The sequence occurs toward the end of the film where Esmond's father has severed Lorelei (Monroe) financially from Esmond, forcing her to earn her living by performing. In this sequence, having finally found her, Esmond is sitting in the audience watching the show. We thus have the familiar Hollywood situation, where the woman's performing permits her double articulation as spectacle for the male gaze (i.e., she is object of desire for both the male spectator in the diegetic audience and for the spectator in the cinema watching the film). The strategy formalizes the mirror-phase situation by framing the female body both within the stage proscenium arch and the cinema screen.

During this sequence, which starts with Esmond's astonished gaze at Lorelei from the theater seat (presumably he is surprised anew by

Lorelei's sexiness), Lorelei directs her gaze toward the camera that is situated in Esmond's place. The space relations are thus quite simple, there being merely the two spaces of the stage and of the theater audience. We know that the film is being made under the authorial label "Hawkes," that within the diegesis, Monroe and Russell are setting up the action, but that, despite this, the patriarchal world in which they move constrains them and makes only certain avenues available.

When we turn to the video inspired by the Monroe dance sequence, we see that the situation is far more complicated. First, it is unclear who is speaking this video, even on the remote "authorial label" level, since credits are never given in the usual run of things. Is it perhaps Madonna, as historical star subject? Is it "Madonna I," the movie-star protagonist within the "framing" diegesis? Is it "Madonna II," the figure within the musical dance diegesis? Is it the director who has fallen in love with her image and desires to possess her? If we focus first on the visual strategies and then on the soundtrack, you will see that we get different and still confusing answers to the question.

Visually, the director's (D) gaze seems to structure some of the shots, but this is not consistent, as it is in the Monroe sequence. And shots possibly structured by him (or in which he is later discovered to have been present) only occur at irregular intervals. The video begins by foregrounding (perhaps pastiching?) the classical Hollywood male gaze: there is a close-up of the director, played by Keith Carradine (the video thus bows again to the classical film), whom we soon realize is watching rushes of a film starring "Madonna I" with an obsessed, glazed look on his face. "I want her, George," he says; George promises to deliver, as we cut to a two-shot of the men, behind whom we see the cinema screen and Madonna I's image but as yet hear no sound from the performance. The camera closes in on her face, and on her seductive look first out to the camera then sideways to the men around her. As the camera now moves into the screen, blurring the boundaries between screening room, screen, and the film set (the space of the performance that involves the story of the Material Girl, Madonna II), the "rehearsal" (if that is what it was) ends, and a rich lover comes onto the set with a large present for Madonna I.

This then is a desire for the woman given birth through the cinematic apparatus, in classic manner; yet while the sequence seems to *foreground* those mechanisms, it does not appear to critique or in any way comment upon them. In Fredric Jameson's terms, this makes the process pastiche rather than parody and puts it in the postmodernist mode. The blurring of the diegetic spaces further suggests postmodernism, as does the following confusion of enunciative stances, taking the visual track alone. For while the D's gaze clearly constructed the first shot-series, it is not clear that his gaze structures the shot where Madonna I receives the present. We still hear the whirring sound of a projector, as if this were still the screening room space; and yet we are *inside* that screen—we no longer see the space around the frame, thus disorienting the viewer.

We cut to a close-up of a white phone ringing and a hand picking it up, and are again confused spatially. Where are we? Whose look is this? There has been no narrative preparation for the new space or for the spectator address: the phone monologue by Madonna I (the only time in the entire video that she speaks) establishes the space as her dressing room. As she speaks, the camera behaves oddly (at least in standard Hollywood conventions), dollying back slowly to the door of her room, to reveal standing there the D. Was it then his gaze that structured the shot? At the moment of reaching him, the gaze certainly *becomes* his, Madonna I seen to be its object. The phone monologue that he overhears, along with the viewer, establishes that Madonna I has just received a diamond necklace, which causes the D to throw his present into the waste basket that the janitor happens to be carrying out that moment. It also establishes that Madonna I is *not* the "material girl" of her stage role, since she offers the necklace to her (presumed) girlfriend on the phone.

We now cut back to the stage space that we presume is the film set; it is not clear, since the diegesis does not foreground the filming processes, and yet there is no audience space. Rather, Madonna II sets up a direct rapport with the camera filming the rock video, and therefore with the TV spectator, deliberately playing for him/her rather than for the men in frame. But the spatial disorientation continues: there is a sudden cut to the rear of a flashy red car driving into the studio, followed by shots of Madonna I's elegant body in matching red dress (knees carefully visible), of her rich lover bending over her, and of her face and apparently dismissive reply. Whose gaze is this? Who is enunciating here? As Madonna I leaves the car, we discover the D again, but the series of shots could not have been structured by his gaze.

We cut back to the stage/film set for the most extended sequence of the performance in the video. This sequence follows the Monroe "Diamonds" dance closely, and stands in the strange intertextual relationship already mentioned: we cannot tell whether or not the Monroe sequence is being commented upon, simply used, or ridiculed by exaggeration (which sometimes seems to be happening). Things are more complicated by the fact that *Gentlemen Prefer Blondes* is itself a comedy, itself mocking and exaggerating certain patriarchal gender roles. The situation is further confused by occasional play with the image in the video, destroying even the illusion of the stability of the stage/set space; at least once, a two-shot of Madonna II and one of the lovers is simply flipped over, in standard rock-video style but in total violation of classical codes that seek to secure illusionism.

Since there is no diegetic audience, the spectator is now in direct rapport with Madonna's body, as she performs for the TV spectator. There is again no diegetic source of enunciation; the spectator either remains disoriented, or secures a position through the body of the historical star, Madonna, implied as "producing" the video or simply fixed on as a centering force. This is an issue to be taken up shortly.

Most of the camera work in the dance sequence involves sharp images and either long shots (the camera follows Madonna II's movements around the stage) or straight cuts; but toward the end of the dance rehearsal, the style changes to superimpositions and deliberately blurry shots, suggestive perhaps of a heightened eroticism. The camera allows Madonna II's head to be carried by the men underneath itself, so that only her arm remains in view; after some "dazed" shots, the camera pans left along the edge of the set to discover brown stairs with the D standing by them, gazing at the performance. But once again, the sequence was not set up, as it would have been in conventional Hollywood codes, as his structuring gaze; the gaze is only discovered *after* the fact, thus allowing enunciative confusion.

The same disorientation continues in a shot (perhaps a flash forward, although that term suggests the kind of narrative coherence that is precisely missing here) that follows after another dance sequence. Here the D is seen bringing simple daisies to a now smiling and receptive Madonna I, clothed in white (a play on Hollywood signifiers for innocence?), in her dressing room. We cut to the end of the stage performance (there are repeated blurry shots as before, again signifying, perhaps, sexual delirium), before a final cut to the space outside the studio, where the D is seen paying someone for the loan of a car. As Madonna I walks seductively out of the studio, the D ushers her into his car. The last shot is taken through the now rain-sodden glass (inexplicable diegetically) and shows their embrace.

This brief analysis of the main shots and use of diegetic spaces demonstrates the ways in which conventions of the classic Hollywood film, which paradoxically provided the inspiration for the video, are routinely violated. The purpose here was to show how even in a video that at first appears precisely to remain within those conventions—unlike many other videos whose extraordinary and avant-garde techniques are immediately obvious—regular narrative devices are not adhered to. But the video violates classic traditions even more with its sound-image relations.

This aspect of the video brings up the question of the rock video's uniqueness as an artistic form, namely as a form in which the sound of the song, and the "content" of its lyrics, is prior to the creation of images to accompany the music and the words. While there are analogies to both the opera and to the Hollywood musical, neither form prepares for the rock video in which the song–image relationship is quite unique. The uniqueness has to do with a certain arbitrariness of the images used along with any particular song, with the lack of limitations spatially, with the frequently extremely rapid montage-style editing not found generally (if at all) in the Hollywood musical song/dance sequences, and finally with the precise relationship of sound—both musical and vocal—to image. This relationship involves (a) the links between musical rhythms and significations of instrumental sounds, and images provided for them; (b) links between the significations of the song's actual *words* and images conjured up to convey that "content"; (c) links between any one musical phrase and the accompanying words, and the relay of images as that phrase is being played and sung.

This is obviously a very complex topic—far beyond my scope here—but let me demonstrate some of the issues in relation to "Material Girl," where again things are far simpler than in many videos. We have seen that on the visual track there are two distinct but linked discourses, that involving the D's desire for Madonna I (his determined pursuit and eventual "winning" of her), and that of Madonna I's performance, where she plays Madonna II, the "material girl." These discourses are not hierarchically arranged as in the usual Hollywood film, but rather exist on a horizontal axis, neither subordinated to the other. In terms of screen time, however, the performance is given more time.

When we turn to the soundtrack, we find that, after the brief introductory scene in the screening room (a scene, by the way, often cut from the video), the soundtrack consists entirely of the lyrics for the song "Material Girl." This song deals with the girl who will only date boys who "give her proper credit," and for whom love is reduced to money. Thus, all the visuals pertaining to the D–Madonna I love story do not have any correlate on the soundtrack. We merely have two short verbal sequences (in the screening room and dressing room) to carry the entire other story: in other words, soundtrack and image track are not linked for that story. An obvious example of this discrepancy is the shot of Madonna I (arriving at the studio in the flashy car) rejecting her rich lover: Madonna lip-syncs "That's right" from the "Material Girl" song—a phrase that refers there to her only loving boys who give her money—in a situation where the opposite is happening: She *refuses* to love the man who is wealthy!

In other words, the entire video is subordinated to the words with their signifieds that refer in fact only to the stage performance. The common device in the Hollywood musical of having the dance interlude simply an episode in the main story seems here to be reversed: the performance is central while the love story is reduced to the status merely of a framing narrative. Significant here also is the disjunction between the two stories, the framing story being about a "nice" girl, and the performance being about the "bad" girl: but even these terms are blurred by the obvious seductiveness of the "nice" girl, particularly as she walks at the end toward the car in a very knowing manner.

We see thus that the usual hierarchical arrangement of discourses in the classical realist text is totally violated in "Material Girl." While Madonna I is certainly set up as object of the D's desire, in quite classical manner, the text refuses to let her be controlled by that desire. This is achieved by unbalancing the relations between framing story and per-formance story so that Madonna I is overridden by her stage figure, Madonna II, the brash, gutsy "material girl." The line between "fiction" and "reality" within the narrative is thus blurred: this has severe conse-quences just because the two women are polar opposites.

In *Gentlemen Prefer Blondes*, on the other hand, no such confusion or discrepancy exists. From the start, Monroe's single-minded aim is to catch a rich man, and she remains fixed on that throughout. The function of her performances of "Diamonds Are a Girl's Best Friend" is partly simply to express what has been obvious to the spectator, if not to Esmond, all along; but also to let Esmond get the idea, were he smart enough. Lorelei sings a song that expresses her philosophy of life, but we are clear about the lines between the stage-fiction and the context of its presentation, and Monroe as a character in the narrative. Part of the confusion in the Madonna video comes about precisely because the scene of the performance is not made very clear and because the lines between the different spaces of the text are blurred.

The situation in "Material Girl" is even more problematic because of the way that Madonna, as historical star subject, breaks through her narrative positions via her strong personality, her love of performing for the camera, her inherent energy and vitality. Madonna searches for the camera's gaze and for the TV spectator's gaze that follows it because she relishes being desired. The "roles" melt away through her unique presence and the narrative incoherence discussed above seems resolved in our understanding that Madonna herself, as historical subject, is the really "material girl."

It is perhaps Madonna's success in articulating and parading the desire to be desired in an unabashed, aggressive, gutsy manner (as against the self-abnegating urge to lose oneself in the male that is evident in the classical Hollywood film) that attracts the hordes of twelve-year-old fans who idolize her and crowd her concerts. The amazing "look alike" Madonna contests (viz. a recent Macy's campaign in New York) and the successful exploitation of the weird Madonna style of dress by clothing companies attests to this idolatry. It is significant that Madonna's early style is a far cry from the conventional "patriarchal feminine" of the women's magazines—it is a cross between a bordello queen and a bag lady: young teenagers may use her as a protest against their mothers and the normal feminine while still remaining very much within those modes (in the sense of spending a lot of money, time, and energy on their "look"; the "look" is still crucial to their identities, still designed to attract attention, even if provocatively).

In some sense, then, Madonna represents the postmodern feminist heroine in that she combines unabashed seductiveness with a gutsy kind of independence. She is neither particularly male nor female identified, and seems mainly to be out for herself. This postmodern feminism is part of a larger postmodernist phenomenon which her video also embodies in its blurring of hitherto sacrosanct boundaries and polarities of the various kinds discussed. The usual bipolar categories— male/female, high art/pop art, film/TV, fiction/reality, private/public, interior/exterior, etc.—simply no longer apply to "Material Girl."

This analysis of "Material Girl" has shown the ambiguity of enunciative positions within the video that in turn is responsible for the ambiguous representation of the female image. The positioning of a video like "Material Girl," moreover, within the twenty-four-hour flow on this commercial MTV channel, allows us to see that it is *this* sort of ambiguous image that appears frequently, as against any other possible female images, which are only rarely cycled. That the video was directed by a woman, Mary Lambert, does not affect this argument. I would not collapse biological sexuality and ideological position. The postfeminist ambiguous images are clearly the ones sponsors consider "marketable," since they are not only most frequently cycled but also propagated in the ad texts that are interspersed among the video texts.

(from *The New York Times*)

The New York Whats

by Russell Baker

I **had just said** "Madonna who?" when *The New York Times* landed on the doorstep.

"You've got to be kidding," said the kid to whom I had just said "Madonna who?"

"Shove off, kid," said I, picking up the newspaper of record. "It's time to find out who did it to whom in Lebanon again yesterday."

Yes, that's what I really said: "Who did it to whom."

Around civilized people I would be embarrassed to say "Who did it to whom," but this was a kid I was addressing, and kids have to learn how to say things right before they're entitled to say them wrong when saying them right would sound silly.

"Madonna and Her Clones" was the headline that caught my eye in the newspaper of record, and the sentences that exhausted my dwindling supply of patience said:

"She uses only one name, but no matter. Only those who have been residing on the planet Jupiter for the last several years need to ask Madonna who?"

Why? Because she is "rock's hottest female star."

Well, my dear *New York Times*, I have not been on the planet Jupiter these past few years, so I know that rock is a form of popular music which is incredibly loud, has lyrics that are unintelligible though painful to the ear, and breeds a steady supply of stars who exude high levels of heat. The rule is: The more heat the star gives off, the bigger the audience.

Thus, being "rock's hottest female star" means Madonna is raking in plenty of what used to be called moolah, but is probably now called BTU, of which her agent takes 10 percent and governments 50 percent

. . . . **47**

of the remainder, leaving her with only 45 percent of the take, provided she can collect it, which in her line of work can sometimes require lawyers if not people handy with guns.

Admittedly I am showing off a bit here, but only to prove to the reader that I am deeply versed in contemporary American culture. For this reason I resent *The New York Times*'s suggestion that my saying "Madonna who?" means I must have been off the planet for several years.

The more I think about *New York Times* arrogance, the more I sympathize with that wide spectrum of opinion ranging from *The Village Voice* to Accuracy in Media to the *New York Post*, which holds that *The New York Times* simply won't do, and ought to be replaced by superior outfits like *The Village Voice*, Accuracy in Media and the *New York Post*.

Why does the *Times* choose to ridicule those of us who still said "Madonna who?" until we picked up the newspaper of record and read "Madonna and her Clones"? Does the *Times* think we have nothing to keep informed about except the waxing and waning heat of rock stars?

Speaking of waxing and waning heat, I haven't seen anything in the *Times* lately about Prince or Michael Jackson. What is the state of their heat? It is not easy to keep abreast of the rock-star news when the newspaper of record deals with it only sporadically, but I try—Heaven knows, I try.

It seems scarcely a year ago that the hottest of all possible stars was Michael Jackson, but while still digesting that fact I was astonished to discover that tremendous heat was suddenly being exuded by Prince, a male rock star whose wardrobe includes an ankle-length blanket of purple sequins.

"What is this!" I exclaimed. "Michael Jackson has lost his heat, and the heat is now with Prince?"

I was reminded of the first book of Kings, which tells us that after King David became "old and stricken in years" the doctors tried everything, but "he has no heat." Had Michael Jackson become old and stricken in years? The *Times* was mute, as it has been on Prince's thermal condition lately.

All we have is this out-of-the-blue sneer because we have been so busy trying to find the temperatures of Prince and Michael Jackson that we didn't know somebody named Madonna was suddenly at maximum heat.

It is hard to bear, *New York Times*. Hard to bear the proud newspaper's contumely, the more so since we at whom you sneer struggle daily to keep up with who did it to whom again yesterday in Lebanon. Hard to bear from a newspaper on which not a soul, I wager, could tell you, without making a trip to the library, how Russ Columbo died.

(from *Madonna Nudes 1979*)

by Martin Schreiber

(from *Rolling Stone*)

Madonna

by Helen Gurley Brown

During the sixties and seventies, everybody was so pure and dedicated to causes other than themselves. It was a rough time for me because I *am* a materialistic girl. Well, along comes this girl with this great hit record "Material Girl," and that charmed me: I thought, "At last!" She looks fantastic, she's a good actress, and I love her clothes. She also has a great body, which you can actually see some of. I know women who have lovely bosoms, thirty-six-inch bosoms, and you wouldn't even know because they wear turtleneck sweaters. If you have such a lovely body, why not make the most of it? I was not the least bit appalled by her pictures in *Penthouse*. She never pretended to be Miss America. Another thing I love about her is she seems to love men; she has made some men happy, and they have made her happy. Madonna has done a little living.

(from *Spin*)

Madonna

by Henry Rollins

Madonna—she makes me want to drink
beer, she makes me want to drive fast and
go bowling, she makes me want to shop at
Sears, she makes me want to kick vegetarians
When I hear her sing, I know she's
singing to me, she wants to get nasty
with me. When I see her face
when I see her eyes

when I see her lips
talking to me
telling me to come on,
I get to feeling mean
I get to feeling like
I wanna do a whole
lot of pushups
or go to a hardware

store. Then
I have to cool down
I gotta cool down
It's either gonna be:
a cold shower,
or a Bruce Springsteen record.

▶ From *Rolling Stone* Polls, 1985

ARTIST OF THE YEAR

1. Bruce Springsteen
2. Phil Collins
3. Sting
4. Bob Geldof
5. *Madonna*

BEST FEMALE SINGER

1. Tina Turner
2. *Madonna*

SEXIEST FEMALE

1. Tina Turner
2. *Madonna*

BEST-DRESSED FEMALE

1. Tina Turner
2. *Madonna*

WORST-DRESSED FEMALE

1. *Madonna*

(from the *Boston Phoenix*)

Primadonna

by Joyce Millman

Most girls who grew up during the sixties and early seventies learned more about their place in society from Barbie than they did from their mothers. Barbie was the madonna/whore complex molded into shapely plastic, a mute ideal of wholesome yet suggestive beauty emphasized in adorable-sexy clothes designed to turn Ken's head its full 360 degrees. She could be outfitted for a range of glamorous fantasy careers or rewarding helpmate ones. And, having no genitals, she was an archetype of chastity. Of course, the most coveted item in the Barbie wardrobe was a voluminous white lace wedding gown. So in 1984, when Madonna Louise Ciccone, Barbie's most apt pupil, posed in a (punky) white wedding gown for the laughably literal madonna/whore cover of her second album, *Like a Virgin*, the little girls—and a lot of us big girls—understood. Madonna was not out to attack traditional institutions or soil traditional daydreams (how could the glowing romantic-rebirth imagery of "Like a Virgin" have been so seriously misread?). No, she was as staunchly middle-class as the most loyal of her fans; like them, she was shaped by the pop culture that Barbie reflected—parents' Fab Fifties stability mixed with the fallout of sixties social change and the trickle-down of seventies permissiveness. For the young girls who bought *Like a Virgin* in droves and made her the most popular (and notorious) white female singer of her time, Madonna is the last word in attitude and fashion, the epitome of cool. Madonna is the video generation's Barbie.

And those girls couldn't have a smarter or spunkier role model. Madonna injects middle-class ideas of femininity with examples of what feminism means to her, and it means simply "equal opportunity." Instead of Barbie's teasing aloofness, she offers an aggressive sexuality that implies it's acceptable for women not only to initiate relationships (and she does in "Physical Attraction," "Borderline," "Crazy for You," "Into the Groove," etc.) but also to enjoy them. Barbie had the land-of-make-believe carte blanche (not to mention the costumes) to be all things at once, but Madonna does it for real. A singer, songwriter, actress, comedienne, and now—on her latest, nerviest, and most assured album, *True Blue* (Sire)—a record producer, Madonna exemplifies the women's-movement slogan that any girl can grow up to be whatever she wants to be (though, not surprisingly, *Ms.* magazine didn't have the guts to make her its token rocker in its 1985 Women of the Year roundup, favoring instead the nearly presexual and less explicitly feminist Cyndi Lauper); in songs like "Over and Over" ("You try to criticize my drive") and, of course, "Material Girl," she asserts that nice girls no longer have to sublimate ambition. Most tantalizing (and controversial) is her insistence that a woman—even a professional woman—ought to be able to act flirty, sexy, or sentimental without being written off as an airhead. Like (the more buttoned-up) Chrissie Hynde, Madonna refuses to suppress her female sensibilities and urges to make it in a man's world.

Director Susan Seidelman knew what she was doing when she cast Madonna as the woman Everywoman wanted to be in *Desperately Seeking Susan*; with her independence, earthy good humor, and the-hell-with-fashion sense of style, Madonna has always suggested the brave bohemian that all the other girls admired, emulated, and whispered about in high school. Maybe that's why she's made such a persuasive pied piper. Her legion of wannabes demonstrate that things haven't really changed—girls and women are still slaves to fad and fashion, they still wait to be told what to do. But Madonna isn't merely this year's girl, like a Farrah, or a Princess Diana (whom she impersonated with such girls-play-dress-up glee on *Saturday Night Live*). She's an idol with clout, and every public move she's made since the centerfold uproar last summer shows that she's considering her power carefully. The message she delivers in her warm, lowbrow way—the balloons that fell on the audience during her *Like a Virgin* concerts read "Dreams Come True"—is no Cinderella story of passivity; it's an illustration that, yes, dreams come true *if* you work for them.

Part of Madonna's appeal is the way she sounds so carefree. Her unabashedly disco-derived singles (a string that *True Blue* continues) are tailored for maximum fun and the top ten. Madonna may have worked with a succession of (male) songwriting partners and producers for her three albums (on *True Blue*, she gets her first production credit, as an equal with Pat Leonard and Stephen Bray), but her sound is her own; her voluptuous voice, sometimes sugary and high, sometimes steamy and low, delivers a vitality, a *humanness*, that's more bewitching than any of her glamour-girl poses and more luminous than her fame. She has the flair for finding outside material that meshes with her own sentiments, and the instinct for zooming in on the pith of a song with some of the most evocative fadeouts this side of Smokey Robinson. Many of her original lyrics may be little more than romantic clichés ("You must be my lucky star," "You must be an angel"), but like girl-group divas Ronnie Spector, Darlene Love, and Mary Weiss (the Shangri-Las), Madonna uses her wholehearted singing to enrich her words. She always sounds as if she has absolute faith in her fairy tales—a faith, she understands, that binds her to her fans. Indeed, in the video for her new single "Papa Don't Preach," wearing faded jeans, a bottle-blond gamine hairdo, and an "Italians Do It Better" T-shirt, Madonna looks like your average teenage girl from Medford or Chelsea; she looks at home walking through an aging neighborhood of cramped two-family houses, opening an ornately grilled screen door, entering a family room filled with plaid furniture and her own baby pictures.

Yes, Madonna is the girl group of the eighties, sympathetically articulating the turbulent teenage emotions sparked by awakening sexuality, class consciousness, and individuality (not to mention peer pressure and parental clampdown), with bubble-gum dance trappings adding an unmistakably urban working-class ambiance. (As Regina's "Baby Love," E. G. Daily's "Say It," and Alisha's "Baby Talk," among others, attest, she's even inspired a Madonna Sound.) And the big-hearted *True Blue* is her most girl-groupish album yet, from its front-stoop view of love, work, dreams, and disappointments, to its chiming bells and female backing harmonies, to its cast of lovingly rendered Ordinary Joes. The insouciant "Where's the Party" depicts a working girl blowing off the day-to-day grind on the dance floor. In the black-leather-jacket bop "Jimmy Jimmy" (with nods to "Uptown" and "Leader of the Pack"), Madonna admires a neighborhood wiseguy's ambition all the more because she knows he's "just a boy who comes from bad places." And the tranquil "La Isla Bonita" and the Feed-the-World fiesta "Love Makes the World Go Round" are "Up on the Roof"–type imaginary escapes from the city snarl, the kind of Latin-flavored sweets that Blondie could never resist. (Madonna is what Debbie Harry might've become had Blondie not diluted their love of disco and pop with punk-intellectual irony.)

Throughout *True Blue*, Madonna transforms her own marital bliss ("This is dedicated to my husband, the coolest guy in the universe," writes Mrs. Sean Penn on the inner sleeve) into high-school-accessible scenarios of a girl breaking down a bad boy's defenses with some motherly-tender firmness. "I don't want to live out your fantasy / Love's not that easy / This time you're gonna have to play my way," she chirps in "White Heat," a scrappy valentine to James Cagney that blows kisses to the Leader of the Brat Pack as well. "I've had to work much harder than this / For something I want / Don't try to resist me," she warns in her sultriest lower register on "Open Your Heart." And in the endearing title track, Madonna finally goes to the chapel with her guy as bells ring like crazy and a trio of backing Madonnas falls into a "Johnny Angel" swoon.

But on *True Blue*'s boldest number, Madonna ventures into territory no girl group was allowed to explore. "Papa Don't Preach" (written by Brian Elliott, with additional lyrics by Madonna) is the first song she's recorded in which she takes off from her image (and accepts her role) as the voice of girlhood. In the guise of a teenager who's worked up the courage to tell her father about her unplanned pregnancy, Madonna forces her wannabes to consider the risks and responsibilities of their sexuality. She makes them agonize with her over the choice a girl "in trouble" (as the song so girls'-bathroomishly puts it) faces: she can "give it up," as her friends urge (and "give it up" is a term ambiguous enough to suggest adoption and abortion), or, as she wails with frighteningly childish stubbornness, "I made up my mind / I'm keeping my baby." Although the melody is as insistently chugging as "Into the Groove" or "Dress You Up," the mood of "Papa Don't Preach" is tense and claustrophobic, from the melodramatic slashes of strings to the way Madonna's voice wavers between brassy determination and husky uncertainty; there's only the faintest hope of happily-ever-after in her shaky "He says that he's gonna marry me / We can raise a little family / Maybe we'll be all right." And when Madonna unfurls the heartrending cry, "What I need right now is some good advice / *Please* / Papa don't preach," she expresses all the pain of growing up too fast.

On the radio during the past two months, the sparse, sirenic number-one ballad "Live to Tell" (the theme song for Sean Penn's film about terror in the bosom of the family, *At Close Range*) was a chilling riddle, Madonna's hushed singing overwhelming everything else on the top forty with its nameless sadness. What's the lesson she's learned? What's the secret she hides? On *True Blue*, "Live to Tell" makes a provocative companion to "Papa Don't Preach." With Madonna measuring the safety of silence against the urge to unburden herself, "Live to Tell" captures the utter loneliness of those times during adolescence when the world crashes down on you with each new problem, but fear of rejection, punishment, condemnation, of inflicting pain—prevents you from confiding in your parents. And that fear encircles "Papa Don't Preach." The most haunting line of the song isn't "I'm keeping my baby," but the whimper, deep into the fadeout, "Don't you stop loving me daddy." A call for parent-child communication as tortured as the Shangri-Las' "I Can Never Go Home Anymore," "Papa Don't Preach" is Madonna's finest three minutes, not merely because it addresses teen pregnancy but because it suggests that a portion of the blame rests on parents' reluctance to discuss, not lecture about, sex. At a time when pregnancy among American teens is epidemic, "Papa Don't Preach" makes parental insensitivity and unreality seem like the greater evil.

Still, despite its message that parents can no longer afford to ignore their teenagers' sexuality, "Papa Don't Preach" may well be misappropriated by the forces of repression the song scorns, the way "Born in the U.S.A." backfired on Bruce Springsteen. How long will it be before some Right-to-Life organization twists the song ("I'm keeping my baby," indeed) into an anthem? Or before Madonna is attacked by the literal-minded—or misunderstood by some of her fans—as glamorizing teen pregnancy? But, like Springsteen, Madonna trusts her listeners to get the point. Most important, "Papa Don't Preach" opens a long overdue and desperately needed discussion on a topic that, as far as pop-single queens go, has begun and ended with the Supremes' "Love Child" (and, sung from the point of view of the out-of-wedlock child, that song is just an old-fashioned scare story about the dangers of premarital sex). "Papa Don't Preach" (and all of *True Blue*) shows that Madonna has figured out a way to get tough while remaining ravishingly faithful to her fans' concerns, to pop simplicity, and to herself. At last, Barbie has a voice. Female adolescence will never be the same.

(from *Reading the Popular*)

Madonna

by John Fiske

Madonna, who has been a major phenomenon of popular culture throughout the late 1980s, is a rich terrain to explore. Her success has been due at least as much to her videos and her personality as to her music—about which most critics are disparaging. It is also significant that her fans and her publicity materials, along with journalistic reports and critiques, pay far more attention to what she looks like, who she is, and what she stands for than to what she sounds like.

In this chapter, then, I concentrate on Madonna's appearance, her personality, and the words and images of her songs, for these are the main carriers of her most accessible meanings. This is not to say that her music is unimportant, for it is the music that underpins everything else and that provides the emotional intensity or affect without which none of the rest would *matter* to her fans. But it does point to the fact that the pleasures of music are remarkably resistant to analysis, and are equally difficult to express in the words and images that are so important in the circulation of culture.

Before her image became known, Madonna was not a success: at the start, at least, her music was not enough on its own to turn her into a major resource of popular culture. In the autumn of 1984 [sic] she was signed to Sire Records, which is "where Warner Bros. put people they don't think will sell."[1] She got some dance club play for "Borderline" and "Holiday," but the *Madonna* LP was selling only slowly. *Like a Virgin*, her second LP, had been made but not released. Warner Bros. then gave Arthur Pierson a tiny budget to make a rock video of "Lucky Star." He shot it in an afternoon against a white studio backdrop, and the resulting video pushed the song into the top ten. The *Madonna* album's sales followed suit, and *Like a Virgin* was released for the Christmas market.

Both LPs held the number-one position for a number of weeks. The film *Desperately Seeking Susan* was released in March 1985, which added an adult audience to the teenage (largely female) one for the songs and videos. The film worked to support the videos in establishing the "Madonna look," a phrase that the media repeated endlessly in 1985 and one that Madonna capitalized on by establishing her Boy Toy label to sell crucifix earrings, fingerless lace gloves, short, navel-exposing blouses, black lacy garments, and all the visual symbols she had made her own.

A concert tour started in April (in the foyers, of course, items of the Madonna look were for sale) and an old film, *A Certain Sacrifice*, that never made cinema release was dug up for the home video market. Also dug up and published in *Playboy* and *Penthouse* were old art school nude photos, and in August 1985, her wedding to Sean Penn became a worldwide multimedia event, despite its "secret" location. In other words, she was a fine example of the capitalist pop industry at work, creating a (possibly short-lived) fashion, exploiting it to the full, and making a lot of money from one of the most powerless and exploitable sections of the community, young girls.

But such an account is inadequate (though not necessarily inaccurate as far as it goes) because it assumes that the Madonna fans are merely "cultural dopes," able to be manipulated at will and against their own interests by the moguls of the culture industry. Such a manipulation would be not only economic, but also ideological, because the economic system requires the ideology of patriarchal capitalism to underpin and naturalize it. Economics and ideology can never be separated.

And there is no shortage of evidence to support this view. Madonna's videos exploit the sexuality of her face and body and frequently show her in postures of submission (as in "Burning Up") or subordination to men. Her physical similarity to Marilyn Monroe is stressed (particularly in the video of "Material Girl"), an intertextual reference to another star commonly thought to owe her success to her ability to embody masculine fantasy. In the *Countdown* 1985 poll of the top twenty "Sex/Lust Objects" Madonna took third place and was the only female among nineteen males.[2] All this would suggest that she is teaching her young female fans to see themselves as men would see them; that is, she is hailing them as feminine subjects within patriarchy, and as such is an agent of patriarchal hegemony.

But, if her fans are not "cultural dopes," but actively choose to watch, listen to, and imitate her rather than anyone else, there must be some gaps or spaces in her image that escape ideological control and allow her audiences to make meanings that connect with *their* social experience. For many of her audiences, this social experience is one of powerlessness and subordination, and if Madonna as a site of meaning is not to naturalize this, she must offer opportunities for resisting it. Her image becomes, then, not a model meaning for young girls in patriarchy, but a site of semiotic struggle between the forces of patriarchal control and feminine resistance, of capitalism and the subordinate, of the adult and the young.

The field of cultural studies, in its current state of development, offers two overlapping methodological strategies that need to be combined and the differences between them submerged if we are to understand this cultural struggle. One derives from ethnography, and requires us to study the meanings that the fans of Madonna actually *do* (or appear to) make of her. This involves listening to them, reading the letters they write to fanzines, or observing their behavior at home or in public. The fans' words or behavior are not, of course, empirical facts that speak for themselves; rather, they are texts that need "reading" theoretically in just the same way as the "texts of Madonna" do.

This brings us to the other strategy, which derives from semiotic and structuralist textual analysis. This involves a close reading of the signifiers of the text—that is, its physical presence—but recognizes that the signifieds exist not in the text itself, but extratextually, in the myths, countermyths, and ideology of their culture. It recognizes that the distribution of power in society is paralleled by the distribution of meanings in texts, and that struggles for social power are paralleled by semiotic struggles for meanings. Every text and every reading has a social and therefore political dimension, which is to be found partly in the structure of the text itself and partly in the social relations of the reader and the way they are brought to bear upon the text.

It follows that the theory that informs any analysis also has a social dimension that is a necessary part of the "meanings" the analysis reveals. Meanings, therefore, are relative and varied: what is constant is the *ways* in which texts relate to the social system. A cultural analysis, then, will reveal both the way the dominant ideology is structured into the text and into the reading subject, and those textual features that enable negotiated, resisting, or oppositional readings to be made. Cultural analysis reaches a satisfactory conclusion when the ethnographic studies of the historically and socially located meanings that *are* made are related to the semiotic analysis of the text. Semiotics relates the structure of the text to the social system to explore *how* such meanings are made and the part they play within the cultural process that relates meanings both to social experience and to the social system in general.

So Lucy, a fourteen-year-old fan, says of a Madonna poster:

> She's tarty and seductive . . . but it looks alright when she does it, you know, what I mean, if anyone else did it it would look right tarty, a right tart you know, but with her its OK, it's acceptable. . . . with anyone else it would be absolutely outrageous, it sounds silly, but it's OK with her, you know what I mean. [3]

We can note a number of points here. Lucy can only find patriarchal words to describe Madonna's sexuality—"tarty" and "seductive"—but she struggles against the patriarchy inscribed in them. At the same time, she struggles against the patriarchy inscribed in her own subjectivity. The opposition between "acceptable" and "absolutely outrageous" not only refers to representations of female sexuality, but is an externalization of the tension felt by adolescent girls when trying to come to terms with the contradictions between a positive feminine view of their sexuality and the alien patriarchal one that appears to be the only one offered by the available linguistic and symbolic systems. Madonna's "tarty" sexuality is "acceptable"—but to whom? Certainly to Lucy, and to girls like her who are experiencing the problems of establishing a satisfactory sexual identity within an oppressing ideology, but we need further evidence to support this tentative conclusion. Matthew, age fifteen, not a particular fan of Madonna, commented on her marriage in the same discussion. He thought it would last only one or two years, and he wouldn't like to be married to her "because she'd give any guy a hard time." Lucy agreed that Madonna's marriage would not last long, but found it difficult to say why, except that "marriage didn't seem to suit her," even though Lucy quoted approvingly Madonna's desire to make it an "open marriage." Lucy's problems probably stem from her recognition that marriage is a patriarchial institution and as such is threatened by Madonna's sexuality; the threat of course is not the traditional and easily contained one of woman as whore, but the more radical one of woman as independent of masculinity. As we shall see later, Madonna denies or mocks a masculine reading of patriarchy's conventions for representing women. This may well be why, according to *Time*, many boys find her sexiness difficult to handle and "suspect that they are being kidded."[4] Lucy and Matthew both recognize, in different ways and from different social positions, that Madonna's sexuality *can* offer a challenge or a threat to dominant definitions of femininity and masculinity.

"Madonna's Best Friend," writing to *Countdown* magazine, also recognizes Madonna's resistance to patriarchy:

> I'm writing to complain about all the people who write in and say what a tart and a slut Madonna is because she talks openly about sex and she shows her belly button and she's not ashamed to say she thinks she's pretty. Well I admire her and I think she has a lot of courage just to be herself. All you girls out there! Do you think you have nice eyes or pretty hair or a nice figure? Do you ever talk about boys or sex with friends? Do you wear a bikini? Well according to you, you're a slut and a tart!! So have you judged Madonna fairly?
> Madonna's Best Friend, Wahroonga, NSW[5]

Praising Madonna's "courage just to be herself" is further evidence of the felt difficulty of girls in finding a sexual identity that appears to be formed in their interests rather than in the interests of the dominant male. Madonna's sexualization of her navel is a case in point.

> The most erogenous part of my body is my belly button. I have the most perfect belly button—an inny, and there's no fluff in it. When I stick a finger in my belly button I feel a nerve in the centre of my body shoot up my spine. If 100 belly buttons were lined up against a wall I would definitely pick out which one was mine.[6]

What is noticeable here is both her pleasure in her own physicality and the fun she finds in admitting and expressing this pleasure: it is a sexual-physical pleasure that has nothing to do with men, and in choosing the navel upon which to center it, she is choosing a part of the female body that patriarchy has not conventionally sexualized for the benefit of the male. She also usurps the masculine pleasure and power of the voyeur in her claim to be able to recognize her navel, in all its proudly proclaimed perfection, among a hundred others. Madonna offers some young girls the opportunity to find meanings of their own feminine sexuality that suit them, meanings that are "independent." Here are some other Madonna fans talking:

> She's sexy but she doesn't need men . . . she's kind of there all by herself.

> She gives us ideas. It's really women's lib, not being afraid of what guys think.[7]

The sense of empowerment that underlies these comments is characteristic of her teenage fans. A group of "wannabes," fans dressed in their own variants of Madonna's look, were interviewed on MTV in November 1987 during Madonna's "Make My Video" competition. When asked why they dressed like that, they replied, "It makes people look at us," or, "When I walk down the street, people notice." Teenage girls, in public, are, in our culture, one of the most insignificant and self-effacing categories of people; the self-assertiveness evidenced here is more than mere posturing—it is, potentially at least, a source of real self-esteem. The common belief that Madonna's "wannabes" lack the imagination to devise their own styles of dress and merely follow her like sheep ignores the point that in adopting her style they are aligning themselves with a source of power.

The "Make My Video" competition showed how frequently the pleasures offered by Madonna to her fans were associated with moments of empowerment. In the competition fans were invited to make a video for the song "True Blue," and MTV devoted twenty-four hours to playing a selection of the entries. Many of the videos played with the theme of power, often at an unachievable, but not unimaginable, level of fantasy, such as one in which schoolgirls overpowered and tied up a teacher who denigrated Madonna; only by admitting her brilliance was he able to earn his freedom. Another took power fantasy to its extreme: it began with home-movie-type shots of two toddlers playing on a beach; the girl is suddenly wrapped up in a towel in the form of the U.S. flag, while the boy is wrapped in one in the form of the hammer and sickle. The video shows the American girl and Russian boy growing up in their respective countries, all the while telephoning and writing constantly to each other. Eventually she becomes president of the United States and he of the USSR, and they prevent an imminent nuclear war by their love for each other.

Another, less extreme video made much closer connections between the empowered fan and her everyday life. The heroine sees her boyfriend off at a train station, then turns and joyfully hugs her female friend waiting outside. They dance-walk down the street and shop for clothes in a street market. At home, the friend dresses up in various Madonna-influenced outfits while the heroine looks on and applauds. Each outfit calls up a different type of boy to the door—all of whom are rejected, to the delight of the two girls. The heroine's boyfriend returns, and the final shot is of the three of them, arms interlinked, dancing down the street—then the camera pulls back to reveal one of the rejected boys on the friend's other arm, then continues pulling back to reveal in sequence each of the rejected boys hanging on her arm in a long line. The video shows girls using their "look" to control their relationships, and validating girl-girl relationships as powerfully, if not more so, as girl-boy ones.

In this video, as with the live "wannabes" interviewed in the same program, control over the look is not just a superficial playing with appearances; it is a means of constructing and controlling social relations and thus social identity. The sense of empowerment that Madonna offers is inextricably connected with the pleasure of exerting some control over the meanings of self, of sexuality, and of one's social relations.

But, like all pop stars, she has her "haters" as well as her fans:

> When I sit down on a Saturday and Sunday night I always hear the word Madonna and it makes me sick, all she's worried about is her bloody looks. She must spend hours putting on that stuff and why does she always show her belly button? We all know she's got one. My whole family thinks she's pathetic and that she loves herself. Paul Young's sexy sneakers.[8]

Here again, the "hate" centers on Madonna's sexuality, expressed as her presenting herself in whorelike terms, painting and displaying herself to arouse the baser side of man. But the sting comes in the last sentence, when the writer recognizes Madonna's apparent enjoyment of her own sexuality, which he (the letter is clearly from a masculine subject, if not a biological male) ascribes to egocentricity, and thus condemns.

Madonna's love of herself, however, is not seen as selfish and egocentric by girls; rather, it is the root of her appeal, the significance of which becomes clear when set in the context of much of the rest of the media addressed to them. McRobbie has shown how the "teenage press" typically constructs the girl's body and therefore her sexuality as a series of problems—breasts the wrong size or shape, spotty skin, lifeless hair, fatty thighs, problem periods—the list is endless.[9] The advertisers, of course, who are the ones who benefit economically from these magazines, always have a product that can, at a price, solve the problem.

This polarization of Madonna's audience can be seen in the 1986 *Countdown* polls. She was top female vocalist by a mile (polling four times as many votes as the second-place singer) and was the only female in the top twenty "Sex/Lust Objects," in which she came third. But she was also voted into second place for the Turkey of the Year award. She's much loved or much hated, a not untypical position for a woman to occupy in patriarchy, whose inability to understand women in feminine terms is evidenced by the way it polarizes femininity into the opposing concepts of virgin-angel and whore-devil.

Madonna consciously and parodically exploits these contradictions:

> "When I was tiny," she recalls, "my grandmother used to beg me not to go with men, to love Jesus and be a good girl. I grew up with two images of women: the virgin and the whore. It was a little scary."[10]

She consistently refers to these contradictory meanings of woman in patriarchy: her video of "Like a Virgin" alternates the white dress of Madonna the bride with the black, slinky garb of Madonna the singer; the name Madonna (the virgin mother) is borne by a sexually active female; the crucifixes adopted from nuns' habits are worn on a barely concealed bosom or in a sexually gyrating navel. "Growing up I thought nuns were very beautiful. . . . They never wore any makeup and they just had these really serene faces. Nuns are sexy."[11]

But the effect of working these opposite meanings into her texts is not just to call attention to their role in male hegemony—a woman may either be worshipped and adored by a man or used and despised by him, but she has meaning only from a masculine-subject position. Rather, Madonna calls into question the validity of these binary oppositions as a way of conceptualizing woman. Her use of religious iconography is neither religious nor sacrilegious. She intends to free it from this ideological opposition and to enjoy it, use it, for the meanings and pleasure that it has for *her*, not for those of the dominant ideology and its simplistic binary thinking:

> I have always carried around a few rosaries with me. One day I decided to wear (one) as a necklace. Everything I do is sort of tongue in cheek. It's a strange blend—a beautiful sort of symbolism, the idea of someone suffering, which is what Jesus Christ on a crucifix stands for, and then not taking it seriously. Seeing it as an icon with no religiousness attached. It isn't sacrilegious for me. [12]

The crucifix is neither religious, nor sacrilegious, but beautiful: "When I went to Catholic schools I thought the huge crucifixes nuns wore were really beautiful."

In the same way, her adolescent girl fans find in Madonna meanings of femininity that have broken free from the ideological binary opposition of virgin-whore. They find in her image positive feminine-centered representations of sexuality that are expressed in their constant references to her independence, her being herself. This apparently independent, self-defining sexuality is as significant as it is only because it is working within and against a patriarchal ideology. And the patriarchal meanings must be there for the resisting meanings to work against. *Playboy*, on behalf of its readers, picks up only her patriarchal and not her resistant sexuality:

> Best of all her onstage contortions and Boy Toy voice have put sopping sex where it belongs—front and center in the limelight. [13]

But even as it recognizes Madonna's patriarchal sexuality, *Playboy* has to recognize her parodic undermining of it, the control she exerts over the way she uses the dominant ideology but is not subjected to it:

> The voice and the body are her bona fides, but Madonna's secret may be her satirical bite. She knows a lot of this image stuff is bullshit: she

knows that *you* know. So long as we're all in on the act together, let's enjoy it.[14]

Some of the parody is subtle and hard to tie down for textual analysis, but some, such as the references to Marilyn Monroe and the musicals she often starred in, is more obvious. The subtler parody lies in the knowing way in which Madonna uses the camera, mocking the conventional representations of female sexuality while at the same time conforming to them. Even one of her ex-lovers supports this: "Her image is that of a tart, but I believe it's all contrived. She only pretends to be a gold digger. Remember, I have seen the other side of Madonna."[15]

Madonna knows she is putting on a performance, and the fact that this knowingness is part of the performance enables the viewer to answer a different interpellation from that proposed by the dominant ideology, and thus occupy a resisting subject position. The sensitive man watching her "Material Girl" performance knows, as she does, as we might, that this is only a performance. Those who take the performance at face value, who miss its self-parody, either are hailed as ideological subjects in patriarchy or else they reject the hailing, deny the pleasure, and refuse the communication:

> The *National Enquirer*, a weekly magazine devoted to prurient gossip, quotes two academic psychiatrists denouncing her for advocating teenage promiscuity, promoting a lust for money and materialism, and contributing to the deterioration of the family. Feminists accuse her of revisionism, of resurrecting the manipulative female who survives by coquetry and artifice. "Tell Gloria (Steinem) and the gang," she retorts, "to lighten up, get a sense of humour. And look at my video that goes with Material Girl. The guy who gets me in the end is the sensitive one with no money."[16]

Madonna consistently parodies conventional representations of women, and parody can be an effective device for interrogating the dominant ideology. It takes the defining features of its object, exaggerates and mocks them, and thus mocks those who "fall" for its ideological effect. But Madonna's parody goes further than this: she parodies not just the stereotypes, but the way in which they are made. She represents herself as one who is in control of her own image and of the process of making it. This, at the reading end of the semiotic process, allows the reader similar control over her own meanings.

Madonna's excesses of jewelry, of makeup, of trash in her style offer similar scope to the reader. Excessiveness invites the reader to question ideology: too much lipstick interrogates the tastefully made-up mouth, too much jewelry questions the role of female decorations in patriarchy. Excess overspills ideological control and offers scope for resistance. Thus Madonna's excessively sexual pouting and lipstick can be read to mean that she looks like that not because patriarchy determines that she should, but because she knowingly chooses to. She wears religious icons (and uses a religious name) not to support or attack Christianity's role in patriarchy (and capitalism) but because she chooses to see them as beautiful, sexy ornaments. She makes her own meanings out of the symbolic systems available to her, and in using *their* signifiers and rejecting or mocking *their* signifieds, she is demonstrating *her* ability to make *her own* meanings.

The video of "Into the Groove" demonstrates this clearly. The song is the theme song of the film *Desperately Seeking Susan*, and the video is a montage of shots from the film. The film is primarily about women's struggle to create and control their own identity in contemporary society, and in so doing to shape the sort of relationships they have with men. The viewers of the video who have seen the film will find plenty of references that can activate these meanings, but the video can also be read as promoting the Madonna look, her style. She takes items of urban living, prises them free from their original social and therefore signifying context, and combines them in new ways and in a new context that denies their original meaning. Thus the crucifix is torn from its religious context and lacy gloves from their context of bourgeois respectability, or, conversely, of the brothel; the bleached blond hair with the dark roots deliberately displayed is no longer the sign of the tarty slut, and the garter belt and stockings no longer signify soft porn or male kinkiness.

This wrenching of the products of capitalism from their original context and recycling them into a new style is, as Chambers has pointed out, a practice typical of urban popular culture:

Caught up in the communication membrane of the metropolis, with your head in front of a cinema, TV, video, or computer screen, between the headphones, by the radio, among the record releases and magazines, the realization of your "self" slips into the construction of an image, a style, a series of theatrical gestures.

Between what is available in the shops, in the market, and the imprint of our desires, it is possible to produce the distinctive and the personalized. Sometimes the result will stand out, disturb and shock the more predictable logic of the everyday. . . .

The individual *constructs* her or himself as the object of street art, as a public icon: the body becomes the canvas of changing urban signs.[17]

In this street-produced bricolage of style, the commodities of the capitalist industries are purified into signifiers: their ideological signi- fieds are dumped and left behind in their original context. These freed signifiers do not necessarily mean *something*, they do not acquire new signifieds; rather, the act of freeing them from their ideological context signifies their users' freedom from that context. It signifies the power (however hard the struggle to attain it) of the subordinate to exert some control in the cultural process of making meanings.

The women in *Desperately Seeking Susan* who are struggling to control their social identity and relationships are participating in the same process as subcultures are when they recycle the products of the bourgeoisie to create a style that is theirs, a style that rejects meaning and in this rejection asserts the power of the subordinate to free them- selves from the ideology that the meaning bears.

Madonna's videos constantly refer to the production of the image; they make her control over its production part of the image itself. This emphasis on the making of the image allows, or even invites, an equiva- lent control by the reader over its reception. It enables girls to see that the meanings of feminine sexuality *can* be in their control, *can* be made in their interests, and that their subjectivities are not necessarily totally determined by the dominant patriarchy.

The constant puns in Madonna's lyrics also invite this creative, producerly relation to the text. Puns arise when one word occurs in two or more discourses, and while the immediate context may give one priority, traces of the other(s) are always present. The pun never makes a final, completed sense of the relationship between these various discourses—it leaves them at the stage of collision and invites the reader first to recognize the pun and second to produce her or his sense out of this meeting of discourse. Within a pun, the play of contradictions and similarities is remarkably free and open. "Like a Virgin" opens with the following lyrics:

> I made it through the wilderness
> Somehow I made it through
> Didn't know how lost I was
> Until I found you
> I was beat
> Incomplete
> I'd been had, I was sad and blue
> But you made me feel
> Yeah you made me feel
> Shiny and new
>
> Like a virgin
> Touched for the very first time
> Like a virgin
> When your heart beats next to mine
> Gonna give you all my love boy
> My fear is fading fast
> Been saving it all for you
> 'Cause only love can last.

In *Understanding Popular Culture*, Chapter 5, I note how the semiotic excess of puns makes them particularly common in popular culture.[18] Madonna's lyrics are no exception. Woven through these lines are puns playing with at least four discourses—religion, particularly religious love, sexuality or physical love, romantic love, and a discourse of street wisdom, of urban survival. Thus, *made it* has the street-wise meaning of survived or came out on top, but also the sexual meaning of sexual conquest and, in its association with *wilderness*, echoes of Christ's survival and resistance of temptation. It is absent from the discourse of romantic love. *Wilderness*, too, is, in the religious discourse, the wilderness of the New Testament, but it is also the wilderness of contemporary urban life without true romantic love, the secular equivalent of religious love. So we could continue. *Lost* is sexually "lost," a loose woman whose experience is only of sex, not of romance; it is also lost in the streets, and has echoes of Christ or the Israelites lost in the wilderness. *I've been had* similarly has a street-wise and a sexual meaning. So by the time we get to *virgin*, the word has become a semiotic supermarket—the religious virgin, the sexual virgin (which the singer clearly is *not*), the emotional romantic virgin (which, like the religious virgin, she *is*), and the naive virgin who has "been had" and "lost" in the streets. *Touched* also has religious meanings of "laying on of hands" or "blessing," physical ones of sexuality, emotional ones of true love, and street-wise ones of near madness or loss of control.

The relationship between these discourses is open, unresolved, and requires active, productive readers. The similarities and differences among religious love, romantic love, sexual experience, and street-wisdom are left reverberating and active, not closed off. There is no final meaning that says, for instance, that religious love contradicts sexuality but supports romantic love and invalidates street-wisdom. One cannot simply conclude that street-wisdom and physical sexuality are rejected, and romantic and religious love affirmed. Romantic love may be placed in a negative relationship to sexuality and urban survival, or it may be a development out of them, a growth for which they provide the soil. Puns do not preach: they raise issues, questions, and contradictions, and invite the imaginative participation (and therefore pleasure) of the reader in their resolution.

The form of the pun always resists final ideological closure: the potential meanings provoked by the collision of different discourses is always greater than that proposed by the dominant ideology. Thus, "Boy Toy," the name Madonna has given to her range of products and the media apply to her, can be read as *Playboy* does when it calls her the "world's number one Boy Toy" or "The compleat Boy Toy."[19] In this reading Madonna is a toy for boys, but the pun can also mean the opposite, that the boy is the toy for her, as she toys with the men in "Material Girl." This is the reading that Madonna herself prefers when she says:

I like young boys—15 or 16 year olds are the best. I like them smooth and thin. I want to caress a nice smooth body not a hulk.[20]

The video of "Burning Up" is built around puns, parodic excess, and contradictions. The narrative shows Madonna in a white dress lying writhing on a road, as she sings of her helpless passion for her uncaring lover who is driving toward her in a car, presumably to run over her. Her love for the boy makes her as (apparently) helpless a victim as the stereotyped female tied to the railroad track in many a silent movie. But the last shot of the video shows her in the driver's seat of the car, a knowing, defiant half smile on her lips, with the boy nowhere to be seen. This narrative denial of female helplessness runs throughout the performance as a countertext to the words of the lyric.

So when she sings, "Do you want to see me down on my knees?/I'm bending over backward, now would you be pleased," she kneels on the road in front of the advancing car, then turns to throw her head back, exposing her throat in the ultimate posture of submission. But her tone of voice and her look at the camera as she sings have a hardness and a defiance about them that contradict the submissiveness of her body posture and turn the question into a challenge, if not a threat, to the male.

The puns in "Burning Up" are more subdued and less balanced than those in "Like a Virgin," though they also play with the two discourses of the sexual and the religious. The sexual may be given a greater emphasis in the text, but the discourse of religion is not far below the surface as Madonna sings of kneeling and burning, of her lack of shame and the something in her heart that just won't die. This yoking of sexuality and religion appears to be performing the traditional ideological work of using the subordination and powerlessness of women in Christianity to naturalize their equally submissive position in patriarchy, but, as in "Material Girl," the text provides the reader with ample opportunities to undermine the dominant ideology while wryly recognizing its presence in the representation, for again the representation of women's sexuality includes the means of that representation and therefore questions its ideological effectivity. The introductory sequence exhibits this clearly. In the thirty-three seconds before Madonna is shown singing, there are twenty-one shots:

1. female eye, opening
2. white flowers, one lights up
3. female mouth, made up (probably Madonna's)
4. blue car, lights go on
5. Madonna in white, lying on road
6. male Grecian statue with blank eyes
7. goldfish in bowl
8. closeup of male statue, eyes light up

9. midshot of statue, eyes still lit up
10. extreme closeup of eye of statue, still lit up
11. chain around female neck, tightened so that it pinches the flesh
12. blurred close-up of Madonna, with the chain swinging loose
13. laser beam, which strikes heavy bangles, manaclelike on female wrist
14. laser beam on goldfish in bowl
15. Madonna removing dark glasses, looking straight at camera
16. Madonna sitting on road
17. Madonna removing dark glasses
18. Madonna lying on her back on the road
19. the dark glasses on the road, an eye appears in one lens, greenish electronic effects merge to realistic image of eye
20. Madonna sitting on road, facing camera
21. close-up of Madonna on road, tilting her head back

This sequence has two main types of image, ones of looking and ones of subordination or bondage. Traditionally, as the eyes of the Greek statue tell us, looking has been a major way by which men exercise power over women, and the resulting female subordination is shown by Madonna's submissive postures on the road. The goldfish caught in the bowl is an ironic metaphor for the woman held in the male gaze. But the laser beam is a modern "look," impersonal, not the traditional male eye beam, and this can cut the female free from her bonding manacles, free the goldfish from the bowl. Similarly, Madonna's singing frees the chain that has previously been tightened around her neck. Later in the video, as Madonna sings of wanting her lover, and wanting to know what she has to do to win him, she tightens and then loosens the same chain about her neck; the next shot is a collage of male eyes, into which Madonna's lips are inserted as she sings. The pattern is repeated; her performance shows how women can be free from the look and the power of the male. Removing the dark glasses as she looks at us is a sign of her control of the look: we see what she allows us to. The glasses replace her lying on the road, but instead of her apparent submissiveness, they gain an active, electronic, all-seeing eye.

Similarly, the video of "Lucky Star" opens and closes with Madonna lowering and raising dark glasses as she looks at the camera, again controlling what we see. In "Borderline," the male photographer is a recurring image, as Madonna parodies the photographic model she once was while singing of her desire for freedom. The resulting photograph is shown on the cover of a glossy magazine (called *Gloss*!) being admired by men.

Madonna knows well the importance of the look. This is a complex concept, for it includes how she looks (what she looks like), how she looks (how she gazes at others, the camera in particular), and how others look at her. Traditionally, looking has been in the control of men; Freud even suggests it is an essentially masculine way of exerting control through an extension of voyeurism, but Madonna wrests this control from the male and shows that women's control of the look (in all three senses) is crucial to their gaining control over their meanings within patriarchy.

The ideological effectivity of this is evidenced in a student essay:

> There is also a sense of pleasure, at least for me and perhaps a large number of other women, in Madonna's defiant look or gaze. In "Lucky Star" at one point in the dance sequence Madonna dances side on to the camera, looking provocative. For an instant we glimpse her tongue: the expectation is that she is about to lick her lips in a sexual invitation. The expectation is denied and Madonna appears to tuck her tongue back into her cheek. This, it seems, is how most of her dancing and groveling in front of the camera is meant to be taken. She is setting up the sexual idolization of women. For a woman who has experienced this victimization, this setup is most enjoyable and pleasurable, while the male position of voyeur is displaced into uncertainty. (Robyn Blair, nineteen-year-old fan)

The look (in all senses of the word), meanings of self and of social relations, and power or powerlessness are interdetermined concepts— each one requires the other two to complete it. Madonna offers her fans access to semiotic and social power; at the basic level this works through fantasy, which, in turn, may empower the fan's sense of self and thus affect her behavior in social situations. This sort of empowering fantasy is pleasurable to the extent that it reverses social norms, and, when the fantasy can be connected to the conditions of everyday life—when, that is, it is a relevant fantasy—it can make the ideal into the achievable. The first two fan videos described above may be wish-fulfillment fantasies, but the third brings the fantasized ideal within reach of the everyday. The first two evidence the desire for empowerment; the third explores ways of achieving it. Fantasy is not adequately described by writing it off as mere escapism; it can, under certain conditions, constitute the imagined possibilities of small-scale social change, it may provide the motive and energy for localized tactical resistances. Madonna's popularity is a complexity of power and resistances, of meanings and countermeanings, of pleasures and the struggle for control.

▶ Notes

1. Madonna, quoted in *Countdown*, Special Annual, 1985, p. 2.

2. Poll of top twenty "Sex/Lust Objects," *Countdown*, December 1985, p. 35.

3. Lucy (Madonna fan), quoted in *Countdown*, November 1985.

4. John Skow, "Madonna Rocks the Land," *Time*, May 27, 1985, p. 47.

5. "Madonna's Best Friend," quoted in *Countdown*, December 1985, p. 70.

6. Madonna, quoted in *Madonna: Close up and Personal* (London: Rock Photo Publications, 1985).

7. Madonna fans, quoted in Skow, "Madonna Rocks the Land," p. 47.

8. Quoted in *Countdown*, Special Annual, 1985, p. 109.

9. A. McRobbie, "*Jackie*: Anthology of Adolescent Femininity," in B. Wattes, T. Bennett, and G. Martin, eds. *Popular Cultures: Past and Present* (London: Croom Helm/Open University Press, 1982), pp. 263–283.

10. Madonna, quoted in *National Times*, August 23–29, 1985, p. 9.

11. Ibid.

12. Ibid., p. 10.

13. "Madonna," *Playboy*, September 1985, p. 122.

14. Ibid., p. 127.

15. Chris Flynn, quoted in *New Idea*, January 11, 1986, p. 4.

16. *National Times*, August 23–29, 1985, p. 10.

17. I. Chambers, *Popular Culture: The Metropolitan Experience* (London: Methuen, 1986), p. 11.

18. John Fiske, *Understanding Popular Culture* (London: Unwin Hyman, 1989).

19. "Madonna," *Playboy*, September 1985, pp. 122, 127.

20. Madonna, quoted in *Madonna: Close up and Personal* (London: Rock Photo Publications, 1985).

(from *U and I*)

On Updike on "True Blue"

by Nicholson Baker

At some point, then, at several points, John Updike must have felt that panic that the founder of any highly successful entrepreneurial concern feels, when his business has grown so big that he can't remember all of his employees' names. The very sensation of that overfertile sump of your own previous usages, a vast dying sea just on its own, never mind the rest of the marine world, begins to force you in the direction of simplicity: you can see this force operating, for example, in an essay Updike wrote for *Esquire* in 1987, about listening to the radio. (I remember the essay well because, though it didn't say what I wanted to say, it still came too close to an essay I was doing on the same subject for me to finish mine.) In it, Updike remembers how in the cold car of his childhood (the same car as in *The Centaur*), he would "lean into the feeble glow of the radio dial as if into warmth," and he brings his radio affections up to date by saying that he likes a certain tune by Madonna ["True Blue"], and he closes the sentence of approval with a colon and a single word: "catchy." A thirty-year-old Updike would never have resorted to that word because calling a tune "catchy" isn't on its own interesting enough: the Updike of that era would have exerted himself to find a more refulgent dinglebolly of an adjective as diligently as Whitney Balliet, that tireless prodigy, still does in writing about music. But Updike has chosen "catchy," and it satisfies us in its setting, because he feels and we feel the inversion of word frequency that happens over the course of a life of careful writing, as the near-to-hand and superficially uninteresting become interesting through relative neglect. If you begin as something of a mannerist and phrasemaker, you offer yourself the hope of gradually disgusting yourself into purity and candor; if on the other hand you start by affecting a direct Saxon scrubbedness, then when a decade or so later you are finally ready to cut through the received ideas to say something true, the simplicity will feel used up and hateful and you'll throw yourself with a wail on the OED and bring up great dripping sesquipedalian handfuls while your former admirers shake their chignons in pity. I know perfectly well that I should not be using inkhorners like "florilegia" when I mean "collection" and "plenipotentiary" when I mean "stand-in" at my age (b. 1957)—and though the latinate conscripts were indeed the ones that first sprang to mind as I was typing those sentences, I did look askance at them on the screen a minute after I used them, for two reasons. First, because their eager scholasticism made me wonder if others would wonder whether my choices had leaped from a thesaurus or one of those maddening block calendars that offer a new vocabulary word every day. (I *still* find the deracinated adjacency of the thesaurus objectionable, and never use one, and feel guilty when I try to make a dictionary serve the same slatternly function, and I am only tempted to seek one out in the reference section if I strongly suspect that a reader may say "Florilegia?—right, sure, he just looked up *anthology*, the fraud," and I need to assure myself that the word I used is not sitting right there three words over from the word I think the reader will sneerily suppose I was wishing to avoid, and even then I resist the urge, because if I do find that the word I want to use is there and I avoid it I will be operating under the influence of Roget's, too. Yet at the same time I hate all this over-scrupulousness and I am drawn to Updike's honest picture of himself in "Getting the Words Out" as "paw[ing]" through dictionaries and thesauruses, and I similarly admired Barthelme when at the Berkeley writers' conference he blew Leonard Michaels's (pale yellow) socks off by casually saying in a question-and-answer session that *sure* he used a thesaurus, *absolutely*; I love both Updike's and Barthelme's implied boredom with the purist's pretense that every word he uses has to have been naturally retrieved from a past passage. So I agree with Updike that a thesaurus isn't intrinsically evil, and yet I can't use one—and I even feel slightly guilty when I use a certain word whose placement I have admired in something by Updike in roughly the same way he uses it: for instance, I wrote the phrase "consorted in the near vestibules of my attention" in my second novel, and I used "consorted" because one morning I was reading a review of a novel (can't remember which one) in *Hugging the Shore* and was struck by a lovely use of "consort" ["... better consorts with our sense of what a writer should be" in a review of

Beckett's *Mercier and Camier*] and again worried, just as I had all those years ago when I read "absurdly shook my head No" that I would never write as well as Updike. But now that I know from *Self-Consciousness* that Updike regularly uses thesauruses, I'm drawn to show the same dismissiveness toward "consort" that I worry others will direct at my use of "florilegia": it ("consort" I mean) now feels as if he found it under "adjacency" or some other big rubric, when honestly he could have found it in a thousand places—Henry James is a frequent consorter, for example. And, second, I looked askance at "florilegia" and "plenipotentiary" because I felt a needle jump in my déjà vu–meter that might indicate that I'd used them both before, and I didn't like the idea of people (i.e., Updike) thinking, "Florilegia *again*? It wasn't that great the first time! He's pretending his vocabulary is a touch-me-anywhere-and-I'll-secrete-a-mot-juste kind of thing, when it turns out to be this cribbed little circle of favored freaks that he uses over and over hoping nobody will notice!" So what I have to do now is to search the disks that hold my two novels for the words "florilegia" and "plenipotentiary"— an activity that has to be as artificial as any thesaurus search. Each novel I write will introduce another layer of this vocabularistic panic, and increasingly I will come to recognize the utility of words and phrases that don't make waves, since their very commonness keeps them from being noted as events that can or cannot be unintentionally repeated; and eventually, one morning when I'm fifty or so, I will be trying to work up my long-abandoned notes for a pop music essay, and I'll want simply to say that a certain song is good, and the adjectives will line up for the casting session, and one by one I will nod as they twirl past in the half-lit stage, saying I used you, too old, too young, I used you, I used you, I didn't use you for x reason, I didn't use you for y reason, and finally, like Hope following all the evils that flap out of Pandora's box, the word "catchy" will flutter up, "Like a virgin, touched for the very first time," as Madonna would say, and I will think, Hey!—but then, because I quoted it to illustrate the whole problem of vocabulary management in this essay, I will remember that Updike already used it and that it is off-limits, and, in a wistful non sequitur, I will find myself wishing that I had been Updike's friend. Catchy, catchy: it *is* a beautiful word.

The Seven Ladies of ASCAP

Betty Comden, Madonna, Carole King, Gloria Gaither, Reba McEntire, Valerie Simpson and Marilyn Bergman

by Hirschfeld

▶ From *Rolling Stone* Polls, 1986

ARTIST OF THE YEAR

1. Bruce Springsteen
2. Peter Gabriel
3. Phil Collins
4. *Madonna*

BEST FEMALE SINGER

1. *Madonna*

WORST ALBUM

1. *Eat 'Em and Smile*, David Lee Roth
2. *Heartbeat*, Don Johnson
3. *True Blue, Madonna*

WORST SINGLE

1. "Heartbeat," Don Johnson
2. "Dancing On the Ceiling," Lionel Ritchie
3. "Walk This Way," Run-DMC
4. *"True Blue," Madonna*

WORST FEMALE SINGER

1. Cyndi Lauper
2. *Madonna*

BEST ALBUM COVER

1. *Eat 'Em and Smile*, David Lee Roth
2. *Third Stage*, Boston
3. *5150*, Van Halen
4. *True Blue, Madonna*

WORST VIDEO

1. "Yankee Rose," David Lee Roth
2. "True Colors," Cyndi Lauper
3. "Heartbeat," Don Johnson
4. "Goin' Crazy," David Lee Roth
5. *"True Blue," Madonna*

BEST-DRESSED FEMALE

1. Tina Turner
2. *Madonna*

WORST-DRESSED FEMALE

1. Cyndi Lauper
2. *Madonna*

SEXIEST FEMALE

1. *Madonna*

Critics' Poll

BEST SINGLE

1. "Kiss," Prince and the Revolution
2. "Walk This Way," Run-DMC
3. *"Papa Don't Preach," Madonna*

(from *The New York Times*)

In Search of Madonna's Persona

by Vincent Canby

On the evening of Thursday, August 6, approximately ten thousand people, according to police estimates, crowded into the lower section of Times Square to watch the arrival of Madonna for the premiere of her new film, *Who's That Girl*. The next day, at noon, at the first regularly scheduled performance of the film at the 1,151-seat Ziegfeld Theater. I counted less than sixty people in the house when the show began.

In this age of electronically enhanced personality, fame may be fleeting, but it doesn't disappear overnight. It took Tiny Tim more than a decade to fade away and the Sex Pistols a couple of years (and one murder). *Howard the Duck* lasted four weeks. Madonna was as big an attraction on Friday at noon as she had been on Thursday evening but, apparently, her stardom on records, in music videos, in concert and as a free show in Times Square is *not*, as they say, translating to the box office of movie theaters.

With its usual bluntness, *Variety* stated the facts. *Who's That Girl*, the trade paper reported last week, is "a loser."

Ever since she first came on the music scene three years ago, there's been a certain amount of hype surrounding the ascent of Madonna— actually Madonna Louise Veronica Ciccone from Bay City, Michigan— to the top of the record charts. The voice is small, the musicianship not super, and the personality a kind of electronically enhanced variation on those of other people.

Yet that was then and this is now, when Madonna, the singer and knockout music-video performer, and, more recently, movie actress, has developed a public personality that is decidedly and wittily her own.

Largely through the sexy, parodistic music videos directed by Mary Lambert, and Susan Seidelman's *Desperately Seeking Susan*, her first theatrical feature, Madonna has shaped up as a character in her own right.

She's a knowing, shrewd, pragmatic young woman, a performer of invigorating energy who still looks a lot like Marilyn Monroe, even with short hair, but who has much more in common with the enthusiastic, unembarrassed, comic tartiness of Jean Harlow, somehow let loose on the streets of New York in the eighties.

Little of this would you be able to guess from *Who's That Girl* the film, which is halfway over before the "real" Madonna emerges, and none at all from the "Who's That Girl" music video, which, though its purpose is to promote the film, promotes everything that's least attractive about it.

What you're witnessing is a film career that's terrifically promising, drainwise. You might even suspect that there's a Cyndi Lauper "mole" among her advisers, someone bent on wrecking a career before it's decently gotten started and gained any momentum.

Who's That Girl doesn't duplicate the folly of last year's *Shanghai Surprise*, in which Madonna was cast against type (as a missionary in pre–World War II China), before that portion of the theatrical movie audience that doesn't see music videos knew what her type was supposed to be.

Who's That Girl, in fact, is a good deal better than its own distributors thought it was when they refused to screen it in advance to the press. It's an eighties comedy that qualifies as screwball, with a promisingly nutty screenplay by Andrew Smith and Ken Finkleman.

It's about a yuppie Manhattan lawyer, played straight and very comically by Griffin Dunne, whose assignment is simply to pick up Madonna, newly paroled on a murder rap, at a prison gate and put her on a bus to Philadelphia. The forty-five-minute drive turns into twenty-four hours of lunacy involving a wild cougar, mobsters, a society wedding, an interview with the fussy members of a co-op board, car chases, and larceny at Cartier's.

Under the direction of James Foley, and also, perhaps, of the producers, Madonna plays the first half of the movie at a fever pitch of inappropriate (for her) mannerisms, including an adenoidal accent, a supposedly comic "little girl" walk, shrewish temper tantrums, and coy facial expressions, none of which has anything to do with the sophisticated, self-aware Madonna of music videos and concert stage. In the second half of the film, when she's allowed to play at her own insinuating pace, Madonna at last emerges and is a delight.

The "Who's That Girl" music video catches none of this quality at all, concentrating instead on the hysterically off-putting personality that the star is required to play in the early scenes. It appeals neither to people who've never seen her before nor to anyone who's admired the sometimes brazenly erotic and funny performer Madonna is in her best music videos.

It may be, as has been suggested by my colleague Jon Pareles, that there's simply too much "free" Madonna available on television, in her music videos, for the star to attract fans to movies theaters that charge as much as six dollars a ticket. Movies, too, are not the "events" that her sell-out concert appearances are. Yet she's never even been seen dancing and singing in a movie. Hollywood has busily been giving a *new* image to someone whose initial image hasn't yet been formed, at least as far as movies are concerned.

Before Madonna makes another film, her producers might do well to study the creature as she's been defined in her best music videos. Chief among these is the extraordinarily provocative, impressionistic "Open Your Heart," which, in a brisk, haiku-like four minutes and twenty-two seconds, presents Madonna as every adolescent boy's wildest, sweetest fantasy. It's a tiny, comic, sexy classic, directed by Jean-Baptiste Mondrino, photographed by Pascal Lebegue, with smashing production design by Richard Sylbert (*Carnal Knowledge* among other films).

In Madonna, Hollywood has a potent, pocket-sized sex bomb. So far, though, all it does is tick.

(from "McRock: Pop as Commodity," in *Facing the Music*)

On Madonna vs. Bruce

by Mary Harron

Before considering the ways in which video has changed the face of hype, we should return to the question of what pop and rock really mean. As both encompass many musical styles, it is easier to assess them in terms of the values they represent.

Pop stands for mutability and glitter. Its mode is the 45 single and the pinup, and its value is measured by record sales and the charts. Pop is about dreams and escapism and ecstatic moments; it believes in clichés and its philosophy is "give the people what they want." It is egalitarian by nature—anyone can make it—and capitalist.

Rock is about the search for permanence within the free-floating values of the marketplace. It is about tradition (blues, country, and folk roots), and it is hierarchical in that it believes in geniuses and heroes. Its mode is the long-playing album and the in-depth interview. Rock wants deep emotion and catharsis and truth; it has a religious element that pop does not. Rock believes in originality and self-expression in defiance of crass commercialism.

If this seems to suggest that pop means shallow and rock means depth, consider which is the more profound experience—Smokey Robinson's "The Tracks of My Tears" or Led Zeppelin's "Stairway to Heaven"? And yet the one is a pop, the other a rock classic. And far from being rigid categories, pop and rock often intertwine—where would you put "River Deep Mountain High"? Where would you put Prince? How do you classify punk?

To take the most successful examples from each category, rock in the 1980s is exemplified by Bruce Springsteen, pop by Madonna. Springsteen, dressed in worker's denim, eschewing glamour, proclaiming his loyalty and affection for his lower-middle-class New Jersey roots, is a byword for authenticity. His songs deal with humble lives and his music is a synthesis of the great traditions of the past, in rock 'n' roll, rhythm and blues, and country ballads. He rarely gives interviews and seems appalled by hype. Madonna, of course, embraces hype like an old-fashioned Hollywood starlet (her obvious role model) and has had a success that is due as much to her "bad girl" style, her use of the press, and—above all—her videos, as it is to her music.

But rather than stressing the obvious differences between Bruce Springsteen and Madonna, let's see what they have in common. The most obvious shared quality is their striving. Both are known to work out, both present their live shows as heavy athletic achievements. Behind this lies the old show business ethic of giving the audience their money's worth, and being seen to do so. Madonna's manager explained on an early tour that she would play medium-size venues, not stadiums, because he wanted the audience to see her sweat.

But the striving wouldn't mean much if the performers weren't also seen to be making it. Neither failure nor the hippy indifference to the work ethic are popular in the eighties. Both Madonna and Springsteen represented success—working hard for it, then finding it—and holding out the promise, through their example, that you can get it too. And they offer something of a formula for how to get it: Madonna's vegetarianism and strict athletic regime, Springsteen's refusal to take drugs and indifference to alcohol. You can make it if you try. This gives their material a paradoxical quality when either one sings about failure. When Madonna sings about heartbreak and vulnerability in love, she still holds before us the image of the sex symbol, the tough ambitious girl who clawed her way to the top. Springsteen sings about the poor and defeated in triumphant, soaring rock 'n' roll songs that also hold before us the image of his own success. A crucial factor here is the way video has changed the public response to a song—it holds the artist's image in mind while you listen, so that the image and the song's message become confused and intertwined.

No pop artist can be successful *at the wrong time,* or by running totally counter to the popular mood, and the eighties mood was in favor of guilt-free, well-earned success. Springsteen, with his concern for the working man, his classic liberal values, his evocation of Woody Guthrie et al., would seem in absolute opposition to the spirit of the Reagan age. But what an artist says and what he is actually *projecting* can be very different things. A classic example is the use of the American flag on *Born in the U.S.A.* as the backdrop to a close-up of Springsteen's ass, clad in torn jeans, with an old baseball cap hanging out of one pocket. As Springsteen himself explained to Kurt Loder in *Rolling Stone*: "I didn't have any secret message. I don't do that very much. We had the flag on the cover because the first song was called 'Born in the U.S.A.,' and the theme of the record kind of follows from the themes I've been writing about for the last six or seven years. But the flag is a powerful image, and when you set that stuff loose, you don't know what's gonna be done with it."[1]

There is no need to call this cynicism or calculation. Springsteen has always been temperamentally conservative (his music is steeped in the past) although politically liberal, and he is the most consciously American artist of recent years. But that contradiction allowed him to sing songs of liberal social protest, and yet be the most popular mainstream rock 'n' roll artist of a deeply reactionary age. Dave Marsh, in *Glory Days*, castigates CBS correspondent Bernard Goldberg for declaring:

> Bruce Springsteen sings about Americans—blue-collar Americans trapped and suffocating in old broken-down small towns. His songs are about working-class people, desperate people hanging on to the American dream by a thread. . . . He touches his fans and they touch him. His shows are like old-time revivals with the same old-time message: If they work hard enough and long enough, like Springsteen himself, they can also make it to the promised land.[2]

Goldberg may have misunderstood Springsteen's lyrics, but not his total effect, in which compassion for the defeated means less than his own blinding success. Public perception has always been impossible to measure but what is clear is that now, more than ever before, rock stars have no control over how their images are received. The video onslaught and the general electronic surfeit of images have made it very unlikely that one single message will get through. The September 25, 1986, issue of *Rolling Stone*, the special college issue, had an article devoted to "The Baby Bankers," the new breed of yuppie graduates making fortunes on Wall Street. One of the typical cases they picked on was a chillingly bright-eyed and eager twenty-three-year-old named Harry Nudelman. Harry had a job in mergers-and-acquisitions, proclaimed oil raider T. Boone Pickens to be his personal hero, and had two photographs taped above his desk at work: his parents, and Bruce Springsteen.

For a performer, control over the meaning of what he does has always meant having control over his image, over how his audience will perceive him. This has always been true, but never more so than since the new cynicism about marketing introduced by punk, and the fusion between hit songs and visual images introduced by video. For a performer like Springsteen the more he tries to detach his image from that sales process, the more artificial his image becomes—if only because the maintenance of his integrity requires a continual watchfulness and involvement in overseeing his own marketing process. It is as self-conscious as his decision—as a multimillionaire rock star—to always appear publicly in humble working man's clothes. Madonna, with her unabashed artificiality and calculation is actually presenting a more genuine image of herself and her position than Springsteen, and finds her image easier to control.

But of course no performer can actually control how an audience receives them or their work, and one of the greatest dilemmas for all pop artists (and those with a financial stake in their success) is how to ensure the longevity of their career. The problem lies in the volatility of the pop-rock market, and the answer is to build a personal identification and loyalty that can transcend it. At its most intense a rock star can become, like the greatest movie stars, one of the saints of the electronic age: an icon to be worshiped for themselves rather than for anything they have actually done. The pursuit of the highest level of modern celebrity means developing a persona that can attract this kind of intense personal identification and fascination. This is not the same as selling records: Phil Collins, the most faceless of modern pop stars, regularly goes platinum even though most of his audience probably don't know one personal detail about him—and could care less. No one worships Phil Collins; they have simply made him very rich.

▶ Notes

1. Dave Marsh, *Glory Days* (New York: Pantheon, 1987), p. 208.
2. Ibid., pp. 253–54.

▶ From *Rolling Stone* Polls, 1987

BEST FEMALE SINGER

1. Whitney Houston
2. *Madonna*

WORST FEMALE SINGER

1. Madonna

WORST SINGLE

1. "Bad," Michael Jackson
2. "I Want Your Sex," George Michael
3. "Girls, Girls, Girls," Motley Crue
4. "I Think We're Alone Now," Tiffany
5. "Who's That Girl," Madonna

HYPE OF THE YEAR

1. Michael Jackson
1. U2
3. The Beastie Boys
4. Madonna

BEST SONG FROM A MOVIE

1. "La Bamba," Los Lobos
2. "(I've Had) The Time of My Life," Bill Medley and Jennifer Warnes
3. "Good Times," INXS
4. "Hazy Shade of Winter," Bangles
5. "Who's That Girl," Madonna

BEST LIVE PERFORMANCE

1. U2
2. Pink Floyd
3. *Madonna*

WORST LIVE PERFORMANCE

1. Whitney Houston
2. The Cure
3. *Madonna*

BEST ROCK COUPLE

1. David Coverdale and Tawny Kitaen
2. Jim Kerr and Chrissie Hynde
3. *Madonna and Sean Penn*

BEST-DRESSED FEMALE

1. Whitney Houston
2. Stevie Nicks
3. *Madonna*

WORST-DRESSED FEMALE

1. *Madonna*

SEXIEST FEMALE

1. *Madonna*

(from *Confessions of a Pretty Lady*)

On Madonna Dreams

by Sandra Bernhard

I **have many recurring dreams;** they could be called nightmares, depending on how you view them. I dream about Madonna more than anyone I know (or don't know); somehow she's indelibly written into my subconscious, and the theme is always the same.

She's always very sweet and caring but unavailable. In one dream, I'm at my house in Scottsdale, Arizona, where I went to high school, and all the streets in my desert neighborhood are packed with tourists, as if there was some kind of a bazaar going on. Madonna is there, walking toward me, flanked by two bodyguards, right next to my elementary school, Cocopah. She needs protection so people won't bother her, but I want to be alone with her and become friends, so we start walking around the streets arm in arm, being very cool in black leather jackets, and I'm really trying to impress her and convince her that I'm worthy of her friendship. Then she has to get ready for a dress rehearsal of her show that she's doing in my backyard by the swimming pool. There's a lot of excitement, her show isn't really that great, it needs work and I want to help save her, but I'm having mixed emotions about how to tell her. She's running around in her black-and-red bustier, too preoccupied to notice me.

▶ From *Rolling Stone* Polls, 1988

WORST-DRESSED FEMALE

1. Cyndi Lauper
2. *Madonna*

(from *ADWEEK*)

In Being a Good Corporate Citizen, Pepsi Came to Wrong Conclusion

by Richard Morgan

New York—Guilt by association. Make that two associations.

When Pepsi pulled its Madonna spot last week, it was responding to viewer confusion over the pop star's commercial appearance—for the very first time—and her first video appearance in two years. (That's a long time between bullets, by the way, as Madonna's many "wannabes" will attest.)

But the soft-drink maker was also responding to another association—or so it seemed, anyway—and that's the one headed by Rev. Donald Wildmon.

The persnickety media reverend reports that Pepsi, in addition to yanking the Madonna commercial, promised to pull out of Madonna's forthcoming world tour. The explication is that Wildmon, whose American Family Association claims 380,000 members, instilled the fear of boycott into the sellers not only of soda but, possibly, of all consumer goods.

"We have no comment on that," a Pepsi spokesman said about the tour, "except to say we have had discussions with Wildmon."

The spokesman insisted, however, that Pepsi wasn't caving in to Wildmon. And, as evidence, he recalled how the very same reverend threatened a Pepsi boycott last fall when the world's premier risk marketer sponsored the videocassette version of *E.T.*

Wildmon's reasoning went like this: MCA Universal, which released *E.T.*, also released the controversial movie *The Last Temptation of Christ*. That meant Pepsi, because it sponsored *E.T.*, supported the sacrilege in *Temptation*.

Pepsi responded by telling Wildmon where to get off, and, interestingly, off he got. If only it had taken the same tack this time.

I can sympathize with the heat Pepsi must have taken from its bottlers; I even appreciate its concern over customer confusion. But I can't help thinking that, in trying to be a good corporate citizen, Pepsi came to the wrong conclusion. There is certainly no better time—and there may never be a better opportunity—for responsible advertisers to stand up to irresponsible boycotters.

For starters, the spot in question is testimony to all that's good in advertising. It's a "Mean Joe Greene" for little girls, a media "must-see" for impossible-to-reach teens. It's soft-sell imagery that hits hard, a hometown message that works around the globe. It promised not only to take the sponsor into the hearts of its core drinkers but also to put the endorser before audiences even she might not have reached.

Most of all, the spot had taste—the kind that seems to be increasingly lacking in programming and other "edit" formats (witness the video of the same "Like a Prayer" song used in the commercial). And, ironically, it's the kind of taste that seems to be surfacing, more and more, in advertising.

By pulling the spot, Pepsi denied little girls a simple upbeat scene with, most likely, their favorite star. The void left these kids with a video—a confusing and disturbing array of religious images that, reportedly, Madonna lifted from some ancient French films she loves.

The video ain't the commercial, however, and never will be. Only the chance to figure this out is now lost to millions. In a way, the public has been denied a choice at least as great as the choice Pepsi perennially puts to the "new" or the "next" generation about soft drinks.

Whatever the confusion now, it's certain to get worse this week as the "Like a Prayer" video moves out of MTV exclusivity and onto noncable outlets. Kids who never saw the commercial are bound to think: "Whew! If that's what the video's like, no wonder the spot got canned."

Pepsi, too, may lose by playing it safe. The leader of lifestyle advertising has often been criticized for being content with the most tenuous of connections between itself and its endorsers. Michael

Jackson, for instance, bore no resemblance to the celebrity endorser of yore.

Pepsi took a chance on this "linkage," as music marketer Jay Coleman calls it, and proved to skeptics everywhere that the right association—artfully advertised—can move a product even if the endorser refuses to touch it. Madonna's potential to reinforce this notion is (excuse me) awesome.

The reason it'll never be realized is sad enough for McCann-Erickson's John Dergin, Coke veteran extraordinaire, to comment: "I am not able to chortle over the agony of our competitors in this case."

That reason, again, is guilt by association. Saddest of all, perhaps, is that it's a verdict Pepsi seems to have rendered unto itself.

(from *America*)

Like a Catholic: Madonna's Challenge to Her Church

by Andrew M. Greeley

I **am not sure** whether a discussion of the serious implications of the Madonna rock music video "Like a Prayer" is possible in the contemporary climate of discourse in American Catholicism. Nonetheless, I propose to try. I will discuss the religious theme of "Like a Prayer," Madonna's critique of her religious heritage, and the more general issue of the relationship between sexuality and religious imagination.

Some preliminary comments about the audio and videotapes of "Like a Prayer":

1) Virtually all the rock music critics agree that technically the music and singing of "Like a Prayer" are the best that Madonna has ever done. *Rolling Stone* says that it is "as close to art as pop music gets . . . proof not only that Madonna should be taken seriously as an artist but that hers is one of the most compelling voices of the eighties."

2) The lyrics of the album run from harmless to devout. In the title song, God's voice calls the singer's name, and it feels like home. That "Like a Prayer" is in fact a prayer is evident from the lyrics themselves, from the singer's interpretation of them, and from the critical reaction. In the words of Edna Gunderson in *USA Today*, "Lyrically 'Prayer' is a confessional feast, with Madonna's Catholic upbringing as the main course. Songs are rife with religious overtones, spiritual and hymnal arrangements and a host of references to joy, faith, sin and power."

The Arizona *Daily Star* notes that "it is largely a story of renewal and self-determination and it speaks with authority. You can dance, if you want to, but this time there's a heart and a brain behind the beat."

Only those who come to the music and lyrics with a grim determination to find prurience and blasphemy can miss—and then with considerable effort—the God hunger that animates them.

3) The music video is utterly harmless, a PG-13 at the worst, and by the standards of rock video, charming and chaste. More than that, it is patently a morality play. In the singer's own words it is "a song of a passionate young girl so in love with God that it is almost as though He were the male figure in her life."

The girl in the story witnesses a crime; she sees a black man falsely accused of it; she flees from the criminals and hides in a church; she prays to a black saint (Martin de Porres, one presumes), and falls asleep. She dreams that the saint comes alive and represents God as her lover. She awakens from the dream and realizes that in the power of God's love she can run the risk of doing right. In Madonna's words, "She knows that nothing's going to happen to her if she does what she believes is right." She goes to the police station and obtains the release of the innocent man.

To emphasize the religious themes of the album, it comes steeped in the smell of sandalwood, recalling the church incense of the past and implicitly (if unintentionally) the sandalwood themes of the Song of Songs.

That this is the meaning of the video is clear from its obvious sense, from the testimony of the singer, and from the virtually unanimous reaction of the young people who have watched it. (In my sociology of religion class of 150 students, before any comment from me, 30 percent rated the video PG, 68 percent rated it PG-13, and 2 percent rated it R or X.)

This is blasphemy?

Only for the prurient and the sick who come to the video determined to read their own twisted sexual hang-ups into it. Only for those who think that it is blasphemous to use religious imagery in popular music. Only for those who think that sexual passion is an inappropriate metaphor for divine passion (and thus are pretty hard on Hosea, Jesus, Saint Paul, Saint Bernard of Clairvaux, and Saint Teresa of Avila). Only for those whose subconscious racism is offended at the image of a black saint revealing God's love.

The line between blasphemy (the abuse of the divine) and sacramentality (the search for the Creator in the created) may sometimes be thin. One person's blasphemy may be another person's sacramentality—a Mary crowning is blasphemous for a fundamentalist and sacramental for a Catholic. Fundamentalists may well believe that the use of sexual passion as a metaphor for God's passion, especially in a work of popular art, is blasphemous. Catholics, dedicated as they are to a search for the Creator in creation, can hardly think so.

Even the most rigid fundamentalist or Catholic Jansenist must search desperately to find prurience in "Like a Prayer." Madonna's low-cut dress (or slip)? The tender kiss of the (black) saint (God)? The brief image of sensual satisfaction on the face of the woman in the dream as she's caught up in God's love? These would be an "occasion of sin" for young people?

Someone has to be kidding!

An immensely popular, and now critically acclaimed, singer tells a morality story filled with Catholic imagery, and some Christians respond to it with threats of boycotts against Pepsi-Cola (for whom she has made ads and which has lost $5 million because of its cancellation of the ads). Such a response tells more about those who respond than it does about the work of art itself.

In her interviews about "Like a Prayer" and previous songs, Madonna Louise Veronica Ciccone has repeatedly described the importance of Catholicism in her childhood and the remnants of Catholic guilt that continue to haunt her life: "If you enjoy something, it must be wrong." In the rock video when the girl grabs a knife and cuts herself, causing stigmatalike wounds on her hands, the wounds represent guilt, Madonna tells us. However, it is not guilt but love that leads the girl to do what she knows is right. Madonna seems to be saying that the guilt that obsessed her Catholic childhood is not enough to produce virtue.

She has been less explicit about the love imagery and the sense of sacramentality she has also carried with her from her Catholic childhood. Perhaps she is unaware of this second part of her inheritance. Nonetheless it permeates her work. She says she is not sure whether she is a Catholic or whether she would raise a child as Catholic. That is her own personal problem. In fact she sings "like a Catholic" (especially in "Like a Prayer"), and for our purposes in this article that is what counts.

Perceive the paradox: Catholicism in its present formulation passes on to its children both obsessive and imprisoning guilt and a liberating sense of God's love as sacramentalized in creation and especially in human love. It is a paradox struggling to become a contradiction.

Anyone who listens to the laity knows how bitter are the revulsions of many against their guilt-dominated Catholic childhood and how many of them claim, like Madonna, that they were taught to believe that anything one enjoys must be wrong. Not all Catholics were educated this way; but if we are honest, we must admit that guilt and anger about guilt is widespread among Catholics. That most of them cling to their Catholicism (like Madonna) one way or another is evidence that the appeal of Catholic imagery is stronger than the ugliness of Catholic guilt.

Guilt is the central theme of contemporary Catholicism; the sacramental imagination is transmitted (in fifteen countries that fellow sociologist Michael Hout and I have studied recently) either unintentionally or with the sense that, compared to guilt, it is unimportant. Christian leadership often concentrates on what is peripheral and the result of accidental historical circumstances and ignores what is essential and timeless. And organizes boycotts against those who sometimes have a better sense of the sacramental—the lurking presence of God—than they do.

In my sociology of religion class, the division of reaction to "Like a Prayer" was between fundamentalist Protestants, who were uneasy about the "shock" of the juxtaposition of womanly eroticism and the sacred, and Catholics, who were not disturbed by the blending of the two. "Catholics are more sensual," commented a mainline Protestant student. Surely the sacramental imagination ought to make them so; if they are in this era, however, the reason is that they are able to resist the Jansenism that still perdures.

In the present climate within the Catholic Church, the Irish monks would not have dared to convert an Indo-European intercourse symbol into the Celtic cross representing Jesus and Mary and the union of male and female in God. If she wanted to keep clergy and hierarchy happy, Saint Teresa would not have dared use the powerful erotic imagery of her mystical writings, nor would Saint Bernard have dared to write his commentary on the Song of Songs the way he did. The builders of Romanesque churches would not have (as my colleague at the University of Arizona, Donna Swaim, has told me) used pagan fertility symbols on their altars as signs of vitality to ward off morbidity. Fourth-century Roman liturgists would not have incorporated into the Easter Vigil service a pagan fertility ritual that used a candle and water.

Madonna must be denounced and Pepsi-Cola threatened with boycott because she is a sexually attractive woman who dares to link her sexuality with God and religious images: That, gentle persons, is the heart of the matter.

The link between vitality and fertility, between life and sex, has been so obvious that, until the Reformation and the Counter-Reformation, humankind had no doubts about the pervasive religious imagery of sex and the pervasive sexual imagery of religion. The Irish until the last century used to make love in the fields outside the house where a wake was in process to defy death: Life, continued by sexual union—they told death—is stronger than you are.

It is no accident that Jesus rose from the dead at the time of the Jewish spring fertility festival.

Too often our contemporary Catholic leadership rejects this human experience out of hand. Sex may be necessary for the continuation of the species, but please, lay folk, don't talk about it, don't let its influence seep into your life outside of your bedrooms, don't enjoy it too much, don't let it into your artistic works (especially if they happen to be religious), and don't suggest that the allure of a woman's body in a rock video staged in church can hint at the allure of God.

The novelist Bruce Marshal observed four decades ago that Jansenism is the odd notion that God made an artistic mistake in ordaining the mechanics of human procreation.

The matter is not subject for discussion, as I have learned to my dismay. History, theology, art, archaeology, exegesis—all are simply dismissed as irrelevant when they challenge the deep-seated antipathy toward sexuality that permeates Catholic leadership elites. The laity will be shocked, they tell you, refusing to listen to any other idea. In fact, they are projecting their own reactions into the laity, the vast majority of whom are not shocked.

Those lay folk who suspect, despite the heirs of Cornelius Jansen, that sexual passion may be revelatory will receive little encouragement or enlightenment from their leaders on the subject. They will have to turn to popular artists who manage to grasp the essential Catholic truth that, in the power of God's passionate love, enjoyment does not necessarily make an action sinful and that "nothing will happen to you if you do what you know is right."

(from *Feminine Endings*)

Living to Tell: Madonna's Resurrection of the Fleshly

by Susan McClary

A great deal of ink has been spilled in the debate over pop star Madonna's visual image and the narratives she has enacted for music video. Almost every response in the spectrum has been registered, ranging from unambiguous characterizations of her as "a porn queen in heat"[1] or "the kind of woman who comes into your room at three A.M. and sucks your life out,"[2] to formulations that view her as a kind of organic feminist whose image "enables girls to see that the meanings of feminine sexuality *can* be in their control, *can* be made in their interests, and that their subjectivities are not necessarily totally determined by the dominant patriarchy."[3]

What most reactions to Madonna share, however, is an automatic dismissal of her music as irrelevant. The scorn with which her ostensible artistic focus has been trivialized, treated as a conventional backdrop to her visual appearance, often is breathtaking. For example, John Fiske's complex and sympathetic discussion of the struggle over meaning surrounding Madonna begins, "Most critics have nothing good to say about her music, but they have a lot to say about her image."[4] He then goes on to say a lot about her image, and he too has nothing whatsoever to say about the music. E. Ann Kaplan's detailed readings of Madonna's music videos likewise push the music to the side and treat the videos strictly through the techniques of film criticism.[5]

This essay will concentrate on Madonna, the musician. First, I will locate her within a history of gender relationships in the music world: I hope to demonstrate that Madonna has served as a lightning rod to make only slightly more perceptible the kinds of double binds always presented to a woman who attempts to enter Western music. Second, I will turn to her music and examine some of the ways she operates within a persistently repressive discourse to create liberatory musical images. Finally I will present a brief discussion of the music videos "Open Your Heart" and "Like a Prayer," in which I consider the interactions between musical and visual components.

Throughout this essay, I will be writing of Madonna in a way that assigns considerable credit and responsibility to her as a creator of texts. To be sure, the products ascribed to Madonna are the result of complex collaborative processes involving the input of co-writers, co-producers, studio musicians, video directors, technicians, marketing specialists, and so forth. As is the case in most pop, there is no single originary genius for this music.

Yet the testimonies of co-workers and interviewers indicate that Madonna is very much in control of almost every dimension of her media persona and her career. Even though certain components of songs or videos are contributed by other artists, she has won and fiercely maintains the right to decide finally what will be released under her name. It may be that Madonna is best understood as head of a corporation that produces images of her self-representation, rather than as the spontaneous, "authentic" artist of rock mythology. But a puppet she's not. As she puts it:

> People have this idea that if you're sexual and beautiful and provocative, then there's nothing else you could possibly offer. People have *always* had that image about women. And while it might have seemed like I was behaving in a stereotypical way, at the same time, I was also masterminding it. I was in control of everything I was doing, and I think that when people realized that, it confused them.[6]

I am stressing Madonna's agency in her own self-representation in part because there is such a powerful tendency for her agency to be erased completely—for her to be seen as just a mindless doll fulfilling male fantasies of anonymous puppeteers. This particular strategy for dismissing Madonna has always seemed odd to me because the fantasies she enacts are not very successful at being male fantasies, if that is their objective: they often inspire discomfort and anxiety among men who wish to read her as a genuine "Boy Toy."[7] And I am rather amused when men who are otherwise not conspicuously concerned with feminist issues attack Madonna for setting the cause of women back twenty years—especially because so many girls and women (some of them feminist theorists, including even Betty Friedan[8]) perceive her music and videos as articulating a whole new set of possible feminine subject positions. Furthermore, her spirited, self-confident statements in interviews (several of which are sprinkled liberally throughout this essay) tend to lend support to the interpretations of female fans.

Yet Madonna's agency is not hers alone: even if she wrote everything she performs all by herself, it would still be important to remember that her music and personae are produced within a variety of social discursive practices. Her style is assembled from the musics of many different genres, and her visual images draw upon the conventions of female representation that circulate in film, advertisements, and stage shows. Indeed, in order to be as effective as she unquestionably is, she has to speak intelligibly to the cultural experiences and perceptions of her audience. Her voices are credible precisely because they engage so provocatively with ongoing cultural conversations about gender, power, and pleasure.

Moreover, as will be demonstrated throughout this essay, Madonna's art itself repeatedly deconstructs the traditional notion of the unified subject with finite ego boundaries. Her pieces explore—sometimes playfully, sometimes seriously—various ways of constituting identities that refuse stability, that remain fluid, that resist definition. This tendency in her work has become increasingly pronounced: for instance, in her recent, controversial video "Express Yourself" (which borrows its imagery from Fritz Lang's *Metropolis*), she slips in and out of every subject position offered within the video's narrative context—including those of the cat and the tyrannical master of industry—refusing more than ever to deliver the security of a clear, unambiguous message or an "authentic" self.

Thus I do not want to suggest that she (of all artists!) is a solitary creator who ultimately determines fixed meanings for her pieces. But I will focus on how a woman artist can make a difference within discourse. To strip Madonna of all conscious intention in her work is to reduce her once again to a voiceless, powerless bimbo. In a world in which many people assert that she (along with most other women artists) can't have meant what one sees and hears because she isn't smart enough, claims of intentionality, agency, and authorship become extremely important strategically.

► 1 ◄

Although there are some notable exceptions, women have traditionally been barred from participating in Western music. The barriers that have prevented them from participation have occasionally been formal: in the seventeenth century there were even papal edicts proscribing women's musical education.[9] More often, however, women are discouraged through more subtle means from considering themselves as potential musicians. As macho rock star David Lee Roth (rarely accused of being an ardent feminist) observes: "What if a little girl picked up a guitar and said 'I wanna be a rock star.' Nine times out of ten her parents would never allow her to do it. We don't have so many lead guitar women, not because women don't have the ability to play the instrument, but because they're kept locked up, taught to be something else. I don't appreciate that."[10]

Women have, of course, been discouraged from writing or painting as well, and feminist scholars in literary and art history have already made the barriers hindering women in those areas familiar. But there are additional factors that still make female participation in music riskier than in either literature or the visual arts. First, the charismatic performance of one's music is often crucial to its promotion and transmission. Whether Liszt in his matinee-idol piano recitals, Elvis on *The Ed Sullivan Show*, or the aforementioned David Lee Roth, the composer-performer often relies heavily on manipulating audience response through his enactments of sexual power and desire.[11]

However, for a man to enact his sexuality is not the same as for a woman: throughout Western history, women musicians have usually been assumed to be publicly available, have had to fight hard against pressures to yield, or have accepted the granting of sexual favors as one of the prices of having a career. The seventeenth-century composer Barbara Strozzi—one of the very few women to compete successfully in elite music composition—may have been forced by her agent-pimp of a father to pose for a bare-breasted publicity portrait as part of his plan for launching her career.[12] Women on the stage are viewed as sexual commodities regardless of their appearance or seriousness. Brahms pleaded with the aging Clara Schumann (provocatively dressed, to be sure, in widow's weeds) to leave off her immodest composition and concertizing.[13] One of Madonna's principal accomplishments is that she brings this hypocrisy to the surface and problematizes it.

Second, musical discourse has been carefully guarded from female participation in part because of its ability to articulate patterns of desire. Music is an extremely powerful medium, all the more so because most listeners have little rational control over the way it influences them. The mind/body split that has plagued Western culture for centuries shows up most paradoxically in attitudes toward music: the most cerebral, nonmaterial of media is at the same time the medium most capable of engaging the body. This confusion over whether music belongs with mind or with body is intensified when the fundamental binary opposition of masculine/feminine is mapped onto it.[14] To the very large extent that mind is defined as masculine and body as feminine in Western culture, music is always in danger of being perceived as a feminine (or effeminate) enterprise altogether.[15] And one of the means of asserting masculine control over the medium is by denying the very possibility of participation by women. For how can an enterprise be feminine if actual women are excluded?

Women are not, of course, entirely absent from traditional music spectacle: women characters may even be highlighted as stars in operas. But opera, like the other genres of Western music, is an almost exclusively male domain in that men write both libretti and music, direct the stage action, and interpret the scores. Thus it is not surprising that operas tend to articulate and reinforce precisely the sexual politics just described. The proceedings are controlled by a discourse organized in accordance with masculine interests—a discourse that offers up the female as spectacle while guaranteeing that she will not step out of line. Sometimes desire is articulated by the male character while the passive, domesticated female simply acquiesces. In such instances, the potential violence of male domination is not necessarily in evidence: the piece seems to unfold in accordance with the "natural" (read: patriarchal) sexual hierarchy.

But a kind of desire-dread-purge mechanism prevails in operas in which the tables are turned and a passive male encounters a strong, sexually aggressive female character. In operas such as *Carmen*, *Lulu*, and *Salome*, the "victimized male" who has been aroused by the temptress finally must kill her in order to reinstate social order.[16] Even in so-called absolute music (instrumental music in which there is no explicit extramusical or programmatic component), the themes conventionally designated as "feminine" must be domesticated or eradicated for the sake of narrative closure.

The ways in which fear of female sexuality and anxiety over the body are inscribed in the Western music tradition are obviously very relevant for the would-be (wannabe?) woman musician. First, women are located within the discourse in a position of both desire and dread— as that which must reveal that it is controlled by the male or which must be purged as intolerable. Many male attacks on Madonna unself-consciously locate their terror in the fact that she is not under masculine control. Like Carmen or Lulu, she invokes the body and feminine sexuality; but unlike them, she refuses to be framed by a structure that will push her back into submission or annihilation. Madonna interprets the problem as follows:

> I think for the most part men have always been the aggressors sexu-ally. Through time immemorial they've always been in control. So I think sex is equated with power in a way, and that's scary in a way. It's scary for men that women would have that power, and I think it's scary for women to have that power—or to have that power and be sexy at the same time.[17]

Second, the particular popular discourse within which Madonna works—that of dance—is the genre of music most closely associated with physical motion. The mind/body–masculine/feminine problem places dance decisively on the side of the "feminine" body rather than with the objective "masculine" intellect. It is for this reason that dance music in general usually is dismissed by music critics, even by "serious" rock critics. Recall the hysterical scorn heaped upon disco when it emerged, and recall also that disco was the music that underwrote the gay movement, black urban clubs, *Saturday Night Fever*'s images of working-class leisure, and other contexts that did not conform to the cherished ideal of (white, male, heterosexual, middle-class) rebel rock.[18] Similar dismissals of dance music can be found throughout the critical history of Western "serious" music. To the extent that the appeal is to physicality rather than abstracted listening, dance music is often trivialized at the same time that its power to distract and arouse is regarded with anxiety.[19]

Madonna works out of a discursive tradition that operates according to premises somewhat different from those of mainstream Western music. Her musical affiliations are with African-American music, with a culture that places great value on dance and physical engagement in music. It also is a culture that has always had prominent female participants: there are no white equivalents of Bessie Smith or Aretha Franklin—women who sing powerfully of both the spiritual and the erotic without the punitive, misogynist frame of European culture.[20] In critiquing Madonna's music, Dave Marsh (usually a defender of Madonna) once wrote, "A white Deniece Williams we don't need."[21] But perhaps that is precisely what we *do* need: a white woman musician who can create images of desire without the demand within the discourse itself that she be destroyed.

the libretti you mean?

► **2** ◄

Madonna writes or co-writes most of her own material. Her first album was made up principally of her tunes. She surrendered some of the writing responsibility on *Like a Virgin* (interestingly, two of the songs that earned her so much notoriety—"Material Girl" and "Like a Virgin"—were written by men). But in her third album, *True Blue*, she is credited (along with her principal collaborators, Stephen Bray and Patrick Leonard) with co-production and with the co-writing of everything except "Papa Don't Preach." She co-wrote and co-produced (with Bray, Leonard, and Prince) all of the songs on her most recent album, *Like a Prayer.* It is quite rare for women singers to contribute so much to the composition of their materials, and it is almost unheard of for them to acquire the skills required for production. Indeed, very few performers of either sex attain sufficient prestige and power within the recording business to be able to demand that kind of artistic control.

Madonna's music is deceptively simple. On one level, it is very good dance music: inevitably compelling grooves, great energy. It is important to keep in mind that before she even presented her scandalous video images to the public, she had attracted a sizable following among the discerning participants of the black and gay disco scenes through her music alone. She remains one of the few white artists (along with George Michael) who regularly show up on the black charts.

Her music deliberately aims at a wide popular audience rather than at those who pride themselves on their elite aesthetic discrimination. Her enormous commercial success is often held against her, as evidence that she plays for the lowest common denominator—that she prostitutes her art (and, by extension, herself).[22] Moreover, the fact that her music appeals to masses of young girls is usually taken as proof that her music has absolutely no substance, for females in our culture are generally thought to be incapable of understanding music on even a rudimentary level. But surely Madonna's power as a figure in cultural politics is linked to her ability to galvanize that particular audience—among others.[23]

To create music within a male-defined domain is a treacherous task. As some women composers of so-called serious or experimental music are discovering, many of the forms and conventional procedures of presumably value-free music are saturated with hidden patriarchal narratives, images, agendas. The options available to a woman musician in rock music are especially constrictive, for this musical discourse is typically characterized by its phallic backbeat. It is possible to try to downplay that beat, to attempt to defuse its energy—but this strategy often results in music that sounds enervated or stereotypically "feminine." It is also possible to appropriate the phallic energy of rock and to demonstrate (as Chrissie Hynde, Joan Jett, and Lita Ford do so very well) that boys don't have any corner on that market. But that beat can always threaten to overwhelm: witness Janet Jackson's containment by producers Jimmy Jam and Terry Lewis in (ironically) her song "Control."[24]

Madonna's means of negotiating for a voice in rock resemble very much the strategies of her visual constructions; that is, she evokes a whole range of conventional signifiers and then causes them to rub up against each other in ways that are open to a variety of divergent readings, many of them potentially empowering to girls and women. She offers musical structures that promise narrative closure, and at the same time she resists or subverts them. A traditional energy flow is managed—which is why to many ears the whole complex seems always already absorbed—but that flow is subtly redirected.

The most obvious of her strategies is irony: the irony of the little-girl voice in "Like a Virgin" or of fifties girl-group sentiment in "True Blue." Like her play with the signs of famous temptresses, bustiers, and pouts, her engagement with traditional musical signs of childish vulnerability projects her knowledge that this is what the patriarchy expects of her and also her awareness that this fantasy is ludicrous. Her unsupervised parody destroys a much-treasured male illusion: even as she sings "True Blue, baby, I love you," she becomes a disconcerting figure—the woman who knows too much, who is not at all the blank virginal slate she pretends to present. But to her female audience, her impersonation of these musical types is often received with delight as a knowing wink, a gesture of empowerment.[25]

Madonna's engagement with images of the past is not always to be understood as parody, however. Some of the historical figures she impersonates are victims of traditions in opera and popular culture that demand death as the price for sexuality.[26] Principal among the victims she invokes are Carmen and Marilyn Monroe, both highly desired, sexual women who were simultaneously idolized and castigated, and finally sacrificed to patriarchal standards of behavior. It is in her explicit acknowledgment of the traditional fate of artistic women who dare be erotic and yet in her refusal to fall likewise a victim that Madonna becomes far more serious about what have been referred to as "sign crimes."[27] If the strategy of appropriating and redefining conventional codes is the same in these more serious pieces as in the "True Blue" parody, the stakes are much, much higher.

▶ 3 ◀

In order to account for the radical quality of the music in "Live to Tell" (and later, "Like a Prayer"), I must refer to the assumptions that guarantee the tonal narratives of the masculine canon since the seventeenth century. Tonal music is narratively conceived at least to the extent that the original key area—the tonic—also serves as the final goal. Tonal structures are organized teleologically, with the illusion of unitary identity promised at the end of each piece. But in order for pieces to have any narrative content, they must depart from the tonic and enact an adventure in which other key areas are visited (theorists sometimes say "conquered") and in which the certainty of tonal identity is at least temporarily suspended. Otherwise there is no plot. Yet with the exception of a few pieces in the nineteenth century and early twentieth that deliberately call into question the premises of this narrative schema, the outcome—the inevitable return to tonic—is always known in advance. To the extent that "Other" keys stand in the way of unitary identity, they must finally be subdued for the sake of narrative closure. They serve as moments both of desire (because without the apparent longing to approach these other keys, there is only stagnation) and of dread (because they threaten identity).

As we have already seen, such narratives can easily be observed in nineteenth-century symphonies, in which lyrical "feminine" themes are encountered and then annexed (for the sake of closure and generic convention) to the key of the "masculine" theme. The more seductive or traumatic the encounter with the Other, the more violent the "necessary" heroic reaction. Beethoven's symphonies are especially telling in this regard: in the *Eroica*, an unprecedented level of dissonant bashing seems "required" to maintain thematic, rhythmic, and tonal identity. The struggle appears justified in the end, however, when we get to hear the uninterrupted transcendence of the theme in its tonic homeland.[28] In the Ninth Symphony, in which identity is marked as far more tentative, the violence levels are even higher. The arcadian third movement (a rare moment in which Beethoven permits dialogue and freedom of movement without the suggestion of overt anxiety) is self-consciously obliterated by the crashing dissonance introducing the finale's so-called "Ode to Joy."[29]

Most popular music avoids this schema, for songs typically are content with the sustaining of harmonic identity. There is usually no implied Other within these musical procedures, no structural obstacle or threat to overcome. However, all that is required to transform these stable procedures into narratives is for a detail to be problematized—to be construed as Other and as an obstacle to the configuration defined as Self or identity. In such songs, time becomes organized around the expectation of intensified conflict, climax, and eventual resolution. They adopt, in other words, the same desire-dread-purge sequence that characterizes the narratives of so much classical music and literature.

Rock songs that work on the basis of this sequence can be found from Led Zeppelin to The Cult's "Fire Woman [you're to blame]" or

Dokken's "Kiss of Death." I will discuss as examples a couple of songs by the heavy metal band Whitesnake. Several of Whitesnake's songs quite clearly enact within the music the excitement of interacting with the area of the Other (personified in their videos by Tawny Kitaen as temptress) and yet the horror of being sucked in by that area, which precipitates and justifies outbreaks of violence for the sake of identity consolidation.

"Here I Go Again" defines the sixth degree of the scale as the moment of desire and also of potential entrapment. The choice of that scale degree is not accidental: there is a strong gravitational tendency in tonal music for six (a relatively weak position, sometimes referred to as "feminine") to resolve down to five, which belongs to the ("masculine") tonic triad. In pop as in classical music procedures, the tonic is rather boring by itself, and lingering on the sixth degree can create a delicious tension. However, if six threatens to take over, then identity may be destroyed. In "Here I Go Again," so-called deceptive cadences on the sixth degree repeatedly rob the piece of certainty, yet create precisely the sense of nostalgic longing that characterizes the song. Its spectacularly enacted "climax" occurs only after a prolonged episode in which the harmony seems paralyzed on the "feminine" modal degrees, and the violence of the climax permits the return to the progressions that define quintessential masculine cadential control. The piece concludes, however, not with certainty but with a fade; and in the video, the fade is accompanied by images of a devouring Kitaen hauling lead singer David Coverdale over into the back seat of the car he is driving. This is what happens, apparently, when the purge is unsuccessful.

In "Still of the Night," the threat is far more intense, both musically and theatrically. At the end of the first verse (on the words "in the still of the night"), Coverdale strains upward—both vocally and physically, as though in orgasm—to hold onto the sixth degree, before returning decisively to tonic control. The second time through, however, both the heroic Coverdale and the harmony get trapped for what seems an interminable duration in that position which has been so carefully defined as that of desire. The energy drains away, the musical and physical gestures mime impotence, and Kitaen struts about striking menacing poses. For a long time, there seems to be no possibility of escape or return. When the musical energy finally manages to extricate itself from the abyss, the rest of the piece is concerned with attempting violently to purge the contaminating element. In the video, this eradication sequence is dramatized visually as Kitaen is dragged off and tossed into a paddy wagon marked "Sex Police."

What we have here once again—in the abstract symphony as well as these particular metal fantasies—is the playing out in music of the classic schema of Western masculine subjectivity. Of course, music is not the only cultural artifact that operates in this manner. John Fiske has written about how it informs the narrative conventions of popular episodic television shows such as *Magnum P.I.*:

> Like all ideological constructs, masculinity is constantly under threat—it can never rest on its laurels. The threats come internally from its insecure bases in the rejection of the mother (and the guilt that this inspires) and the suppression of the feminine, and externally from social forces, which may vary from the rise of the women's movement to the way that the organization of work denies many men the independence and power that their masculinity requires. Thus masculinity has to be constantly reachieved, rewon. This constant need to reachieve masculinity is one of the underlying reasons for the popularity of the frequent televisual display of male performance.[30]

Likewise, critics such as Teresa de Lauretis, Susan Bordo, and Mieke Bal have written about how the schema is inscribed and transmitted in literature, film, philosophy, theology, science.[31] But our topic here is music, and, as we have seen, a great deal of music too is organized in accordance with this pattern. Indeed, music without words (so-called absolute music) is especially prone to relying on it, to treating it as though it were a design dictated by natural or metaphysical law.

But it is one thing to be aware of this schema and its implications as an analyst and theorist. It is quite another to take the formal procedures conventionally inscribed within these discourses and cause them to tell another story. Especially if one finds oneself always already cast by society in the position of the Other rather than that of the "universal" (i.e., masculine) Self.

► **4** ◄

In the stage performance of "Live to Tell," the backdrop of the stage is filled with a huge projection of Madonna as Monroe, the quintessential female victim of commercial culture. The instrumental introduction sets up a bass pedal on D, performed by an inert synthesizer sonority utterly lacking in warmth. Over the pedal, a series of bleak open fifths mechanically marks the pulses of the metric order as though they are inevitable. This stark image alternates with an energetic pattern that emerges suddenly in the area of the relative major, F. The second sound-image differs from the opening sonority in part because the major key is semiotically associated with hope. Moreover, the bass is active rather than static, and it resists the apparent inevitability of the opening meter by anticipating slightly each of its changes: it seems to possess freedom of motion. However, just as this passage seems on the brink of establishing F major as the principal point of reference, it is recontained by the clanging fifths and the empty pedal on D. A traditional reading would understand D (with its pedal and fifths) as fundamental (as that which defines identity) and F major as the "feminine" region, which—even if it offers the illusion of hope, escape, and freedom—must be contained and finally purged for the sake of satisfactory closure.[32]

When she begins singing the verse, Madonna steps temporarily outside of this dichotomy of D-versus-F to sing over a new pedal on C. As she sings, her voice repeatedly falls lethargically back to the void of the C-pedal, as though she cannot overcome the gravitational pull it and the meter exert. Her text suggests that she has a weighty, long-buried "tale to tell," and her language ("I was not ready for the fall," "the writing on the wall") resonates with biblical references. If she as a woman is necessarily identified as the Other, as she who is held responsible for "the Fall," how is she to enter into narrative? How to step into a musical procedure in which the choices are already so loaded?

With the chorus ("a man can tell a thousand lies"), she opts for the warmer major key of F, her momentum picks up, and she begins to sound as though she will establish this more affirmative region as her tonic or point of reference. However, to close in this second region—conventionally the "feminine" position—is to accept as identity the patriarchal definition of femininity. Moreover, to the extent that F major is not the opening key, to cadence here is to choose fantasy; for while this key is reassuring and nurturing, it is not "reality" as the piece defines it initially. And formal convention would dictate that this second key area must eventually be absorbed and purged. Thus closure here is revealed as perilous. At the last moment before the implied cadence ("it will burn inside of *me*"), she holds to a pitch incompatible with harmonic closure. The age-old contrapuntal norm would dictate that her melodic pitch (once again the sixth degree, the image of desire in the Whitesnake piece) must resolve down to conform with the bass. Instead, her melodic pitch and the harmonic backdrop hold in a standoff until the bass—not the melody—moves to conform to the melody's (that is, to *her*) will.

The pitch cadenced on, however, is D; and while it defies immediate closure, it also strikes the common tone that permits the pitiless pedal of the beginning to return. As before, Madonna steps outside the dilemma to C for a verse in which she wearily comments on her subjective knowledge of beauty, warmth, truth, light even in the face of this apparent no-win situation. But eventually she must rejoin the world in which she has to engage with the choice between F and D, and once again she works to avoid closure in either.

Finally, after this escape-recontainment process has occurred a couple of times, the bottom suddenly drops out. It sounds as though the piece has ended in the foreordained defeat of the victim—she who is offered only the second-position slot in the narrative schema. In her live performance, at this point Madonna sinks to the floor and lies motionless for what seems an interminable length of time. There is silence except for the low, lifeless synthesizer drone on D. For someone like myself who is used to this scenario as the inevitable end of my heroines, witnessing this moment from a performer who has been so brash, so bursting with erotic energy and animation, is bitter indeed. But then she rises from the floor, bearing with her the ghosts of all those victims—Marilyn most explicitly, but also Carmen, bare-breasted Barbara Strozzi, and all the others who were purged for the sake of social order and narrative closure—and begins singing again.

In order to take charge of the narrative procedure, Madonna begins to oscillate strategically between the two tonal poles on D and F. As she sings "If I ran away, I'd never have the strength," she sings over a bass that moves up and down indecisively between D and A (mediant of F, but dominant of D), suggesting a blurred region in which both keys cohabit. When the opening dilemma returns, she prevents the recontainment gesture of the fifths by anticipating their rhythmic moment of reentry and jumping in to interpose the F-major refrain instead. So long as she manages thus to switch back and forth, she can determine the musical discourse. To settle for an option—either option—is to accept a lie, for it is flexibility in identity rather than unitary definition that permits her to "live to tell." The piece ends not with definitive closure but with a fade. As long as we can hear her, she continues to fluctuate.

This extraordinary song finally is not about unambiguous triumph: triumph would be easy to simulate, since this is what tonal pieces conventionally do. Yet given the premises of this song, triumphant closure would be impossible to believe. Moreover, it would merely reproduce the structure of oppression that informs narrative convention. Rather it is about staying in motion for the sake of survival, resisting closure wherever it lies in wait.[33]

By thus creating songs that refuse to choose between identity and Other—that invoke and then reject the very terms of this schema of narrative organization—Madonna is engaged in rewriting some very fundamental levels of Western thought. In "Live to Tell," the two clear regions of the traditional narrative schema seem to be implied. Semiotically, the unyielding fifths are "masculine," the lyrical, energetic refrain, "feminine," and the early part of the piece reveals that the fifths are formally designed to contain the excess and relative freedom of the refrain. But to the extent that identification with the feminine moment in the narrative spells death, the piece cannot embrace this space as reality without losing strategic control. Thus the singer risks resisting identification with "her own" area, even if it means repeated encounters with that which would contain her. In a sense, she sets up residence on the moments of the harmonic context that fluctuate between desire and dread on the one hand and resolution on the other. Rather than deciding for the sake of secure identity (a move that would lapse back into the narrative of masculine subjectivity), she inhabits both and thus refuses closure.

Formulations such as this are all the more remarkable because the ideological implications of musical narratives are only now beginning to be analyzed by cultural critics. The fact that some of Madonna's music enacts models of organization that correspond to formulations of critics such as Teresa de Lauretis need not suggest that Madonna is a connoisseur of critical theory. Yet to the extent that de Lauretis and Madonna inhabit the same historical world and grapple with the same kinds of problems with respect to feminine identity, their similarities are not entirely coincidental either. And Madonna is as much an expert in the arena of musical signification as de Lauretis is in theoretical discourse. It seems clear that she has grasped the assumptions embedded within these basic musical mechanisms and is audaciously redirecting them.

It must be conceded that male musicians could construct forms along these lines if they wanted to do so—there is nothing essentially feminine about what Madonna is doing in this piece. But most men would not perceive that there was a problem in the standard narrative, would not enact struggles that involve resistance to purging the alien element.[34] The strategies of Madonna's songs are those of one who has radically conflicting subject positions—one who has been taught to cheer for resolutions in cultural narratives, but who also realizes that she is of the sort that typically gets purged for the sake of that resolution. Madonna's refusal of definition (which infuriates many a critic) goes beyond the paradox of her name, her persona, her visual imagery. It also produces brave new musical procedures.

▶ **5** ◀

Having thus been converted to Madonna as a musician who dares to create liberatory visions, I find the necessity of reading her music videos all the more urgent. Visual images seem to speak much louder than music—at least critics of Madonna's videos have found it difficult to notice the music, given the provocative nature of the pictures. Yet it is generally accepted that music in film covertly directs the affective responses of viewers far more than they know. I would suggest that the *music* in music videos is largely responsible for the narrative continuity and the affective quality in the resultant work, even if it is the visual images we remember concretely.[35]

I was acquainted with the song "Open Your Heart" long before I saw the video attached to it. While affectively much more upbeat than "Live to Tell," the musical imagery of "Open Your Heart" shares many of its resistant qualities: up against the shimmering, pulsating energy of the backup, Madonna avoids conforming to the beat; and, at cadences, she subverts expected points of arrival. But unlike in "Live to Tell," in which resistance indicates sheer survival, the play with closure in "Open Your Heart" creates the image of open-ended jouissance—an erotic energy that continually escapes containment.

By contrast, the video of "Open Your Heart" begins not in a visual field of open erotic joy but rather in the confined environment of a peep show. Madonna sings the song from the center of a carousel that revolves to display her to the gazes of customers peering safely from their cubicles. Here she becomes Marlene Dietrich in *The Blue Angel*, her usually exuberant motion restrained to what she is able to accomplish with her only prop: a stationary chair. At one point in the first segment of the video, she is filmed dancing; but the camera is almost still, and her motions are confined to the small range the static camera can take in.

This confinement is especially noteworthy given the extraordinary exhilaration of the music: the tension between the visual and musical dimensions of the video is extremely unsettling. Only when she disappears from the carousel and reappears to run away from her patriarchal boss with the young boy do the music and visuals begin to be compatible. In other words, two very different narrative strata are present in the video: that of the relatively consistent rhythmic energy in the music versus that of the transformation from patriarchal puppet to androgynous kid in the visuals.

Like many of Madonna's strategies, the one she attempts in this video is quite audacious. For instance, the peep show situation is shot in such a way that the leering patrons are rendered pathetic and grotesque, while she alone lays claim to subjectivity: thus, the usual power relationship between the voyeuristic male gaze and object is here destabilized. Likewise, the young boy's game of impersonating the femme fatale and Madonna's transvestism at the end both refuse essentialist gender categories and turn sexual identity into a kind of play. Still, the video is risky, because for all those who have reduced her to "a porn queen in heat," there she is: embodying that image to the max. Those features of the video that resist a reductive reading of this sort—the nonfit of the music, the power inversions, the narrative of escape to androgyny—can easily be overlooked. This is, of course, always the peril of attempting to deconstruct pornographic images: it becomes necessary to invoke the image in order to perform the deconstruction; but, once presented, the image is in fact there in all its glory.

In this video, Madonna confronts the most pernicious of her stereotypes and then attempts to channel it into a very different realm: a realm where the feminine erotic need not be the object of the patriarchal gaze, where its energy can motivate play and nonsexual pleasure. The end of this video is as tenuous as the transcendent pitch in "Live to Tell": it speaks not of certainty, but of horizons, of possibilities, of the hope of survival within available discursive practices.

▶ 6 ◀

These themes—survival, pleasure, resistance to closure—are reengaged most dramatically in Madonna's recent song and video, "Like a Prayer." In contrast to the relationship between sight and sound in "Open Your Heart," the tensions she is putting into play in this music video are virtually all audible within the music itself, prior to the visual images. Moreover, many of the tensions that have always surrounded her personae are here made explicit.

The central dichotomy she inevitably invokes is that of the virgin and the whore.[36] Her name (actually, fortuitously, her given name: Madonna Louise Veronica Ciccone), her apparently casual flaunting of crucifixes and rosaries as accessories, and her overtly erotic dress and behavior have consistently thrown into confusion the terms of that standard binary opposition; but what precisely she means by this play of signs has never been obvious. Indeed, many critics have taken her use of religious imagery to be a prime example of what Fredric Jameson calls "blank pastiche": the symbols are seen as detached from their traditional contexts and thus as ceasing to signify.[37] However, Madonna's insistence on the codes of Catholic iconography has always at least potentially engaged with the sedimented memory of that tradition, even if only negatively—as blasphemy. In "Like a Prayer," the religious connotations of her entire project are reactivated and reinterpreted. But although this set of issues is finally foregrounded, her treatment of these highly sensitive themes is quite unexpected and, as it turns out, highly controversial.

The song draws upon two very different semiotic codes associated with two very different forms of Christianity: Catholicism and the black Gospel church. These codes would seem at first glance to be incompatible. But Madonna is tapping into a tradition of Catholicism that has long been suppressed: that of the female mystics such as Saint Teresa who claimed to have experienced mystical union with Christ.[38] In Saint Teresa's writings, religious ecstasy is described through images of sexual ecstasy, for the intensity of her relationship with the deity could only be expressed verbally to other human beings through metaphors of submission, penetration, even orgasm. In the seventeenth century, composers of sacred music freely borrowed images of desire and eroticism from the steamy operatic stage for purposes of their devotionals and worship services, for these experiences were thought to be relevant to the new forms of personalized faith encouraged by both the Reformation and the Counter-Reformation.[39]

After the seventeenth century, this strain of religious erotic imagery was purged from most mainstream Christian denominations, only to reemerge occasionally during moments of intense emotional revivalism. Certain forms of charismatic fundamentalism since the eighteenth century have employed erotic imagery for purposes of inducing personalized meditation or even trance states and speaking in tongues. Both Bach's pietistic bride-and-groom duets (see Cantata 140) and Jerry Lee Lewis's evangelical rock 'n' roll ("Whole Lot of Shakin' Goin' On") testify to this phenomenon. However, the semiotic connections between religious and sexual ecstasy are most consistently apparent in the black Gospel churches. Throughout its history (as preserved on recordings), Gospel has freely borrowed musical and poetic styles from the secular music of its day: witness, for instance, the mergers with jazz, blues, funk, and rap evident on present-day Gospel radio stations—or, for that matter, the entire career of Aretha Franklin. Moreover, the Gospel church continually produces new generations of black pop musicians whose music is fueled by the fervent energy of that spiritual context.

"Like a Prayer" opens with an invocation of stereotyped mystical Catholicism: with the halo of a wordless (heavenly) choir and the fundamental accompaniment of a "timeless" pipe organ as she sings of how "Life is a mystery." But with the words "When you call my name" (when, in other words, she is hailed as a new kind of subject), Madonna breaks into ecstatic, funky, Gospel-flavored dance music. These two moments are distinguished for narrative purposes through the same harmonic contrast between D minor and F major as in "Live to Tell." What seems to be a struggle between mystical timelessness on D minor and exuberant, physical celebration on F major ensues. This time, however, she is not afraid to embrace F as tonic, especially when halfway through, on the words "your voice can take me there," she lands decisively on that pitch.

But D minor does not disappear entirely—it reenters for a long, rather sinister return of the beginning material in the middle of the song. Eventually, however, the music is channeled back to F major for more celebration. Gradually D minor comes to serve only for "deceptive" cadences. Traditionally deceptive cadences spell disappointment, a jarring intervention at the promised moment of identity. But in "Like a Prayer," they provide the means of avoiding closure and maintaining the dance. Finally, in the long, ecstatic coda to the song, F major and D minor at cadences become in a sense interchangeable: no longer self and Other, they become two flickering moments in a flexible identity that embraces them both, that remains constant only insofar as both continue to be equally present.

This is similar to the strategy of "Live to Tell," except that here the music itself does not involve the suggestion of threatened annihilation. But the controversial video released with the album sets up something like the external threats of containment articulated in "Live to Tell." The video is organized in terms of an inside and an outside. Outside the church is the world of Ku Klux Klan cross-burnings, of rape and murder, of racist authority. One of the most striking moments in the video occurs when Madonna dances provocatively in front of the burning crosses, aggressively defying those who burn crosses to contain her and her sexuality as well. And, indeed, Madonna has testified to having planned originally to present an even more extreme scenario: "I had all these ideas about me running away with the black guy and both of us getting shot by the KKK."[40] Video director Mary Lambert says of the segment with the burning crosses: "That's an ecstatic vision. The cross is a cautionary symbol and Madonna's performance throughout has been tortured and emotional. The inference of Ku Klux Klan racism is there, but the burning cross is an older symbol than the Klan. Saints had it. It symbolizes the wrath of God."[41]

But inside the church is the possibility of community, love, faith, and interracial bonding. The references to Catholic mysticism and the black Gospel church are made explicit in the visuals, with a heady mixture of a miraculously weeping statue, the stigmata, the Saint Teresa–like union between the saint and the believer, and the highly physical musical performance by the Andraé Crouch choir. Within the security of the church, difference can be overcome and the boundless joy of the music can become reality.[42] As in "Live to Tell," this song is about survival rather than simple triumph. And it is about the possibility of creating musical and visual narratives that celebrate multiple rather than unitary identities, that are concerned with ecstatic continuation rather than with purging and containment.[43]

In a world in which the safe options for women musicians seem to be either denying gender difference or else restricting the expression of feminine pleasure to all-women contexts, Madonna's counternarratives of female heterosexual desire are remarkable. The intelligence with which she zeroes in on the fundamental gender tensions in culture and the courage with which she takes them on deserve much greater credit than she usually is given. That she manages both to outrage those who would have her conform and to delight those who are still trying to puzzle out their own future options within this society indicates that her strategies are by and large successful. If Madonna does, in fact, "live to tell"—that is, survive as a viable cultural force—an extraordinarily powerful reflex action of patriarchy will have been successfully challenged.

▶ Notes

1. J.D. Considine, "That Girl: Madonna Rolls Across America," *BuZZ* 2, no. 11 (September 1987): "According to the PMRC's Susan Baker, in fact, Madonna taught little girls how to act 'like a porn queen in heat' " (p. 17). E. Ann Kaplan describes her image as a combination of bordello queen and bag lady. See *Rocking Around the Clock: Music Television, Postmodernism, and Consumer Culture* (New York: Methuen, 1987), p. 126. See also pages 39–46 in this book.

2. Milo Miles, music editor of the Boston *Phoenix*, as quoted in Dave Marsh, "Girls Can't Do What the Guys Do: Madonna's Physical Attraction," *The First Rock & Roll Confidential Report* (New York: Pantheon, 1985), p. 161. Compare the imagery in Considine, "That Girl": "By some accounts—particularly a notorious *Rolling Stone* profile—Madonna slept her way to the top, sucking her boyfriends dry, then moving on to the next influential male" (p. 16). Both Marsh and Considine refute this image, but it is a fascinating one that combines the predatory sexuality of the vampire and succubus with the servile masochism of the female character in *Deep Throat*. For a reasonably detailed (if positively slanted) account of Madonna's early career, see Debbi Voller, *Madonna: The Illustrated Biography* (London: Omnibus Press, 1988). See also pages 31–38 in this book.

3. John Fiske, "British Cultural Studies and Television," *Channels of Discourse*, ed. Robert C. Allen (Chapel Hill: University of North Carolina Press, 1987), p. 297. See also pages 58–75 in this book.

4. Ibid., p. 270.

5. See Kaplan, *Rocking Around the Clock*, especially pp. 115–27; and "Feminist Criticism and Television," *Channels of Discourse*, pp. 211–53.

6. Mikal Gilmore, "The Madonna Mystique," *Rolling Stone* 508 (September 10, 1987), p. 87. I wish to thank Ann Dunn for this citation.

7. In his interview with Madonna in *Rolling Stone* 548 (March 28, 1989), Bill Zehme says: "Maybe you noticed this already, but a number of songs on the new album [*Like a Prayer*] have sort of antimale themes." Her response: "[*Surprised*] Well, gee, I never thought of that. This album definitely does have a very strong feminine point of view. Hmmm. I've had some painful experiences with men in my life, just as I've had some incredible experiences. Maybe I'm representing more of the former than the latter. I certainly don't hate men. No, no, no! Couldn't live without them!" (p. 180). Madonna is caught typically in a double bind in which she is chastised at the same time for being a passive doll and for being an aggressive man-hater. See again the citations in note 1.

8. On a special MTV broadcast called "Taboo Videos" (March 26, 1988), Betty Friedan states in an interview: "I tell you, Madonna—in contrast to the image of women that you saw on MTV—at least she had spirit, she had guts, she had vitality. She was in control of her own sexuality and her life. She was a relatively good role model, compared with what else you saw."

9. Jane Bowers, "Women Composers in Italy, 1566–1700," *Women Making Music: The Western Art Tradition, 1150–1950*, ed. Jane Bowers and Judith Tick (Urbana: University of Illinois Press, 1986): "On 4 May 1686 Pope Innocent XI issued an edict which declared that 'music is completely injurious to the modesty that is proper for the [female] sex, because they become distracted from the matters and occupations most proper for them.' Therefore, 'no unmarried woman, married woman, or widow of any rank, status, condition, even those who for reasons of education or anything else are living in convents or conservatories, under any pretext, even to learn music in order to practice it in those convents, may learn to sing from men, either laymen or clerics or regular clergy, no matter if they are in any way related to them, and to play any sort of musical instrument' " (pp. 139–40).

An especially shocking report of the silencing of women performers is presented in Anthony Newcomb, *The Madrigal at Ferrara, 1579–1597* (Princeton: Princeton University Press, 1980). The court at Ferrara had an ensemble with three women virtuoso singers who became internationally famous. Duke Alfonso of Ferrara had the "three ladies" sing for Duke Guglielmo of Mantua and expected the latter to "praise them to the skies." "Instead, speaking loudly enough to be heard both by the ladies and by the Duchesses who were present [Duke Guglielmo] burst forth, 'ladies are very impressive indeed—in fact, I would rather be an ass than a lady.' And with this he rose and made everyone else do so as well, thus putting an end to the singing" (p. 24).

See also the examinations of the restrictions placed on women as musicians and performers in Richard Leppert, *Music and Image: Domesticity, Ideology and Sociocultural Formation in Eighteenth-Century England* (Cambridge: Cambridge University Press, 1988); and Julia Kosa, "Music and References to Music in *Godey's Lady's Book*, 1830–77" (Ph.D. dissertation, University of Minnesota, 1988).

10. David Lee Roth, cited in Marsh, "Girls Can't Do," p. 165. I might add that this is a far more liberal attitude than that of most academic musicians.

11. This is not always an option socially available to male performers, however. The staged enactment of masculine sensuality is problematic in Western culture in which patriarchal rules of propriety dictate that excess in spectacles be projected onto women. Thus Liszt, Elvis, and Roth can be understood as effective in part because of their transgressive behaviors. This distinction in permissible activities in music theater can be traced back to the beginnings of opera in the seventeenth century. See Robert Walser, "Running with the Devil: Power, Gender, and Madness in Heavy Metal Music" (Ph.D. dissertation, University of Minnesota, forthcoming).

12. Ellen Rosand, "The Voice of Barbara Strozzi," in *Women Making Music*, p. 185. See also Anthony Newcomb, "Courtesans, Muses, or Musicians? Professional Women Musicians in Sixteenth-Century Italy," in *Women Making Music*, pp. 90–115; and Linda Phyllis Austern, " 'Sing Againe Syren': The Female Musician and Sexual Enchantment in Elizabethan Life and Literature," *Renaissance Quarterly* 42, no. 3 (Autumn 1989), pp. 420–48. For more on the role of Renaissance courtesans in cultural production, see Ann Rosalind Jones, "City Women and Their Audiences: Louise Labé and Veronica Franco," *Rewriting the Renaissance: The Discourses of Sexual Difference in Early Modern Europe*, ed. Margaret W. Ferguson, Maureen Quilligan, and Nancy J. Vickers (Chicago: University of Chicago Press, 1986), pp. 299–316.

13. See the excerpts from Clara's diary entries and her correspondences with Robert Schumann and Brahms in Carol Neuls-Bates, ed. *Women in Music: An Anthology of Source Readings from the Middle Ages to the Present* (New York: Harper & Row, 1982), pp. 92–108; and Nancy B. Reich, *Clara Schumann: The Artist and the Woman* (Ithaca: Cornell University Press, 1985). *Women in Music* contains many other documents revealing how women have been discouraged from participating in music and how certain of them persisted to become productive composers nonetheless.

14. For examinations of how the mind/body split intersects with gender in Western culture see Genevieve Lloyd, *The Man of Reason: "Male" and "Female" in Western Philosophy* (Minneapolis: University of Minnesota Press, 1984); Susan Bordo, "The Cartesian Masculinization of Thought," *Signs* 11, no. 3 (1986), pp. 439–56; and Evelyn Fox Keller, *Reflections on Gender and Science* (New Haven: Yale University Press, 1985).

For discussions of how these slipping binary oppositions inform music, see Geraldine Finn, "Music, Masculinity and the Silencing of Women," in *New Musicology*, ed. John Shepherd (New York: Routledge, forthcoming); and my "Agenda for a Feminist Criticism of Music," *Canadian University Music Review*, forthcoming.

15. This binary opposition is not, of course, entirely stable. Imagination, for instance, is an attribute of the mind, though it was defined as "feminine" during the Enlightenment and consequently becomes a site of contestation in early Romanticism. See Jochen Schulte-Sasse, "Imagination and Modernity: Or the Taming of the Human Mind," *Cultural Critique* 5 (Winter 1986–87), pp. 23–48. Likewise, the nineteenth-century concept of "genius" itself was understood as having a necessary "feminine" component, although actual women were explicitly barred from this category. See Christine Battersby, *Gender and Genius* (London: Women's Press, 1989).

The common association of music with effeminacy is only now being examined in musicology. See Leppert, *Music and Image;* Linda Austern, " 'Alluring the Auditorie to Effeminacie': Music and the English Renaissance Idea of the Feminine," paper presented to the America Musicological Society, Baltimore (November 1988); Jeffrey Kallberg, "Genre and Gender: The Nocturne and Women's History," unpublished paper; and Maynard Solomon, "Charles Ives: Some Questions of Veracity," *Journal of the American Musicological Society* 40 (1987), pp. 466–69.

16. See Catherine Clément, *Opera, or the Undoing of Women,* trans. Betsy Wing (Minneapolis: University of Minnesota Press, 1988).

17. Quoted in Gilmore, "The Madonna Mystique," p. 87. Nevertheless, Madonna is often collapsed back into the stereotype of the *femme fatale* of traditional opera and literature. See the comparison between Madonna and Berg's Lulu in Leo Treitler, "The Lulu Character and the Character of *Lulu,*" *Music and the Historical Imagination* (Cambridge, Mass.: Harvard University Press, 1989), pp. 272–75.

18. See Richard Dyer, "In Defense of Disco," *On Record: Rock, Pop, and the Written Word,* ed. Simon Frith and Andrew Goodwin (New York: Pantheon Press, 1990), pp. 410–18.

19. See, for instance, Theodor W. Adorno's hysterical denouncements of jazz in "Perennial Fashion—Jazz," *Prisms,* trans. Samuel Weber and Shierry Weber (Cambridge, Mass.: MIT Press, 1981), pp. 121–32: "They [jazz fans] call themselves 'jitterbugs,' bugs which carry out reflex movements, performers of their own ecstasy" (p. 128).

20. However, I have often encountered hostile reactions on the part of white middle-class listeners to Aretha Franklin's frank sensuality, even when (particularly when) it is manifested in her sacred recordings such as "Amazing Grace." The argument is that women performers ought not to exhibit signs of sexual pleasure, for this invariably makes them displays for male consumption. See the discussion in John Shepherd, "Music and Male Hegemony," in *Music and Society: The Politics of Composition, Performance and Reception,* ed. Richard Leppert and Susan McClary (Cambridge: Cambridge University Press, 1987), pp. 170–72.

21. Marsh, "Girls Can't Do," p. 162.

22. See Mary Harron's harsh and cynical critique of rock's commercialism in general and Madonna in particular in "McRock: Pop as a Commodity," in *Facing the Music,* ed. Simon Frith (New York: Pantheon Books, 1988), pp. 173–220. At the conclusion of a reading of Madonna's "Open Your Heart" video, Harron writes: "The message is that our girl [Madonna] may sell sexuality, but she is free" (p. 218). See also Leslie Savan, "Desperately Selling Soda," *The Village Voice* (March 14, 1989), p. 47, which critiques Madonna's decision to make a commercial for Pepsi. Ironically, when her video to "Like a Prayer" (discussed later in this essay) was released the day after the first broadcast of the commercial, Pepsi was pressured to withdraw the advertisement, for which it had paid record-high fees. Madonna had thus maintained her artistic control, even in what had appeared to be a monumental sellout. See also pages 93–95 in this book.

23. See the discussion of the responses to Madonna of young girls in Fiske, "British Cultural Studies," pp. 269–83. See also the report of responses of young Japanese fans in Gilmore, "The Madonna Mystique," p. 38. Madonna's response: "But mainly I think they feel that most of my music is really, really positive, and I think

they appreciate that, particularly the women. I think I stand for everything that they're really taught to *not* be, so maybe I provide them with a little bit of encouragement." Considine, "That Girl," quotes her as saying: "Children always understand. They have open minds. They have built-in shit detectors" (p. 17).

24. When Jackson first signed on with Jam and Lewis, the music for this song was already "in the can" awaiting an appropriate singer. The mix throughout highlights the powerful beats, such that Jackson constantly seems thrown off balance by them. At one point the sound of a car collision punctuates her words, "I never knew what hit me"; and the ironic conclusion depicts the crumbling of her much-vaunted control. Not only was Jackson in a more dependent position with respect to production than Madonna, but the power relations *within the song itself* are very diferent from those Madonna typically enacts.

25. "There is also a sense of pleasure, at least for me and perhaps a large number of other women, in Madonna's defiant look or gaze. In 'Lucky Star' at one point in the dance sequence Madonna dances side on to the camera, looking provocative. For an instant we glimpse her tongue: the expectation is that she is about to lick her lips in a sexual invitation. The expectation is denied and Madonna appears to tuck her tongue back into her cheek. This, it seems, is how most of her dancing and groveling in front of the camera is meant to be taken. She is setting up the sexual idolization of women. For a woman who has experienced this victimization, this setup is most enjoyable and pleasurable, while the male position of voyeur is displaced into uncertainty." Robyn Blair, quoted in Fiske, "British Cultural Studies," p. 283.

26. For the ways women performers have been seen as inviting tragic lives, see Robyn Archer and Diana Simmonds, *A Star Is Torn* (New York: E.P. Dutton, 1986); Gloria Steinem, *Marilyn* (New York: Henry Holt, 1986). For an analysis of Hitchcock's punishments of sexual women, see Tania Modleski, *The Women Who Knew Too Much: Hitchcock and Feminist Theory* (New York: Methuen, 1988). For treatments of these issues in classical music, see my "The Undoing of Opera: Toward a Feminist Criticism of Music," foreword to Clément, *Opera*, pp. ix–xviii.

27. In Gilmore, "Madonna Mystique," Madonna states: "I do feel something for Marilyn Monroe. A sympathy. Because in those days, you were really a slave to the whole Hollywood machinery, and unless you had the strength to pull yourself out of it, you were just trapped. I think she didn't know what she was getting herself into and simply made herself vulnerable, and I feel a bond with that. I've certainly felt that at times—I've felt an invasion of privacy and all that—but I'm determined never to let it get me down. Marilyn Monroe was a victim, and I'm not. That's why there's really no comparison" (p. 87). The term "sign crimes" is from Arthur Kroker and David Cook, *The Postmodern Scene: Excremental Culture and Hyper-Aesthetics* (New York: St. Martin's Press, 1986), p. 21.

28. For an excellent narrative account of the *Eroica*, see Philip Downs, "Beethoven's 'New Way' and the Eroica," in *The Creative World of Beethoven*, ed. Paul Henry Lang (New York: W.W. Norton, 1970), pp. 83–102. Downs's interpretation is not inflected, however, by concerns of gender or "extramusical" notions of alterity.

29. For other readings of the Ninth Symphony, see Leo Treitler, "History, Criticism, and Beethoven's Ninth Symphony" and "'To Worship That Celestial Sound':

Motives for Analysis," in *Music and the Historical Imagination*, pp. 19–66; and Maynard Solomon, "Beethoven's Ninth Symphony: A Search for Order," *19th-Century Music* 10 (Summer 1986), pp. 3–23.

30. Fiske, "British Cultural Studies," p. 262. For more on constructions of masculine subjectivity, see Arthur Brittan, *Masculinity and Power* (London: Basil Blackwell, 1989), and Klaus Theweleit, *Male Fantasies*, vols. I and II, trans. Stephen Conway, Erica Carter, and Chris Turner (Minneapolis: University of Minnesota Press, 1987 and 1989). I owe my knowledge of and interest in metal to Robert Walser. I wish to thank him for permitting me to see his "Forging Masculinity: Heavy Metal Sounds and Images of Gender," in *Sound and Vision*, ed. Simon Frith, Andrew Goodwin, and Lawrence Grossberg (forthcoming).

31. See again the citations in note 14; Teresa de Lauretis, "Desire in Narrative," *Alice Doesn't* (Bloomington: Indiana University Press, 1984), pp. 103–57, and "The Violence of Rhetoric: Considerations on Representation and Gender," in *Technologies of Gender* (Bloomington: Indiana University Press, 1987), pp. 31–50; and Mieke Bal, *Lethal Love: Feminist Literary Readings of Biblical Love Stories* (Bloomington: Indiana University Press, 1987).

32. Compare, for example, the opening movement of Schubert's "Unfinished" Symphony, in which the tune we all know and love is in the second position and is accordingly quashed. George Michael's "Hand to Mouth" (on the *Faith* album) is a good example of the same imperatives at work in popular music. In both the Schubert and Michael, the pretty tune represents illusion up against harsh reality. My thanks to Robert Walser for bringing the Michael song to my attention.

33. This strategy of always staying in motion is advocated in Teresa de Lauretis, "The Technology of Gender," especially pp. 25–26. See also Denise Riley, *"Am I That Name?": Feminism and the Category of "Women" in History* (Minneapolis: University of Minnesota Press, 1988); and Kaja Silverman, "Fragments of a Fashionable Discourse," in *Studies in Entertainment: Critical Approaches to Mass Culture*, ed. Tania Modleski (Bloomington: Indiana University Press, 1986), pp. 150–51.

34. Some of the so-called Minimalist composers such as Philip Glass and Steve Reich also have called the conventions of tonal closure into question, as did Debussy at an earlier moment. See my "Music and Postmodernism," in *Contemporary Music Review* (forthcoming).

35. Andrew Goodwin advances a similar argument in "Music Video in the (Post) Modern World," *Screen* 18 (Summer 1987), pp. 39–42.

36. In the souvenir program book from her 1987 tour, Madonna is quoted as saying: "Madonna is my real name. It means a lot of things. It means virgin, mother, mother of earth. Someone who is very pure and innocent but someone who's very strong." Needless to say, this is not how the name has always been received.

37. For a cynical interpretation, see Steve Anderson, "Forgive Me, Father," *The Village Voice*, April 4, 1989: "Madonna snags vanguard attention while pitching critics into fierce Barthesian discussions about her belt buckles. Certainly she's an empire of signs, but the trick behind the crucifixes, opera gloves, tulle, chains, and the recent rosary-bead girdle is that they lead only back to themselves, representing *nothing*" (p. 68).
But see also the complex discussion in Fiske, "British Cultural Studies," pp.

275–76, which quotes Madonna as saying: "I have always carried around a few rosaries with me. One day I decided to wear [one] as a necklace. Everything I do is sort of tongue in cheek. It's a strong blend—a beautiful sort of symbolism, the idea of someone suffering, which is what Jesus Christ on a crucifix stands for, and then not taking it seriously. Seeing it as an icon with no religiousness attached. It isn't sacrilegious for me." Fiske concludes that "her use of religious iconography is neither religious nor sacrilegious. She intends to free it from this ideological opposition and to enjoy it, use it, for the meanings and pleasure that it has for *her* and not for those of the dominant ideology and its simplistic binary thinking."

38. For excellent discussions of the Catholic tradition of female saints and erotic imagery, see Caroline Walker Bynum, "The Female Body and Religious Practice in the Later Middle Ages," in *Zone: Fragments for a History of the Human Body*, ed. Michel Feher et al. (New York: Zone, 1989), pp. 160–219; and Julia Kristeva, *Tales of Love*, trans. Leon S. Roudiez (New York: Columbia University Press, 1987), especially pp. 83–100 and pp. 297–317.

This association is in line with many of Madonna's statements concerning Catholicism, such as her claim that "nuns are sexy" (Fiske, "British Cultural Studies," p. 275). However, she need not be aware of Saint Teresa in order for these kinds of combinations of the sacred and erotic to occur to her. Once again, her experiences as a woman in this culture mesh in certain ways with the traditional symbolism of holy submission in Christianity, and thus her metaphors of spirituality are similar in many ways to Saint Teresa's. She also intends to create this collision in the song and video. In Armond White, "The Wrath of Madonna," *Millimeter* (June 1989), Mary Lambert (director of the "Like a Prayer" video) states: "Madonna and I always work together on a concept. We both felt the song was about sexual and religious ecstasy" (p. 31). The black statue in the church is identified as Saint Martin de Porres. I wish to thank Vaughn Ormseth for bringing this article to my attention.

39. See the many settings of texts from the Song of Songs by composers such as Alessandro Grandi and Heinrich Schütz. The sacred erotic likewise influenced the literary and visual arts. See Bernini's sculpture of, or Richard Crashaw's poem concerning, Saint Teresa. I am at the moment writing a book, *Power and Desire in Seventeenth-Century Music* (Princeton: Princeton University Press, forthcoming), that examines this phenomenon.

40. Quoted in Liz Smith's column, *San Francisco Chronicle*, April 19, 1989, E1. I wish to thank Greil Marcus for bringing this to my attention. Lydia Hamessley first pointed out to me the significance of inside and outside in the organization of the video.

41. White, "The Wrath of Madonna," p. 31.

42. For an excellent discussion of the political strength of the music, rhetoric, and community of the black church today, see the interview of Cornel West by Anders Stephanson in *Universal Abandon? The Politics of Postmodernism*, ed. Andrew Ross (Minneapolis: University of Minnesota Press, 1988), pp. 277–86. Madonna speaks briefly about her identification with black culture in Zehme, "Madonna," p. 58.

43. For another sympathetic discussion of the politics of this video, see Dave Marsh, "Acts of Contrition," *Rock & Roll Confidential* 67 (May 1989), pp. 1–2.

(from *Personality Comics Presents Madonna #1*)

by Stephen Spire III, Jimmy Palmiotti, and Dave Sharpe

(from *Esquire*'s "Women We Love" 1989 issue)

Madonna, Girl of a Thousand Faces

Lady.
Broad.
Bitch.
Angel.
Virgin.
Whore.
Stripper.
Dame.
Hussy.
Flapper.
Blonde.
Brunette.
Wife.
Divorcée.
Hard.
Soft.
Acts bad.
Sings good.
Likes boys.
Likes men.
Says, You can
have me.
Says, I can
take you.
Sue us, we like
complications.

(from *Musician*)

The Decade in Madonna: Ascension of the Catholic Schoolgirl

by Mark Rowland

As the decade draws to a close the votes are tabulated and the winner is . . . Madonna. She, not Bruce Springsteen, is the biggest. She, not Michael Jackson, is the baddest. She, not Prince, is the nastiest. She, not Pepsi-Cola, is the shrewdest. She, not The Who, has earned our respect.

To talk about Madonna is to discover how words like *reductionism* ("a procedure or theory that reduces complex data or phenomena to simple terms"—Webster's) get coined. You can't argue with her triumph. It is complete. Even when her films blow dead air or her marriage breaks up or her records bomb—that's never happened—she's the winner. You can open your heart, as the song goes, and accept Madonna, or you can lump it. But there's not gonna be a recount. She *is* the winner. Though you might, at some point, wonder why.

Wondering why I've accepted Madonna in my heart got me thinking about Martin Scorsese's *The Last Temptation of Christ*. Scorsese is clearly someone who took his Catholic upbringing very seriously—at one point he studied for the priesthood—and many of his movies are animated by the sort of emotional conflicts Catholic upbringings so frequently inspire. *Last Temptation* was his great labor of love in this regard, a devout meditation on the life of Christ. The result: theaters bombed, boycotts, home video under the counter.

Then there is Madonna, who also obviously grew up Catholic, titled her bust-out record *Like a Virgin* and appeared on the LP cover wearing a crucifix, a sexy bodice, and a belt that read "Boy Toy." The record sold millions, and the yahoos haven't touched her yet.

The difference, I think, is that Scorsese pays attention to the ideals of Catholicism, like how growing up in a church that tries to make you feel guilty about sex makes sex all the more exciting. Suggesting that on MTV is not so dangerous. But it's nervy enough to qualify as sharp entertainment.

Of course Madonna is sharp. More reductionism: If Dan Quayle had seventeen straight top ten hits, he'd be sharp too. She image-borrows from Marilyn and Marlene and even Judy Holliday (in the dreadful movie *Who's That Girl*), all bombshells and extremely bright women. Madonna's luster doesn't shimmer naturally like theirs. Where she excels as an artist is her ability to pull together a whole reference shelf of favored styles into a pastiche that feels fresh, hip, even original. In that sense she embodies the reigning imperative of eighties pop music.

One thing you gotta admire about Madonna is that she made it by combining the power of pop's new format, the MTV video, with its oldest, the dance single. By contrast, her albums seem uneven and shapeless, carrier-paks for fans too lazy to buy the individual hits. Almost all her singles have ace melodic hooks, beats at once funky and aerobic, are well-produced (meaning that pros like Nile Rodgers and Reggie Lucas knew enough to serve *her* vision), and thanks to video, hang together like the episodes of a long-running serial in which the heroine changes with the scenery.

Thus Madonna segues from glamourpuss ("Like a Virgin") to streetwise urchin ("Into the Groove") to pregnant teenager ("Papa Don't Preach") to whatever it was she was up to in "Like a Prayer." Rivals as theatrical as Michael Jackson and Prince end up playing themselves in front of a camera, which inevitably becomes kind of a snore. Madonna can't match their talent, but she takes more chances with her personality, which makes her more likely to hold your attention. Which is the point.

For all her attitude and ambition, Madonna comes off pretty regular. Not like she'd be your friend—she's too driven to hang out with nobodies. But if the opportunity arose, you could relate. Like Barbie, the basic Madonna model is surprisingly free of gimcracks and weirdness. She's fun for the whole family—a savvy woman, entering her thirties, who sings like a little girl and likes to stir things up. Good/bad, but not evil.

The first time I paid attention to Madonna, just before she got real famous, was at a semi-seedy health club we both worked out at in New York. When she was there I spent most of my time watching her, not because her navel is so swell but because I have never seen anyone, before or since, work out so long and so hard. It actually seemed a little nutty at the time. But—you've seen the results.

Which is why, in the end, Madonna is the winner. She worked the hardest, or at least she worked out the hardest. For a while in the 1980s, it was the same American Dream.

▶ From *Rolling Stone* Polls, 1989

BEST ALBUM

1. *Full Moon Fever,* Tom Petty
2. *Steel Wheels,* the Rolling Stones
3. *Disintegration,* the Cure
4. *Like a Prayer, Madonna*

WORST ALBUM

1. *Hangin' Tough,* New Kids on the Block
2. *Batman,* Prince
3. *Girl You Know It's True,* Milli Vanilli
4. *Like a Prayer, Madonna*

BEST FEMALE SINGER

1. Paula Abdul
2. *Madonna*

WORST FEMALE SINGER

1. *Madonna*

BEST VIDEO

1. "Sowing the Seeds of Love," Tears For Fears
2. *"Express Yourself," Madonna*

WORST VIDEO

1. *"Like a Prayer," Madonna*
2. "If I Could Turn Back Time," Cher
3. "Hangin' Tough," New Kids on the Block
4. "Love in an Elevator," Aerosmith
5. *"Cherish," Madonna*

WORST ALBUM COVER

1. *Steel Wheels*, the Rolling Stones
2. *Like a Prayer, Madonna*

BEST-DRESSED FEMALE

1. Paula Abdul
2. *Madonna*

WORST-DRESSED FEMALE

1. Cher
2. *Madonna*

SEXIEST FEMALE

1. Paula Abdul
2. *Madonna*

Critics' Poll

BEST VIDEO

1. *"Like a Prayer," Madonna*

(from *Egg*)

Madonna Eats L.A.

by Anita Sarko

Los Angeles has finally discovered a truly sane way to rate restaurants. Forget that silly New York method of relying on a few taste-bud-jaded critics who base their opinions on obscure slimy bits cooked to perfection. Who really cares about how velvety the sweetbreads are, or how silky the brains, or tender the stomachs? Gross me out! Europe is no better. All those hard-earned stars, and for what? Nothing you'd ever want to see with the lights on, let alone eat.

L.A.'s new yardstick may still rely on a star system, but it's much more simplified and literal. At this moment, what Lana Turner was to Schwab's drugstore, what David Hockney's pool is to the Hollywood Roosevelt Hotel, what *Rebel Without a Cause* is to the Observatory, "Madonna eats here" is to L.A. cuisine. It was at the seventy-one-year-old Musso & Frank—whose one-liner ID (a cool local custom) is "It's the oldest restaurant in Hollywood"—where I was first hit with "Madonna eats here." By the time I left, five days later, I felt positively slapped silly with this fact and became convinced her only real competition was the infamous cockroach that ate Cincinnati. Considering Madonna's voracious appetite for fame, it won't surprise me if she acquires the film rights to *The Metamorphosis*.

But we're being piggy. Rather, we should salute the woman who is going to do for restaurants what George Washington once did for inns. It's no wonder she jogs so damned much.

► **1** ◄

Morton's (8800 Melrose Ave.)

Dines with her manager, Freddie DeMann, and CAA agent Ron Meyer. Is on best behavior at best table. "If Morton's were a stage, they'd be on the apron."

Campanile (624 S. La Brea Ave.)

Allegedly had kitchen create three desserts in three different colors to taste. Rejected them all in a fit of petulance suffered while sharing them with George Michael. One dessert was yellow.

Columbia Bar & Grill (1448 N. Gower St.)

Records in area. Has her own booth in back section known as the Grill. "She's the nicest, politest, sweetest person to wait on. She calls if she's late."

Chan Dara (1511 N. Cahuenga Blvd.)

The Hollywood Chan Dara relies on self-importance as much as on the cuisine of Bangkok. "Madonna comes in here to have her private time." (We thought rest rooms were only for paying customers.)

Le Dome (8720 Sunset Blvd.)

Allegedly ordered steak and had food fight.

Shane (2932 Beverly Glen Cir.)

Seen at this Italian restaurant, described as Santa Fe meets Milan.

Pazzia (755 N. La Cienega Blvd.)

" '*Baciami il culo*'—'kiss my ass' in Italian—is something she likes to say all the time. She has a wonderful sense of humor."

▶ 8 ◀

Hymie's Fish Market (9228 W. Pico Blvd.)

"She's a real nice lady. She eats salmon or whitefish. She orders what you recommend, nothing fancy. She trusts what I tell her."

▶ 9 ◀

Ben Frank's (8585 Sunset Blvd.)

"She was real domineering. She told Warren what to order. It was as if she ordered for him. They ordered junk food. Greasy food, like onion rings and quesadillas."

▶ 10 ◀

Cafe Mambo (707 Heliotrope Ave.)

Brought multicolored Necco wafers with her for dessert.

▶ 11 ◀

Mirabelle (8768 Sunset Blvd.)

"When Sean and Madonna got married and nobody knew where they were, they were in the secret booth, the back booth on the side where all the celebrities want to be. Celebrities go to other places to dine. They come here to eat."

▶ 12 ◀

Chaya Brasserie (8741 Alden Dr.)

"Hasn't been here in a long time."

▶ 13 ◀

City Restaurant (180 S. La Brea Ave.)

Eats here with Warren and Sandra all the time. A few weeks ago, she came in with her beau, and the host addressed them as Mr. Beatty and Madonna. She said, "Why does everyone call him Mr. Beatty and just call me

Madonna?" Ms. Ciccone (pronounced Chi-ko-nee) shrugged and then proceeded to go on about it for an hour, obviously so upset that she forgot to sit on Mr. Beatty's lap, as is her custom. When Ms. Ciccone left, nobody called her anything.

▶ 14 ◀

Musso & Frank (6667 Hollywood Blvd.)

"I don't think the owners would approve, joking about that in a newspaper."

▶ 15 ◀

The Source (8301 Sunset Blvd.)

"Hasn't been here in a long time."

▶ 16 ◀

Muse (7360 Beverly Blvd.)

"Has black bean soup every time she comes in."

▶ 17 ◀

The Ivy (113 N. Robertson Blvd.)

They hung up on me.

▶ 18 ◀

Atlas Bar & Grill (3760 Wilshire Blvd.)

Restaurant received phone call on Friday asking when it was most crowded. When informed that the hottest time was 8:30, the caller identified himself as Warren and made reservations for four at 8:30. Arrived and put on grand show of affection for customers.

▶ 19 ◀

Sushi on Sunset (8264 Sunset Blvd.)

Reported to be first public appearance with Sean. "Walked in looking like the cat swallowing the canary."

Costume Sketch

(from the Blond Ambition Tour)

by Jean-Paul Gaultier

(from *The New Republic*)

Unlike a Virgin

by Luc Sante

After two or three months of ceaseless barrage upon the American continent, the winds of Madonna have shifted and besieged Europe. Not that the American public is likely to banish her from memory for even a second, especially since The Movie is playing in every minimall and multiplex and is still being considered from every angle in Sunday supplements throughout the land, and The Album is prominently on display in retail outlets of every demographic. The Tour, however, has left these shores, taking with it the unilateral media saturation that brought Madonna into every room of every house and caused her to hover in the periphery, at least, of every consciousness. Is there anyone, at large or in stir, who does not know the details of Madonna's latest look, with its kewpie-doll ponytail and dominatrix affectations, its nose-cone brassieres, and pin-striped suits with breast slits? Or of her stage show, complete with tubular-breasted males, wriggling mermen, and a kickline of Dick Tracys?

Of course, Madonna dwells among us at most times, and her presence is felt in record shops and T-shirt boutiques and on MTV and in the sheets and rags that draw all their material from speculation on the hidden lives of celebrities. But in this late-century version of the dog-and-pony show, her face and body and the attributes of her legend appeared on and in every general-interest magazine and newspaper and magazine-format television program, her name was heard as a reference and a figure of speech in the routines of comedians, the banter of TV news co-anchors, the fulminations of media moralists, in bar-talk and gym-talk and water-cooler-talk and supermarket-line-talk. In the night sky of the American imagination, Madonna looms.

•   •   •

For the time being, at least. Will she endure as a figure to color forever our idea of fame, to become the little picture accompanying the definition of "media star" in the illustrated dictionaries of the future? Will she enter the domain of clip-art imagery as a badly printed blob on shopping bags and paper place mats whose muddy outlines are nevertheless as instantly recognizable as those of the Marilyn of the dress-flipping-up-over-steam-vent or the Brando of the peaked cap and motorcycle jacket?

Such, after all, is her ambition. Madonna is not out for mere money or mere glory; even less is she in pursuit of the perfect beat or the sublime hook. It is not for her to achieve international respect and then disappear into genteel privacy in Switzerland or New Mexico, to define a song or a movie role and then suffer that title's parenthetical accompaniment of her name in every printed citation. She does not want to make her pile and cut out—she does not want to cut out. Madonna wants to conquer the unconscious, to become indelible.

She has already taken steps toward this end. There is, for example, the matter of the single name, which in America is usually an abbreviation conferred by the public over time as an accolade and a sign of affection. Madonna has taken the shortcut of lopping it off herself. And there is the image. In her canny way Madonna realized that in this day and age success results less often from imposing a spectacular figure on the public than from erecting a screen upon which the public can project its own internal movies. So she invented herself as a mutable being, a container for a multiplicity of images. She could be anything, with only the one unchanging grace note: the mole just above her lip.

Madonna Louise Veronica Ciccone hails from Michigan, came to New York in the late 1970s or early 1980s, studied dance, hung out heavily, began her career as a photographer's model (some mildly dirty pictures from this period surfaced a few years ago, and some of the tabloids were weak-minded enough to think they could make a scandal out of them), appeared in a small role in at least one low-grade exploitation movie, and then began making a name as a "track singer" (a lost term from that brief interregnum between live performance and the total electronic environment, referring to vocalists who appeared in clubs singing to taped accompaniment).

On the New York club scene she appears to have gone from decorative nobody to new face on the rise in a sort of Ruby Keeler minute. She persuaded Mark Kamins, a deejay at Danceteria, the club of that hour, to produce a song for her ("Everybody"), then persuaded Seymour Stein, the godfather of New York "new wave," to issue it on his Sire Records label, and it hit the charts. In those days (1982), when Reaganism was still young, dance-party records made by ambitious white semibohemians might be viewed as artistic and even political statements merely by virtue of their genre. By eschewing rock-'n'-roll jingoism in favor of bass out front, wide backbeat, and lyrics that in essence always said, "Let's everybody party down," they made a gesture of calling out to the whole world, especially to its third part. It was a year or two before this stance became generic.

So it was that Madonna's early records, blasting out over such stations as WBLS in New York, stations that were then just beginning to be referred to by the demographic euphemism "urban contemporary," sounded like more than mere product. The very simple lyrics of her second 45, "Holiday" ("We should take a holiday, some time to celebrate . . ."), had a utopian flavor, however soft. Her voice, with its nasal tough-girl inflection by Ronnie Spector out of Minnie Mouse and related by blood or marriage to the throw-down quality exuded by such chanteuses as Teena Marie and Evelyn "Champagne" King, made the invitation sound uncompromising, almost brave. After three or four hits in succession, Madonna was a downtown singer with proven crossover ability.

Still, the likelihood of her achieving any further distinction seemed remote. Madonna, however, was not one to accept any predetermined view of her career. She immediately raised the stakes, and in rapid order began advancing one marketing theme after another, in the process revealing that while she had a small talent as a pop singer, as an image strategist she possessed something approaching genius. Her first order of business was to jettison the appealing but limited waif look featured on the cover of her eponymous first album, to replace its whisper with a shout. For this purpose she initiated a hostile takeover of the sartorial repertoire of her older rival Cyndi Lauper, an original who had taken the hippie-punk scavenger aesthetic to an extreme point and assembled herself as a living collage of old and new styles, clashing colors, mismatched fabrics, accessories contrived from the most unlikely objects.

Madonna, of course, was no original; she was, like her role model David Bowie, a magpie with a flair for highlighting the critical elements of the styles she appropriated. She dispensed with the self-mockery implicit in Lauper's presentation and zeroed in on its fetishistic sexual aspect. Hence the bras-as-outerwear, the "Boy Toy" belt buckles, the junk jewelry by the pound. The look titillated boys of all ages, while teenage girls found in it a form of rebellion that could be safely assumed and doffed outside parental ken, since it involved nothing drastic or irreversible. The look instantly propelled Madonna into the national image bank. She had taken her first beachhead.

A measure of the success of this image was that it lasted much longer in the consciousness of the public than it did in Madonna's own career. Its early crudity can be assessed in her *Virgin Tour* video, which shows her looking askew and even a bit chunky, missing notes and flailing around on stage, but evidently learning on the job. This, however, was her live show. At the same time, she was displaying a precocious understanding of the nascent power of the video clip, becoming one of the first pop stars to issue songs that were inseparably entwined with the visual imagery of their MTV illustrations in the minds of consumers.

Her first successful salvo in this direction was "Like a Virgin." "Should go over big in Italy," quipped a friend of mine at the time; sure enough, the video was shot in Venice, and it contained the first glimmers of her now-trademark Catholic-transgression sideline. Of course, it also possessed all of the grace of a "Girls of the Adriatic" *Playboy* feature, along with the patented MTV significance-trigger of staggering slo-mo; but it can be said to have made its point. Her follow-up was "Material Girl," which may have sounded a bit like Carmen Miranda. What everybody noticed, however, was the video, in which Madonna shamelessly reinvented the wheel, lifting wholesale Marilyn's courtroom dance sequence from *Gentlemen Prefer Blondes* and flushing it of its satire. Subtlety, Madonna well knew, butters no parsnips in the pop marketplace. "Material Girl" was crass, vulgar, obvious, charmless, and virtually definitive of the grasping zeitgeist of 1984. It was, naturally, her biggest hit to date, and probably remains so.

Around the same time she was fortunate enough to be handed an opportunity well beyond her own contrivance. Susan Seidelman, a little-known but enterprising filmmaker apprenticing, as Madonna had, in the Manhattan bohemia career institute, cast her in *Desperately Seeking Susan* as the mystery woman of the title. The film was halting, turgid, and as instantly irrelevant as any Gidget vehicle. But in its tame exploitation of the downtown-scene mystique it somehow rang the safe-rebellion chime for millions of middle-class youth. Madonna was ideally suited to her role, which called for her to look sultry and jaded and not say a whole lot. The movie earned many times its budget, its title entered the catch-phrase arsenal of headline writers everywhere, and Madonna emerged from the experience having attained a new rung of celebrity, along with a reputation, soon shown to be utterly unfounded, as a major box-office attraction.

The rest, as they say, is history. She married the troubled Sean Penn and succeeded in profiting from his bad press, appeared in a couple of cinematic bombs (*Shanghai Surprise* and *Who's That Girl*, in case you've forgotten) that did not leave her terribly scathed, issued many song-and-video packages that each involved a new look and a new attempt at a veneer of meaning, made a stab at artistic respectability by appearing in a sub-par David Mamet play, raised middle-American hackles with further Catholic-transgression affectations in the "Like a Prayer" video, and with a mock-Sapphic Mutt-and-Jeff talk-show routine with Sandra Bernhard, promptly began being seen with Warren Beatty in as many simultaneous locations as Saint Anthony of Padua, and then embarked on an entirely new round of publicity with The Tour, The Movie, and The Album.

This dawn broke in early spring, as the tour started in Japan and immediately began spinning off magazine spreads. The stage show looked scary in these pictures, a late-modernist casino spectacular involving elements from the Cabaret Voltaire, Salvador Dali's 1939 World's Fair show, *A Clockwork Orange*, Ken Russell movies, and the Alternative Miss World pageant. Madonna's hairstyle, for which she acknowledged the influence of the mid-1960s Tressy doll (you squeezed her stomach and pulled an endless lock through a hole in the top of her head), at the same time suggested styles current on late-night cable-TV commercials for Dial-a-Mistress. The Jean-Paul Gaultier outfits were similarly daunting, redolent of Brunhilde and Attack of the Amazons and the homey-sinister allure of the 1950s bondage accoutrements immortalized in those little books published by Irving Klaw. Has she gone too far this time? you were supposed to ask.

The show itself was a wink and a nudge, a dance number and a blackout routine. Indeed, in its erotic display it was probably one of the most traditional stage shows to follow the circuit since everybody stopped wondering who killed burlesque. The degree of sexuality present in its set pieces was entirely allusive, twice-removed, and all but obliterated by the massive inverted commas that enclosed every aspect of the production. As a spiritual heir to Barnum, Madonna was in essence executing her version of the sign he famously put up reading "This Way to the Egress," which lured scores of people with active imaginations and small vocabularies right out the door.

For the record: she mock-kicked her female dancers around the stage while insulting them and complaining about the New York attitude (or at least that was the line at the Nassau Coliseum), mimed sodomizing various parties (though you would have missed the allusion had you been thinking Ziegfeld), allowed herself to be mock-ravished by male dancers gotten up as eunuchs during a faux-Oriental version of "Like a Virgin" and by an unseen deity while she struck ecstasy-of-Saint-Teresa poses during "Like a Prayer." There was also a song (included on the current album) whose lyrics and production number were devoted to spanking. Oh, yes, and there were those male dancers adorned with breasts that flopped like so many pairs of flaccid phalli while her own set looked like armor-plated projectiles.

There might be said to be a recurring theme here. If truth be told, Madonna herself does not precisely exude sexuality. What she exudes is more like will, iron self-discipline, and, of course, punctuality, that courtesy of monarchs. In her "Ciao, Italia" video, decked out in various gymnastic outfits and body-pumping to the screams of tens of thousands in a soccer stadium in Turin, Madonna looks perfectly able to make the trains run on time. (Do not mistake this for an ethnic slur: her last name could just as easily be O'Flanagan and the setting Oslo or Kalamazoo.) Between the teasing simulation of carnality and the real passion for efficiency lies Madonna's bona-fide erotic territory.

All the sexual imagery in the show, behind its rococo and vaudeville trappings, was single-mindedly fixated on power and its representations. The reason that Madonna does not possess much intrinsic sexual appeal, in spite of having raided the symbolic vanity cases of every icon from Harlow to Dietrich to Hayworth to Monroe (and throwing in Elvis for good measure), is that she lacks any trace of vulnerability, a quality that, it should be noted, is essential to the charms of both sexes. Pout and pant and writhe though she might, Madonna is not sexually convincing because her eyes do not register. They are too busy watching the door.

If, at this point, there is any aspect of Madonna's act that seems independent of calculation, it is her preoccupation with the Catholic mysteries. Just such treading of the line between sacred and profane in the "Like a Prayer" video, you will recall, curtailed her lucrative career as a Pepsi-Cola spokesmodel. It seems there was this thing that happened between her and (apparently) Saint Martin de Porres, and then she acquired a case of stigmata, and then . . . Somehow various people took offense at this rather conventional set of images straight out of the Symbolist fakebook and put pressure on her corporate sponsors to suppress a commercial that by all accounts (it was broadcast exactly once) featured a very different, rather family-oriented storyline, even though it was set to the same tune as the video. This incident did not, however, prevent Madonna from including in her stage show a routine suggesting a musical-comedy version of *The Devils of Loudun*, complete with candles, crosses, stained glass, censers, and dancers garbed in minicassocks. While it makes for natural theater and automatic naughtiness, and comes equipped with a rich vocabulary of props, costumes, and buzzwords, it is also, how shall we say, parochial, an odd liability for one attempting so earnestly to cover as broad a consumer base as possible.

Perhaps the whiff of scandal accounts for the gusto with which Madonna throws herself into the exploitation of sacerdotal iconography. During her tour in Toronto, plainclothes cops put in an appearance, apparently following up a complaint of lewdness, and although they took no action, Madonna's parent company, Warner Bros., took the incident and ran with it, generating even more publicity from a noncase of censorship manqué. This occurred, with superb commercial timing, within a week of a more serious occasion: the action by the Broward County (Florida) sheriff's office to ban sales and performances of 2 Live Crew's witless but entirely traditional party record. A week or two after that, the National Endowment for the Arts chose to disregard the advice of its own nominating panel and withheld funds from four performance artists whose very earnest and noncommercial work happens to address the concerns of sexual minorities. Meanwhile, in Italy, Madonna succeeded in garnering more publicity from condemnations of her act by religious authorities, and their disapproval either affected ticket sales or provided a cover for sluggish trade. Presumably, Madonna is now free to title her next opus *Like a Martyr.*

And what of the other two legs of Madonna's media-assault troika? The album, *I'm Breathless*, is a departure for her, although not necessarily a very good idea. It functions as a sort of subsidiary sound track tie-in to *Dick Tracy*, and three of the songs included are featured in the movie. The whole is therefore imbued with a 1930s pastiche quality (all except "Vogue," which is fairly generic dance music but possesses considerably more vigor than any of the other tracks). But the current idea of what the 1930s sounded like bears about the same relation to the real thing as the kind of music that is played by men wearing straw boaters and candy-striped shirts and is called "Dixieland" bears to New Orleans jazz.

Whatever interest the songs might themselves contain is disfigured by an excess of cute fillips, the sort of fripperies that at the time were restricted to novelty records. The three songs appearing in the movie are by Stephen Sondheim, which is fine if you happen to share that kind of taste, although it should be pointed out that his penchant for chromatic eccentricities does no favor to Madonna, whose limited vocal equipment is inadequate to the task at hand. As yet another attempt to expand her horizons, this move by Madonna seems ill-advised, as it neither bears her triumphantly into a new area nor capitalizes on her actual strengths—but the thing currently sits at number four on the charts, so who is to say?

The impossibility of second-guessing the vagaries of the American public is emphasized by the appearance of *Dick Tracy*, a film graced by moments of enormous pictorial beauty that otherwise lurches woodenly along—a Red Grooms construction devised by computer or committee—and yet is the hit movie of the summer. Madonna plays one of the four principal roles not calling for grotesque facial prostheses, although Breathless Mahoney is an animated graphic with all the soul of a rubber stamp. Madonna's job is to look, once again, sultry and jaded. Unfortunately she has been given entirely too much to say, and even though her lines consist of strung-together femme fatale clichés sampled and resequenced from somebody's memory of the works of Mae West, poor Madonna does not manage even a cartoonish conviction. She simply utters, and the lines fall from her mouth and drop on the floor. "I was wondering what a girl had to do to get arrested," she says, with the same inflection she might use to convey her intention of seeing if the mail has arrived.

Madonna, then, is a bad actress, a barely adequate singer, a graceless dancer, a boring interview subject, a workmanlike but uninspired (co-)songwriter, and a dynamo of hard work and ferocious ambition. She has thus far been brilliant at imposing herself on the attention of the world, but there is no telling how long she can keep it up. Her pool of ideas, derived from a diligent study of iconology, is limited. There are only so many more myths she can recut to her fit. Her ability to titillate will wane with time; there is a certain age past which pop stars need to affect a serious demeanor or else find another line of work, and perhaps *I'm Breathless*, for all its many teases, represents a rehearsal for this eventuality, a record made for people who stay home at night.

Actually, it is entirely possible that Madonna will be able to coast from wild youth into eminence without an inordinate amount of exertion. To judge by the audience at her recent stage shows, the largest part of her constituency is made up of teenage girls who may not think she's a genius but admire her as a workhorse and a career strategist (and because she scares teenage boys). To these consumers she is already a fixture, who may ultimately be accorded the sort of permanent landmark status currently enjoyed by enigmas like Bob Hope. For the remainder of the public, much of Madonna's success to date has resulted from her function as a readymade, albeit a very self-willed readymade. If other decades possessed their blond bombshell superstars, is it not fitting that the present era should have one of its own? From this perspective, Madonna is a star the way Ivory is a soap and Broadway is a street. But while endurance comes naturally to statues, it requires speed and fluidity of humans, and in ever increasing amounts. Madonna cannot afford to sleep.

(from the *Los Angeles Times*)

Of Savages and Their Wild Goddess

by Art Buchwald

My friend Walla Dubois, from Tanzania, came to see me. When I visited his country, Walla entertained me at a tribal music festival in his village, and I thought it only fair to reciprocate.

"Would you like to go to Disney World?"

"No," Walla replied, "I want to go to a rock concert and be with the real people of America."

I had no choice but to get tickets for a Madonna concert.

Walla was terribly excited. "Wait until my people back home hear that I went to see Madonna. Is she still going with Warren Beatty?"

We entered the stadium where thousands of fans were naked to the waist, waving their shirts in the air.

Walla whispered to me: "Do you think they'd mind if I took pictures of them? My people will not believe it."

"I'm sure they won't mind," I told him. "Rock concert fans are always posing for tourists."

Walla snapped away as Madonna writhed all over the stage.

The fans had their arms stretched up in the air in some sort of fascist salute. I said to Walla: "How does this compare to home?"

"We never get this primitive," he confided. "Our tribal dancing requires discipline and some sense of decorum. This is the first time I've seen so many savages in one place."

"They're not savages," I assured him. "They are just our children doing their own thing with our money."

"Madonna loves her body, doesn't she?" Walla remarked.

"If our kids couldn't yell and scream and wave their hands they would feel cheated, and they might go out and trash all of Queens. You must understand our customs, Walla. They may seem strange to you, but they have been part of our way of life for twenty years."

"I have just figured out the main difference between our music and yours."

"What is it?"

"Our performers play on drums and yours play on loudspeakers."

"That's true. But notice how sexual Madonna is when she is singing to the audience: It's almost as if she is making love to the entire world."

"In my country we're forbidden by the Supreme Tribal Council to do that. They no longer allow anyone to get too carried away by the passion of the moment. If Madonna comes to Tanzania she will have to put some clothes on, or they will run her out of the country."

"She couldn't. What makes her a great artist is that everyone is turned on by her costumes."

Walla asked: "What do these fans do when they are not at concerts screaming and dancing in the aisles?"

"They repair computers, perform heart surgery, fill prescriptions, fix cars, and develop intercontinental ballistic missile systems. You wouldn't know it to look at them, but a lot of these folks are in charge of air traffic safety."

He said: "It figures."

(from the Cheap Art Store, San Francisco)

Madonna Symposium Survey

Results compiled by

Sarah Williams and

Jennifer Martinez

How will you meet Madonna?

"I'll meet her in a campervan."

"By killing Vice President Quayle for her."

"We'll meet in the bathroom of a restaurant. I'll hand her toilet paper under the stall because hers has none."

"When I visit New York I will go to her favorite clubs as long as my money holds out."

"By assassinating all members of the Supreme Court."

"By interviewing her."

"Gala opening."

"After our deaths, in hell, saying, 'What's a nice girl like you doing in a place like this?' "

What will you say when you meet Madonna?

" 'We love you—please slap me.' "

"I will thank her for all the inspiration and tell her that I love her."

"I will say nothing, just give a knowing psychic glance."

" 'Touch me.' "

" 'You are my idol and inspiration.' "

" 'Bite me.' "

Favorite hairdo?

"*Playboy:* dark head and body hair."

"Madonna's hairdos are all great in context."

"Marilyn Monroe."

"The one with her in the big hat."

"The blond ponytail for the Blond Ambition tour."

"*Like a Prayer* hair."

"Short-platinum."

"In the MTV 'Vote!' commercial."

"Curly black."

"Straight brown."

Describe a peak Madonna-worshiping experience:

"When she leans back in the 'Lucky Star' video."

"Any of several Madonnathons I have been affiliated with. They involve 24, 48, or 72 hours in a row of being in a room covered wall to wall with Madonna posters and pictures, watching Madonna videos, and listening to Madonna."

"During her recent concert I almost fainted when the lights went on and she appeared onstage. I cried several times and it was a revelation."

"During all videos I am transformed and transfixed and transported and transfused."

"I was in the front row of her concert. She looked down and winked at me!"

"Every time she grabs her crotch."

"During the Broadway show *Speed-the-Plow,* I was up in the tenth row cheering for 'my lady' Madonna and having her see me."

"I went to my sister's twelfth birthday party. They were playing *Like a Virgin* there. I saw the album cover. It was orgasmic."

Dreams you've had? Sexual fantasies?

"I was dressed in a tutu and she was slapping me—it felt so gooood!"

"A long marriage ceremony of me to Madonna."

"I was in a room full of gold-framed pictures of her."

"Many—once talking to twin Madonnas."

"My mother revealed to me that Madonna was the child she had given up for adoption."

"Me and Madonna in Jell-O."

" 'Let me be your dog.' "

"Riding in a white limo with her."

"I dream our nervous systems become perfectly in tune and I make her come at will."

"Big big macaroons and Madonna."

"I dreamt she was a makeup person at Payless."

Feelings about Madonna's taste in men:

"Bad."
"Yucky."
"Lousy."
"Ick."
"Skanky."

Bad and ignorant things you've heard people say about Madonna:

"She's just trying to be like Marilyn Monroe."
"Slut."
"She's a slut."
"She's boring."
"She doesn't matter."
"No talent."
"That she can't act."
"That she's a 'fake' blonde."
"She's a bitch."
"She fucked her way to the top."
"She's from Worcester, Mass."
" 'She's a slut.' I say, 'Oh, please!' "

Madonna quotes that have given you guidance:

"Everybody get up and do your thing."
"Living in a material world."

"Her attitude about sexuality and AIDS."

"Touch me."

"Hi, I'm Madonna . . . MADONNA."

"I don't know how to sing or dance but I don't let that stop me."

"You're a superstar."

"God knows I have my bad side."

"Live now."

"When you have a vision, you follow it. You don't need opinions or advice if you have that vision."

"I DON'T BAKE."

(from *Forbes*)

A Brain for Sin and a Bod for Business

by Matthew Schifrin

with Peter Newcomb

She has just finished a rigorous song and dance routine in Nice, France. Madonna Ciccone, the thirty-two-year-old bleached-blond pop star, walks across the stage and pretends to rough up her background vocalists. Clad in an ivory-colored bustier and trousers from a business suit, Madonna then looks out at the crowd of thirty-five thousand fans, grabs her crotch, raises her fist, and yells, "I'm the boss around here." The crowd roars.

This routine was repeated at almost every Madonna performance this summer, but it's more than play-acting. She is the boss. She is the president and sole owner of a multimillion-dollar corporate organization that in peak season has hundreds of employees and operates through nearly half a dozen entities, including Boy Toy Inc., Siren Films, and Slutco.

Congratulations, Madonna. The critics may attack you, but you are one heck of a moneymaker. The nation's top-earning female entertainer for 1990, Madonna brought in an estimated $39 million in pretax earnings. She has staying power, too. While performers like Whitney Houston and Cyndi Lauper rise fast and fade fast, Madonna has stayed near the top for all five years *Forbes* has compiled its list of America's highest-earning entertainers. Since 1986 Madonna has earned at least $125 million.

For Time Warner, the giant entertainment firm, Madonna has meant more than a half-billion dollars in record sales. Then there are concerts, videos, motion pictures, and other merchandise, which added hundreds of millions more for other companies.

People who work with Madonna agree that she is a rarity among entertainers: a star who runs her own business affairs. "She has a very strong hand in dealmaking and financing of her enterprises. Nothing gets done without her participation," says Jeffrey Katzenberg, the chairman of Disney Studios, who dealt with her during the production of *Dick Tracy*. He adds that she uses her lawyers and accountants and advisers "as aides in making her own judgment, as opposed to having them run her life."

Yet if there is one thing that drives Madonna up the wall, it's being described in print or on the tube as a calculating businesswoman. That's not the image she sells. She refused to talk to *Forbes* for this article, and apparently instructed her entire organization to clam up. Managers, accountants, investment advisers, dancers, hairdressers, and makeup artists all refused to speak for the record.

A close business associate of Madonna's made the mistake of speaking to *Forbes* about the performer without getting her permission. The next day he called back pleading with us not to quote him by name. "I could get into a lot of trouble. I have a family." He sounded panicky.

Actually the associate had given away no secrets. He had been highly complimentary. He merely confirmed that she was very "business-oriented" and had "an excellent sense of sell." Is that a sin? No, but Madonna wants rigid control of her own publicity, and being a shrewd businesswoman might be incompatible with the naughty image she has so carefully crafted.

Born on August 16, 1958, in Bay City, Michigan, she's a natural brunette with alabaster skin and blue eyes, one of eight children in a strict middle-class Roman Catholic family. In high school she got mostly A's. But even then she enjoyed standing out from the crowd: As a high school cheerleader she refused to shave her armpits.

This tendency to show off has taken her far. She first came to fame in late 1983 with her premiere album, *Madonna*, which sold nearly 9 million copies. Her look was trampy and punk: She was clad in skimpy black clothes, her navel was exposed, and her dyed-blond hair showed obvious dark roots. Her music was for dancing and her vocal sound was girlish. Her songs were upbeat and oozed sex. She wore lots of bracelets and large crucifix earrings.

By the time her second album, *Like a Virgin*, hit the stores in 1984, she had switched to a silk wedding dress with a belt buckle that read "Boy Toy." She also wore her underwear as outerwear, starting a fashion craze. In a video for the song "Material Girl" on that album, Madonna dressed up as Marilyn Monroe and spoofed Monroe's infamous "Diamonds Are a Girl's Best Friend" number from the movie *Gentlemen Prefer Blondes*. The album sold 11 million copies.

By 1986 Madonna had completely shed the trampy sex kitten look and sound for a more old-fashioned and feminine appearance. She began singing in a deeper, more serious voice, and in a video from her third album wore honey-blond hair and a demure flowered dress. In July 1987 she got herself on the cover of *Cosmopolitan* as a glamorous blonde, and in May 1988 she graced the cover of *Harper's Bazaar* as a prim brunette. Her *True Blue* album of that period sold nearly 17 million copies, and she sold more albums among the over-twenty crowd than ever.

Last year it was time for another model changeover. The cover on Madonna's 1989 album, *Like a Prayer*, featured her looking like a cross between a gypsy and a hippie. The album sold 11 million copies.

Madonna went for a complete makeover in 1990: a futuristic look, her blond hair tied back severely, a modern microphone unit strapped to her head, and her body adorned with bustiers that look more like armor than underwear.

"Where Detroit seems to have a difficult time retooling and turning out a new product line every couple of years to stimulate its customers, Madonna does not," says an entertainment executive who knows her well. "She comes out with new lines with all sorts of new gizmos, options and flashing lights."

She knows, too, the value of controversy: If you make the older generation disapproving enough, the younger generation will pay attention to you. Hence Madonna makes a business of pressing America's moral hot buttons. She has written songs about Catholicism, censorship, and teenage pregnancy.

Her late 1980s breakup with tough-guy actor Sean Penn got almost as much publicity as her marriage to him in August 1985. Later, on TV, she hinted at a lesbian love affair with comedian Sandra Bernhard, but then said she was kidding. On another TV appearance she discussed the sexual pleasure of being spanked.

Madonna's much reported affair with *Dick Tracy* costar Warren Beatty hasn't hurt *Dick Tracy's* box office revenues, which surpassed $100 million this summer. Playing the media like a musical instrument, Madonna garnered herself more ink by agreeing to do the movie role of Breathless Mahoney for union scale ($1,440 per week)—she was that anxious to get the part. The tabloids didn't report that she also negotiated a percentage of gross box office revenues from the film, video, and merchandise sales that will probably put $5 million in her pocketbook. On top of that, she will most likely make $14 million from the *Dick Tracy* soundtrack, which she released as her own album through Time Warner.

Target marketing? Since Madonna's market includes a substantial number of Hispanic and black teenagers, she sings verses of her songs in Spanish and made a video about racial discrimination.

Judging by accounts of her past, Madonna appears to be skilled at meeting and cultivating people who can advance her career. When she first arrived, almost penniless, in New York City in late 1978 she was a dancer, having trained at, but not graduated from, the University of Michigan. According to those who knew Madonna, she soon realized that there was no money in dancing and that success was easier to achieve in pop music. Before long Madonna became romantically involved with a struggling rock musician who taught her to play guitar and drums.

Her next major friendship was with one of New York City's best-connected dance-club disc jockeys, John (Jellybean) Benitez. Benitez got her gigs at Manhattan clubs and helped produce her first album.

In 1985, already a star, she married actor Sean Penn. He introduced her to Warren Beatty, who got her the role in Disney's *Dick Tracy*. Now Madonna is working with Disney on the movie version of *Evita*.

Madonna is a workaholic. In both her Hollywood Hills home and her Manhattan apartment, she has offices equipped with facsimile machines and multiline telephones. She spends several hours each day making business calls. She has been quoted as saying she sets time aside each day for creativity, which she says she can turn on and off at will. Since her physical appearance is crucial to marketing, she has a personal trainer and spends three hours each morning working out.

"What she lacks in formal business education, she more than makes up for with street smarts," says Harry Scolinos, a Los Angeles lawyer who gained insight into Madonna's finances two years ago when one of his clients sued Madonna and then-husband Sean Penn on assault charges. "I would take her street-smart business sense over someone with a Harvard MBA any day."

One key to the durability of Madonna's popularity is her reluctance to be seen as a corporate shill. Unlike Bill Cosby, Paula Abdul, and Michael Jackson, who eagerly hawk products, Madonna refuses to do so. Out of principle? Possibly. More likely she fears it might sully her image as an artist.

The only endorsement Madonna has ever done in the United States was for Pepsi in a short-lived deal last year. It was a disaster for Pepsi, but a complete success for Madonna. For $5 million Madonna was to do three commercials for Pepsi and allow Pepsi to sponsor her tour. The cola company spent millions producing the commercial and hyping its premiere, which was to coincide with the debut of Madonna's new album, *Like a Prayer.* Never mind that Madonna refused to drink the soft drink in the commercial and is seen holding the can only twice; the commercial was to air in prime time and be seen by 250 million people in forty countries.

Madonna got the money, but the commercial aired only once in the United States. Almost immediately after it appeared, Madonna released a video from the new album, showing her kissing a black saint and dancing provocatively in front of burning crosses.

The fans loved it, but thousands of people found it blasphemous. Bottlers lit up the phone lines to Pepsi headquarters. Pepsi canceled the commercial and severed its relationship with Madonna, but paid up. Not only did Madonna pocket the $5 million, but she garnered a few million more in free publicity. As for the people she offended, well, they don't buy pop records anyhow.

Did Madonna deliberately undermine Pepsi's effort? It's hard to say. Roger Mosconi, then senior creative director at BBDO Worldwide advertising agency, worked closely with Madonna filming the commercial. He recalls: "One day Madonna, who liked to joke with me, came up to me and said, 'Hey Roger, are you going to have the burning cross reflecting in the Pepsi can?' And I said what burning cross? And she smiled and said, 'You'll see.'"

Shoemaker Nike, too, ran into trouble with Madonna. Last October Nike began negotiations with Madonna to endorse a new dance shoe. The proffered fee: $4.25 million. The negotiations ended in March, officially because of "scheduling problems." But people directly involved say that during the negotiations, some of which took place in Madonna's Los Angeles home, it became increasingly clear that Madonna wanted to keep her endorsement to an absolute minimum. Says one Nike source, "She wouldn't put them on her feet."

When Nike balked, Madonna then bombarded Nike Chairman Philip Knight with telephone calls in an effort to revive the deal. When that failed, her lawyers called and threatened to sue Nike for the $4.25 million fee, even though no commercial was ever produced. Another deal fell through with Reebok in July.

Like any smart executive, Madonna surrounds herself with capable subordinates. She pays a personal manager up to 10 percent of her income, her business manager another 5 percent and her lawyers around 5 percent, all probably capped at $1 million. And her advisers are top names: Freddy DeMann, her personal manager, handled Michael Jackson during his lucrative *Thriller* days. Her lawyer, Paul Schindler, of New York's Grubman, Indursky & Schindler, is considered one of the best in the business. Business manager Bert Padell is known for his solid-gold client base, despite past problems with fraudulent tax shelters.

Besides these advisers, there are dozens of full-time workers when Madonna is touring, plus a tour agent who gets ten percent of concert revenues. So even if the tour is a sellout, she may lose money.

Madonna knows there is an easier way for a performer to make big money. It's called the movies. Madonna is moving into the movie business in a big way. When she's working on pictures, the studios pick up most of the cost and risk. Movie actors and actresses have fewer people to pay and there is less of a need to come up on your own with a fresh product. In a single movie a performer can make more money than in a year of hard work at concerts. And movies sell just as many record albums as concerts do.

Several of Madonna's movie efforts have been out-and-out disasters. Her sole Broadway performance, in David Mamet's *Speed-the-Plow*, got mixed reviews from the critics. Never mind. Madonna still has the potential to be a major box-office draw. Time Warner's HBO unit reportedly paid $1 million for the rights to broadcast the final concert of her 1990 Blond Ambition Tour. Aired in early August, the concert was HBO's most-watched nonsports event ever.

Why wear yourself out in a string of one-night stands when you can make millions for a single performance? And with the movies you don't need a model changeover every year.

(from *Rock 'n' Roll Comics: Madonna*)

by Todd Loren and Lyndal Ferguson

(from *The Boston Globe*)

Another Image in the Madonna Rolodex

by Ellen Goodman

It's past midnight. The football game is over. The local news is over. Forrest Sawyer is asking the news junkies who are still awake to watch *Nightline:* "Has Madonna finally gone too far?"

On the big screen, the same screen where secretaries of state and terrorists get to say whether they have gone too far, comes a Madonna I've never seen. Conservative black jacket with a collar up to her chin. Power shoulder pads. Gold buttons. Proper little gold earrings. Sleek hair pulled back. Right hand grasping the appropriately serious prop: a pen.

Except for the slim band of dark roots beneath the platinum, except for the voice—early *Working Girls*—she might pass for the CEO of some Wall Street firm. Or she might pass for someone trying to pass for the CEO. That is the thing about Madonna. Look for her identity and you find another image to add to the Rolodex of Madonnas.

Nightline was doing what MTV had refused to do, showing her video, "Justify My Love." And Madonna had come dressed to justify her video by saying: It was, one, artistic and, two, better than the other horrors that grace MTV without such fuss. "Why is it okay," she said, "for ten-year-olds to see someone's body being ripped to shreds?"

To this viewer who refuses to get into the debate about which is worse, sex or violence on TV—lousy choices—the Madonna video was definitely an R but not quite an X. It was clearly fantasy and clearly not the sort of thing you want the kids to find when they're channel-surfing after the *Peter Pan* tape.

But tonight it's not the black-and-white video Madonna fantasies that fascinate me. It's the contrast with the black-dressed and blond-coiffed Madonna.

Madonna the executive is speaking about Madonna the artist, Madonna of the satellite feed is talking about Madonna of the hotel bed. There are other variations on the theme of Madonna, more incarnations in the life of Madonna, more colors to the chameleon.

The woman before me has earned $90 million in four years from the subsidiaries of her own talent: Boy Toy, Siren, and Slutco. The woman has revamped her image every two years like an engine: Material Girl to Blond Ambition. And still she has icon status among those who see her as the bad girl, the sexually assertive woman, the powerful playmogul. Ask for the real Madonna and she would stand up a pantheon of her selves.

Says Lynne Layton, who teaches popular culture at Harvard: "She speaks to many women who feel pushed into one aspect of their femininity—'Don't soil your dress, always be nice.' Madonna has many different versions of femininity and seems comfortable with all of them."

When Madonna first brought her underwear and ambition to the stage, it was said that the multiple Madonna appealed to adolescent girls because they try on identities like lipstick. Years later, she still appeals to young women feeling the stress of expectations. Women who try to be all things to all people: sexy but dressed for success, maternal but independent.

But what bothers me in all this is a belief that she offers the wrong answers to the questions, or the crisis, of identity. Especially female identity.

If the work of growing up is finding a center, integrating the parts, Madonna spotlights the fragments and calls them a whole. If the business of adulthood is finding yourself, she creates as many selves as there are rooms in her video hotel. If we must evolve as grown-ups, she switches instead, like a quick-change artist between acts. And if there is a search among Americans for authenticity, Madonna offers costumes and calls them the real thing.

Multi-Madonna is the survivor of a rough childhood, of religious guilt, and a bad marriage. She has purposely become a female with the nerve to be "bad" and the will to be powerful. She is, in short, sexy and hard-nosed, brassy and vulnerable, S-and-M, victor and victim, dressed in bra and black dress.

But the fight against being "pigeonholed" can also be an excuse for confusion. The star of this show after all makes little attempt to reconcile the contradictions of her life and psyche. She insists instead that all the fragments of a self be accepted.

In the end, watching the Madonnas pass before us over the years is a bit like watching the three faces of Eve—as a role model. That's not an answer for women trying to integrate their lives.

Has Madonna gone too far? Not in a video for adults. But in real life, she has a way to go.

(from *The New York Times*)

Madonna— Finally, a Real Feminist

by Camille Paglia

Madonna, don't preach.

Defending her controversial new video "Justify My Love" on *Nightline* last week, Madonna stumbled, rambled, and ended up seeming far less intelligent than she really is.

Madonna, 'fess up.

The video is pornographic. It's decadent. And it's fabulous. MTV was right to ban it, a corporate resolve long overdue. Parents cannot possibly control television, with its titanic omnipresence.

Prodded by correspondent Forrest Sawyer for evidence of her responsibility as an artist, Madonna hotly proclaimed her love of children, her social activism, and her condom endorsements. Wrong answer. As Baudelaire and Oscar Wilde knew, neither art nor the artist has a moral responsibility to liberal social causes.

"Justify My Love" is truly avant-garde, at a time when that word has lost its meaning in the flabby art world. It represents a sophisticated European sexuality of a kind we have not seen since the great foreign films of the 1950s and 1960s. But it does not belong on a mainstream music channel watched around the clock by children.

On *Nightline*, Madonna bizarrely called the video a "celebration of sex." She imagined happy educational scenes where curious children would ask their parents about the video. Oh, sure! Picture it: "Mommy, please tell me about the tired, tied-up man in the leather harness and the mean, bare-chested lady in the Nazi cap." Okay, dear, right after the milk and cookies.

Mr. Sawyer asked for Madonna's reaction to feminist charges that, in the neck manacle and floor-crawling of an earlier video, "Express Yourself," she condoned the "degradation" and "humiliation" of women. Madonna waffled: "But I chained myself! I'm in charge." Well, no. Madonna the producer may have chosen the chain, but Madonna the sexual persona in the video is alternately a cross-dressing dominatrix and a slave of male desire.

But who cares what the feminists say anyhow? They have been outrageously negative about Madonna from the start. In 1985, *Ms.* magazine pointedly feted quirky, cuddly singer Cyndi Lauper as its woman of the year. Great judgment: gimmicky Lauper went nowhere, while Madonna grew, flourished, metamorphosed, and became an international star of staggering dimensions. She is also a shrewd business tycoon, a modern woman of all-around talent.

Madonna is the true feminist. She exposes the puritanism and suffocating ideology of American feminism, which is stuck in an adolescent whining mode. Madonna has taught young women to be fully female and sexual while still exercising total control over their lives. She shows girls how to be attractive, sensual, energetic, ambitious, aggressive and funny—all at the same time.

American feminism has a man problem. The beaming Betty Crockers, hangdog dowdies, and parochial prudes who call themselves feminists want men to be like women. They fear and despise the masculine. The academic feminists think their nerdy bookworm husbands are the ideal model of human manhood.

But Madonna loves real men. She sees the beauty of masculinity, in all its rough vigor and sweaty athletic perfection. She also admires the men who are actually like women: transsexuals and flamboyant drag queens, the heroes of the 1969 Stonewall rebellion, which started the gay liberation movement.

"Justify My Love" is an eerie, sultry tableau of jaded androgynous creatures, trapped in a decadent sexual underground. Its hypnotic images are drawn from such sadomasochistic films as Liliana Cavani's *The Night Porter* and Luchino Visconti's *The Damned.* It's the perverse and knowing world of the photographers Helmut Newton and Robert Mapplethorpe.

Contemporary American feminism, which began by rejecting Freud because of his alleged sexism, has shut itself off from his ideas of ambiguity, contradiction, conflict, ambivalence. Its simplistic psychology is illustrated by the new cliché of the date-rape furor: " 'No' always means 'no.' " Will we ever graduate from the Girl Scouts? "No" has always been, and always will be, part of the dangerous, alluring courtship ritual of sex and seduction, observable even in the animal kingdom.

Madonna has a far profounder vision of sex than do the feminists. She sees both the animality and the artifice. Changing her costume style and hair color virtually every month, Madonna embodies the eternal values of beauty and pleasure. Feminism says, "No more masks." Madonna says we are nothing but masks.

Through her enormous impact on young women around the world, Madonna is the future of feminism.

Like a Virgin: Madonna's Version of the Feminine

by Lynne Layton

The conflicts around gender arrangements become both the locus for and symbols of anxieties about all sorts of social-political ideas, only some of which are actually rooted primarily in gender relations.

Jane Flax[1]

The civil rights, feminist, and gay rights movements have made the world very different for heterosexual white men, who, for hundreds if not thousands of years, have taken social privilege as their birthright. It is of course still the case that white upper-class males rule the United States economically and politically, but, particularly in the more difficult economic times of the present, it has become much harder for middle- and working-class males to believe that they have a share in the power. The combination of bad economic times and movements in which minorities, gays, and women demand representation and a voice has made white men (and traditional white women) very uneasy about their identity and their social roles, and they are fighting back with violence and repressive legislation; for example, in the past few years, we have seen increased instances of white supremacist attacks on blacks,[2] gay-bashing and the censoring of homosexual art, and the slow whittling away of abortion rights.

In tough economic times, it is to the advantage of the powers that be that white middle- and working-class males take as the source of their oppression not upper-class males but minorities, gays, and women.

Advertisements, songs, films, and other products of popular culture help establish links in the public mind that accomplish this, that pit the powerless against the powerless. Gender difference, for example, is often used in advertisements to cover over other differences, such as class differences, which, if grasped, might be more explosive to the status quo. Judith Williamson finds that alcohol ads that show working-class men in dominant positions over women suggest to a generic male viewer that all men are equally powerful because they all dominate women; what the ads hide are the differences in social and economic power among men of different classes.[3]

Social analysis of popular culture must thus be alert to what gender displays both reveal and conceal. At this time in history, gender battles—such as clashes over the family, abortion rights, women in the workplace, fetal rights—are a bigger motor of social change than class battles. The fact that gender battles are central and the form these battles take, however, results not only from the demands of the women's movement but also from social and economic dislocations that have little to do with gender yet that engender anxieties about identity that get displaced onto "uppity" women.[4]

Madonna's art and its reception by critics and fans reflect and shape some of our culture's anxieties about identity and power inequalities. Madonna disturbs the status quo not only because she is an outspoken, sexy woman but because she has a lot of social and economic power—and she is well aware that this is the case. She asserts that what men find hard to take in her is that she's very sexy but she's not "a bimbo," the assumption made of Marilyn Monroe and other ("dumb") blondes. Sexiness in women has traditionally gone hand in hand with victimization, not power; femme fatales who have power at the beginning of stories, movies or operas (think of Carmen or Salome) are always destroyed by the narrative's end.

Behind male critics' criticisms of her lack of talent, one can often read the kind of rage that suggests it isn't Madonna's talent but her power that motivates the criticism. For example, a male radio talk show host did a show on Madonna in June 1990 and said so many times that he did not begrudge Madonna her millions that it soon dawned on the listener that he did indeed protest too much. Writing in *The Boston Globe* against Madonna's "Hanky Panky," columnist Mike Barnicle mused that perhaps Sean Penn had lost her because he hadn't hit her hard enough. Barnicle's penultimate paragraph refers to her being a multi-millionaire, with a possible "lucrative deal" with Reebok in the offing. Immediately following, he concludes his piece with: "That's great. I wonder if they make a shoe big enough to fit over her fat, sick head?"[5]

Such hostility could not possibly be stirred just by Madonna's lyrics; the train of Barnicle's thought suggests that it is stirred by the mix of her aggressive feminine sexuality and her millions. Thus, Madonna's breaking of sexual taboos, wherein woman refuses a passive sexuality, is part of the disturbance, but the gendered reversal of economic power at a time when men already feel threatened by other men and women prominently operates to draw many women to Madonna and keep many men away.

As the above suggests, understanding Madonna's cultural clout involves understanding what she does with gender, how she weaves together gender and power, and how her and her critics' focus on gender sometimes functions to obscure a focus on power relations. It is thus interesting to look at the relation between Madonna's work and contemporary cultural debates on gender identity, particularly at how she upsets traditional notions of gender and gender arrangements. Madonna presents the perplexing case of someone who accepts the concept of a natural hierarchy of power but attacks that version of the concept that excludes women, gays, and minorities. Several contradictions emerge from Madonna's simultaneous embrace of pluralism and a traditional hierarchy of power, and her mixed reception by feminist critics rests in part on these contradictions. In this essay, I will focus on where and how Madonna enters contemporary debates on gender identity, ending with some speculations on gender and power.

In the first wave of sixties and seventies feminism, Freud's theory and psychoanalysis in general were rejected as sexist and oppressive to women,[6] but as women began to realize that not only power structures but their own unconscious conflicts make change difficult, they turned again to psychoanalysis.[7] One reason for Freud's reinstatement among feminist theorists is that he held that gender identity is socially constructed and not natural or innate; in other words, women may be born anatomically as female but they become women as part of an ongoing social process.[8] In Freud's account, little boys and little girls both begin as little boys, that is, with an active sexuality that is bisexual and polymorphous perverse. Freud (and Jacques Lacan) emphasize the violence done to boys and girls when culture forces them to take their place on one or the other side of the gender divide. Bisexual and nongenital pleasures get repressed but do not disappear; one is never completely at peace with one's gender assignation, and one is definitely never at peace with prescribed and limiting cultural notions of femininity and masculinity.[9]

Less palatable to feminists is Freud's explanation of how little girls come to adopt "normal femininity," that is, a passive position where a girl's active manipulation of the clitoris is replaced by the passive pleasure experienced in vaginal penetration by a man. As is well known, Freud's view is that this transition occurs when girls realize that they and their mothers are defective, inferior beings who lack a penis. Girls then turn away from their mothers and toward their fathers, who, they hope, will give them the cherished penis in the form of a baby. In Freud's story, "masculine" girls, those who continue to pursue an active sexuality by disavowing their lack, become neurotic.

French psychoanalyst and feminist Luce Irigaray has dramatically demonstrated how Freud's notion of sexual difference takes men as the norm and women as the deviation from that norm.[10] It is thus a theory that has no idea of the experience and specificity of women (as Freud acknowledged in his baffled question "What do women want?"). Its view of gender difference is dichotomous, where A = men and $-A$ = women. The minus sign implies not only that women are defined in opposition to men but that they are defined as lacking something, as inferior to men. Irigaray and others assert that difference must take the form not of a dichotomous and hierarchical opposition that depends for its definition on the definition of men but must take the form of A = men and B = women, where women get the chance to define themselves as they speak from their own particular histories, experiences, biologies.

A history of two hundred years wherein bourgeois women have been relegated to the private, domestic sphere and men to the public has created the social component of what theorists define as feminine and masculine gender identity. The two genders have had two entirely different experiences in the world, and these have affected everything from the clothes they wear[11] to the values they hold[12] to the way they define their sense of self. In *The Reproduction of Mothering*, Nancy

Chodorow draws on history and psychoanalysis to discuss the different ways of relating and constituting the self that result from the fact that females, who are devalued in the culture, are the primary caretakers and first identification objects of both male and female children.[13] To become men, boys in this culture must switch their object of identification; not only must they identify with their fathers and other men but, given the cultural devaluation of women, they must *disidentify* with women. In this process, they disavow anything within them that is deemed feminine, including and especially dependency needs. Misogyny thus becomes part of the very process by which a masculine identity is attained and intimacy threatens refusion with the mother and a loss of identity.

Girls do not have to switch their object of identification to establish their gender identity. But mothers have a harder time seeing their daughters as separate, and fathers are likely to discourage daughters' attempts at identification with their autonomy. Female identity thus remains embedded in relationships. As long as only women mother, boys will continue to repress their longings for connection, girls to repress their longings for autonomy.[14] This repression by each gender of a whole side of human experience creates the unconscious conflicts about gender that psychoanalysis illuminates.

To the extent that girls repress aggression and strivings for autonomy and boys repress dependency and strivings for connection, the gender identity that each adopts in accord with cultural prescription is limiting and oppressive and cannot contain the richness of human experience. Carol Gilligan's recent work on adolescent girls discusses the process by which girls at about age twelve begin to suppress what they know and their assertive way of expressing it in order to avoid the kind of conflict that would threaten the continuity of their relationships.[15] So when Madonna sings her anthem "Express Yourself," an explicit call for girls to express themselves and make their boyfriends do the same, we can see why girls are ready to follow her. Madonna's popularity among girls of this age is symptomatic of what is going on in terms of their identity and their gender identity.

Madonna plays out a multitude of gendered roles in her photographs, interviews, songs, and videos, but never does one lose sight of the fact that she plays them as a woman and that she enjoys her own version of femininity, a version which is not the one preferred by the dominant culture.[16] In "Papa Don't Preach," she plays the frightened but determined pregnant teenager to a potentially angry father, searching for the father's approval but not willing to change her behavior to get it. Dressed as a Parisian gamine, she asserts, "But I've made up my mind, I'm keepin' my baby." In "Material Girl," she plays her Marilyn Monroe sexy golddigger role to a horde of adoring, less powerful because interchangeable males. As in so many of her videos, she ironically comments on the main narrative by using a second narrative that throws the first into question. In the second narrative of "Material Girl," the "real" Madonna asserts that money can't buy her love and she falls for the "poor" Keith Carradine, who courts her with daisies and a workman's truck.[17] In "Burning Up," she plays the abject admirer of a man who doesn't know she's alive. "Down on [her] knees," she strikes many poses of panting humiliation, culminating in a road scene where she offers herself up to be run over by the lover's car. Again, a final scene makes a joke of what came before: Madonna is, at the end, behind the wheel of the car, alone, laughing and carefree. In "Like a Prayer," she gives herself stigmata, thereby embodying herself as Christ. By playing a multitude of roles, Madonna restores to consciousness versions of femininity that women and girls are forced to repress in order to get social approval. Three videos, "Like a Virgin," "Express Yourself," and "Justify My Love" best exemplify the complexities of what Madonna does with gender identity.

It was Madonna's videos more than her songs that propelled her into stardom, and "Like a Virgin," one of Madonna's first videos (July 18, 1984), played a major role in bringing her to mass attention. In the video, there is one narrative in which Madonna plays a bride about to be taken to bed by her groom. This narrative is crosscut with scenes where Madonna, in a black tight skirt and top and royal blue tights, sings the song and sexily dances alone in a gondola moving down a Venice waterway. If a sexy, writhing female connotes promiscuity and a bride in white connotes chastity, we can say that what Madonna is doing here is playing with the two social codes that have marked men's views of women since at least medieval times—that is, that women are either virgins or whores. In an interview, Madonna, who went to a Catholic primary school, says that she internalized this view under the tutelage both of school and her religious grandmother: "I grew up with two images of women: the virgin and the whore. It was a little scary."[18] This dichotomous view of Woman has little to do with the complexities of real women[19] except insofar as it has been primarily men who have had the privilege to write the cultural stories, theories, liturgies, and the like that express this dichotomy and that men and women alike grow up internalizing.

As a child, Madonna (whose name already marks her parents' wish that she take her place on the Virgin side of the dichotomy) may have internalized this ideology "whole," and it may still actively operate to limit her personal life; as an adult pop star, however, with the power to manipulate the social code, she spits it back in a new form and tells a different story. "Like" a virgin: the title itself suggests the singer is not a real virgin, despite the white gown. In the sexy scenes Madonna wears her trademark crucifixes and rosary beads, which, again, the social code associates with nuns and chastity. Although no one would believe that the singer has been "touched for the very first time," what is important here is that Madonna claims the right to the soft-focus romance of white gown as well as to an aggressive sexuality.

Madonna explodes culturally limited ways of thinking about female gender identity by wrenching symbols and signs out of their usual contexts and giving them her own meanings, or by confusing meanings in such a way that these old dichotomies are shown to make no sense.[20] To this extent, Madonna deconstructs tired concepts and tired oppositions, oppositions that limit choice for women (and men) not only by allowing no combination of the two, or no third or fourth alternative, but by setting up one side of the opposition as good and the other as evil. Madonna claims the right to be both bad and good and she thus makes us question what's so good about good and what's so bad about bad.

In doing this, Madonna stirs up and gratifies that part of women that always refuses to be a good girl on cultural terms and refuses to take up the middle-class version of femininity, a version in which women are passive and nurturant and always sacrifice career to love, autonomy to connection. Again, I think this partly accounts for why Madonna is so popular with young girls who haven't yet abandoned their assertiveness.

We see the same good girl/bad girl phenomenon in women's attraction to romance fiction. From Du Maurier's *Rebecca* to the Harlequins that line the supermarket shelves, the bad girl, that is, the sexy, feisty, independent, exhibitionistic, loud, and assertive woman who says "I want you" and "I don't want you," and "You'll never dominate me," represents the side of all of us that we are forced to repress to get any kind of social approval (not to mention the economic benefits of wife-hood when there are no other economic alternatives).[21] What fascinates is this other woman, what holds the reader's interest is precisely this tabooed version of femininity. Though the novel, film, or song may ratify the dominant culture's version of femininity in the end, what has been stirred up by the whole narrative is not so easily eradicated. The bad girl continues to haunt good girls in search not only of love but of a self. Alternative versions of femininity, like those that Madonna's art offers (and Roseanne Barr and Joan Collins's Alexis Colby), live in the unconscious; only if they can be integrated can women enjoy being women. Madonna's clear enjoyment of her femininity and sexuality stems from her capacity to play out a variety of gender roles and to break restrictive stereotypes.

Madonna also blurs the line between male and female, animal and human in "Like a Virgin," although the song itself has many elements of the most traditional of romantic, heterosexual narratives. As the song begins, the singer tells us:

> I made it through the wilderness
> Somehow I made it through
> Didn't know how lost I was
> Until I found you

As she sings the first lines, the video shows a lion, which suggests the wilderness but also suggests an identification between herself and the lion, both of whom are "making it through." Beauty is the beast. Later in the video, the groom wears a lion's mask, so an identity is set up between herself and the groom as well as between the wilderness and the sophisticated bridal boudoir. These line blurrings are not to suggest that everything is the same but rather that the distinctions we make, where we draw the lines between man and animal, male and female, are often arbitrary, based in social convention, and designed to preserve power relations as they are.[22]

Those critics who wish to make of Madonna a postmodern decon-structionist do not comment on the traditional boy-girl lyrics, the repeated suggestion that the singer is incomplete without the lover, the belief in love as cure-all for the tribulations of the self. While the videos often ironically comment on such lyrics, the longings expressed in them repeat so often that they demand examination. These contradictions suggest that while Madonna radically undermines fixed and restrictive notions of feminine identity, she is yet one of us in her uncertainties about identity—and perhaps even her uncertainty contributes to her enormous popularity.

In the Blond Ambition Tour of 1990, Madonna did a new version of "Like a Virgin" that has now become a video. (The world premiere was on the MTV *Truth or Dare* special, May 9, 1991.) In this rhythmically Egyptian version, Madonna is dressed in a gold Gaultier corset, lying on a red bed, on either side of her a dancer dressed as a hermaphrodite with cone breasts. (Images of the latter flank both sides of the show's set.) Gender roles and sexual preferences are blurred from the outset as the dancers alternately play with their breasts and then with Madonna's. (In the show, they are even more explicitly sexual with her.) Madonna at first lets herself be pulled this way and that by the slaves, but the "climax" of this video is autoerotic. Crosscut with scenes of Madonna kissing males, females, and the stone on her mother's grave, the video ends with the slaves leaving as Madonna begins wildly to masturbate.

Explaining the concept for this part of the Blond Ambition show in a recent BBC documentary, *Madonna: Behind the American Dream*,[23] Madonna said that as she discovers her own sexuality and shows that she doesn't need men, the voice of the God of the church speaks to condemn her. (The show then moves to "Like a Prayer.") The voice of God finds its echo in male critics, perhaps also disturbed by her self-sufficient enjoyment of her body.

More than just a male-female dynamic, the video and the show itself celebrate the kind of polymorphous perversity and bisexuality that Freud's *Three Essays on Sexuality* proclaims normal in children of both sexes and which live on in the unconscious and in the art of the adult world. Madonna's art makes available again to consciousness the possibilities of gender play and sexuality that we on some level know to be part of us but that society prohibits.

The "Express Yourself" video (May 10, 1989), like its many performance variants, also questions stereotypical female roles, but here Madonna openly takes on a male identity, that of an industrial entrepreneur (and, via choreographic allusion to "Beat It" and "Billie Jean," of Michael Jackson). "Express Yourself," written by Madonna and Stephen Bray, is addressed explicitly to girls and it tells them not to settle for second best in a man. The song insists that a lover be able to express how he feels; if he can't, Madonna makes her point of view clear: "Second best is never enough / You'll do much better baby on your own." To Madonna, a woman without a man is no disgrace—men need to make themselves worthy of a woman's love.

In all performance variants of "Express Yourself," Madonna wears a man's business suit with a corset underneath that shows through both at the top and bottom[24]; in the stage show, a pink Gaultier corset peeks through breast holes in the pinstripe jacket. She removes the jacket to reveal the corset when she sings the lines, "Long stem roses are the way to your heart but / He needs to start with your head," ironically becoming female-sexy at the moment she insists on something more cerebral. (The next line is, "Satin sheets are very romantic, what happens when you're not in bed?")

"Express Yourself" is placed in a context not only of gender but of class difference. The set quotes Fritz Lang's *Metropolis*, a German Expressionist film of the twenties about an underground city of workers enslaved by capitalist entrepreneurs. Eerily larger-than-life black-and-white underground industrial shots of the workers alternate with the penthouse Art Deco color scenes that feature Madonna and the entrepreneur. The workers are chained to a subhuman, mechanical existence, sleeping, it seems, in the sewers. Madonna, first seen in a slinky green gown, inhabits a world of wealth. We see her holding a cat, which she intended as a symbol of femininity and the feminine world. (Her interpretation of the video, she shyly confessed, is that "pussy rules the world."[25]) Indeed, Madonna enters the underground industrial world with her voice/message and her body, disrupting the men's work and the entrepreneur's peace.

Early in the video we see the entrepreneur and the workers anxiously stare at the speaker system as Madonna, still unseen, sings; Madonna has taken control of the airwaves with a plea not to settle for second best, and the entrepreneur does not look pleased. Madonna here clearly plays a traditional feminine role she seems to savor—the redeeming angel who brings together mind (capitalism) and hand (workers) via her necessary ingredient, heart. (Interestingly, the heart is clearly allied with religion in the Lang film.)[26] Scenes of Madonna in bed are crosscut with scenes of a chained worker lying on a steel bed slab slightly above water. Then Madonna, loosely quoting Marlene Dietrich in another German film of the period, *The Blue Angel*, is seen in black underwear behind a screen. The scene in which she sings that if the guy isn't expressing himself, the girl will do better on her own shows Madonna as very sexy, but again in an autoerotic way, touching herself all over.

As her taking over of the airwaves foreshadows, she is not going to remain in the decorative role of the penthouse-kept beauty. Soon we see her in monocle and business suit, singing as the workers awaken (to her message, we assume). Here her moves are aggressive, and they are patterned on Michael Jackson's macho crotch-grabbing in his own videos.[27] But Madonna grabs her crotch in an ambiguous way that at times suggests masturbation, a joy in touching herself, and at times suggests parody of a male exhibiting and/or reassuring himself of what he's got. Madonna also frequently touches her breasts; in her business suit and lace bra one doesn't know whether she is making love to herself as a woman or as a man, but whatever she's doing, her love of her body makes it certain that Madonna cannot be adequately understood by the concept "penis envy." Madonna plays with a variety of stereotypically gendered roles, but she clearly enjoys her embodiment as a woman and makes fun of the notion that women might be lacking anything.

Like "Material Girl," the visuals of "Express Yourself" give off ambiguous messages about both gender and class. The power relations depicted put the male worker sometimes above Madonna, sometimes below her; but the worker is always below the entrepreneur, whereas Madonna, who completely disrupts his work space, is not. The worker's victory over the girl, a typical Madonna motif, is a victory in the sexual realm, but since the male entrepreneur is not competing (he only seems to have eyes for men), it is not really a class victory. Here, as elsewhere, we see that Madonna is much more radical in what she does with gender identity than she is in what she does with either gender or class *relations*, and this is precisely because, in Madonna's world, someone is either above or below the other; never are they equal.

In December 1990, Madonna once again hit the news, this time because MTV had banned her latest video, "Justify My Love." Once again, Madonna was charged with having gone too far in her sexual provocations. MTV had shown "Vogue," which features Madonna in see-through lace that reveals her breasts, but they drew their censorship line at "Justify My Love," which contains nudity and scenes of adults engaged in various kinds of sexual activity. As it happened, Madonna's popularity and the video's notoriety quickly won the video a premiere and Madonna an interview on the "serious" news show *Nightline* (December 3, 1990). The video was considered scandalous because of what I have been here considering radical: Madonna's world of polymorphous perversity, bisexuality, transvestism, and an aggressive female sexuality that refuses the passivity of "normal femininity."

"Justify My Love" begins with the image of a Nijinsky-like androgynous dancer, who weaves his way through the video, possibly representing a world of sexual fantasy. Madonna, exhausted and disheveled, wearing a black raincoat and holding a suitcase, enters a hotel. As she walks down the hall, she passes open rooms with partly naked, heavily made-up people of uncertain gender, who wear leather garb suggestive of the sadomasochistic universe of such films as Liliana Cavani's *The Night Porter*. The song begins with Madonna elaborating some sexual and romantic fantasies she has about her lover. She sings, "I want to kiss you in Paris; I want to hold your hand in Rome." As she sings, she slides to the floor touching herself, revealing garters and black stockings. The lover appears as she tells him it is now time for him to justify her love.

She and the lover next repair to the bedroom where Madonna, in black lace underwear, tells him that she wants to know him; he begins to get on top of her, but she pushes him back. She wants to know him not by making love but by having him tell her his fantasies, dreams, and fears. Thus follow scenes that may (or may not) represent the sexual fantasies of the two lovers. In one, Madonna makes love to what appears to be a woman while her lover watches. In another, the lover is in a suggestively sadomasochistic scene with another male. A third is a group sex scene in which entwined fingers touch. One "message" of the video is the repeated line, "Poor is the man whose pleasures depend on the permission of another." The line is first said as an image of Christ on the cross appears; the line then appears in written form at the end of the video. The suggestion is that the Church has dictated what is normal and what is not, that the Church limits pleasures that are longed for and in reach, and that we are impoverished by the repressed identities forced on us by church and state. MTV, which likes to see itself as an alternative to the adult world of repressive authority, ironically put itself in the same camp as the Church by banning the video.

Except for Madonna and her lover, all of the other figures in the video are heavily made-up and androgynous. In the fantasies, then, assigned gender plays an insignificant role; in fantasy, one alternates between heterosexual and homosexual, passive and aggressive, male and female. The suggestion is that "normal" masculinity and femininity embrace all of the above, that heterosexuality is "turned on" by homosexuality.

In an article titled "Concerning a Psychoanalytic View of Maleness," psychologist Robert May argues that, from birth, we build our sense of self and other by internalizing representations of self and others based on the kinds of relationships we have; May adds that each internal representation of self and other is gendered.[28] Thus, in our fantasy and our relational lives we tend, like Madonna, to play many different gendered roles. We might at times play a powerless little girl in relation to a stern male authority figure; we may play Daddy's girl to a loving father; we may play rough-and-tumble tomboy to an admiring mother. As dreams reveal, our sex hardly limits us to taking on the role of one gender; all characters in any given dream, male or female, reflect some aspect of the dreamer. The point is that we have a multitude of gendered roles within us, and it is cultural prohibition and disapproval—and how they are internalized—that stunt fantasy and distort the form that our desires to play such roles take.

May notes that when people cling to their notion of gender identity, it usually indicates that they are defending against some part of themselves. For example, if a woman relates a dream that contains a character with whom she does not wish to identify, she might exclaim, "That's disgusting. Women don't do that. That's not me!" Yet the dream reveals that this character represents some disavowed part of her; she clings to a cultural notion of femininity as a defense against prohibited longings to be something else.

If gender identity is no more than culturally prescribed notions of femininity and masculinity, then it is a limited and limiting concept. As May argues, against theorists like Erik Erikson, there is no such thing as a sense of unity when it comes to gender identity (or any other aspect of identity); an experience of unity is more than likely to be defensive, that is, a situation in which a person fends off contradictory ways of being and feeling in order to conform to what gets social approval. May writes: "These disparate identifications, these various and shifting images of self and other, this chaotic and contradictory jumble of wishes and worries, *this* is in fact our characterological treasury. The capacity for change and development depends on our having a fund of such contradictory images and fantastic aspirations."

May implies that this is what he views as healthy. In the realm of gender, Madonna's stage persona does indeed present a longed-for disunity that is exciting, fun, and powerful. Madonna clearly stands as an example of someone who is in touch with many of the conflicting pieces that make her up, someone who, extrapolating from May's terms, wears her characterological treasury on her chest.

But May's view of identity is not mainstream, as we can see when we contrast it with syndicated columnist Ellen Goodman's view in a piece about Madonna.[29] Goodman's perspective is shaped by ego psychology, the very theory that May accuses of seeking unity in premature closures. Goodman writes:

> But what bothers me is a belief that she offers the wrong answers to the questions, or the crisis, of identity. Especially female identity.
> If the work of growing up is finding a center, integrating the parts, Madonna spotlights the fragments and calls them a whole. If the business of adulthood is finding yourself, she creates as many selves as there are rooms in her video hotel. If we must evolve as grown-ups, she switches instead, like a quick-change artist between acts. And if there is a search among Americans for authenticity, Madonna offers costumes and calls them the real thing. . . . The star of this show makes little attempt to reconcile the contradictions of her life and psyche. She insists instead that all the fragments of a self be accepted.

Goodman concludes that Madonna is not a good role model for girls because she does not reconcile any of the many parts of herself that she puts on display. Against this, I would argue first that Goodman perhaps confuses the real with the stage Madonna. There are in fact many suggestions that Madonna does not experiment with different facets of herself as playfully as one might wish. Rather, things like her daily two-hour workouts and her repeated hair-dyeing have a driven and/or self-destructive aspect to them that does not suggest the joy in multiplicity of which May writes. (In one interview, her hairdresser warns her that if she dyes her hair one more time it will fall out.)[30] Nonetheless, the stage persona looks as though she enjoys the many aspects of herself, and it is this to which fans respond. Integration here would come from the voice of authority and conformity and not from the voice of free play; integration could only be limiting and dulling.

Second, the fact that one can point to very few grown-ups among adults is at least in part due to cultural restrictions on identity, the narrow view of what it means to be an adult male and an adult female. The ego psychological view of identity is one that smacks of conformity, not health. While it is true that a staggering proportion of the population experiences itself in unhappy fragments, and these people are probably among Madonna's fans, I would guess that they, too, look to Madonna as someone for whom the fragments are not painful but liberating. Goodman and May represent two sides of contemporary debates on identity, one in which fragmentation is lamented and the other in which it is thoughtfully celebrated. Those who lament fragmentation usually dislike Madonna; those, like Lacanian feminists, who celebrate disunity, are wild about her.

Lacanian feminists have focused on gender identity in yet another way, and, here, too, Madonna is exemplary. We have been considering the ways in which gender is represented in a given text, whether the text is a photo, a video, a song, or an interview. In her groundbreaking article of feminist film criticism, "Visual Pleasure and Narrative Cinema," Laura Mulvey examined the way classic Hollywood films are constructed so as to reassure a male viewer that he is a unified, rational self.[31] In Mulvey's view, the way the camera shoots a film and the very form of narrative itself are oppressive to women. (As she puts it, sadism demands a story.) In their concern only with bolstering the ego of the male viewer, the camera and its narrative leave no place for a female spectator; a woman viewer can only choose between a masochistic identification with the female in the fiction or identification with the male character in the fiction and therefore with the male viewer. Thus, films establish a certain fixed pattern of looking relations in which women are coded as "to-be-looked-at" and men are coded as the bearers of the look.

Mulvey's argument is based on the premise that a male-dominant culture requires the continuous reproduction of a male ego that takes itself as rational and as a unity. To do this, it must suppress anything other to itself, anything that raises its anxiety about its wholeness and its dominance. In Freudian and Lacanian theory, the sight of women reminds man that he can be castrated, that there are castrated beings in the world. Women, in other words, remind men of difference and disunity. If men are to feel safe in their positions of dominance, the anxiety this creates must be assuaged, and Mulvey and others feel that all the apparatuses of culture—such as the family, the church, the "rules" of filmmaking—are deployed in the interest of assuaging men's castration anxiety.

Films, according to Mulvey, do this in two ways: They may alleviate anxiety by demystifying the mystery of woman, by examining her or punishing her or saving her; this occurs in most classic Hollywood narratives. Films may also alleviate anxiety by fetishizing woman, by turning her into the penis men fear will be lost; this occurs in close-ups of a woman's face or body wherein she becomes larger than life and stops the narrative altogether. Mulvey concludes with a call for an antirealist, antinarrative cinema, a cinema that would focus attention on its own techniques, rather than hide them, and that would not allow the ego to continue to take itself as a rational unity. Only in such a cinema, she argues, could women, too, find pleasure in spectatorship.

The history of feminist film criticism is in large measure a history of responses to Mulvey's article. Questions that critics have debated include: Is there a female gaze? What would it look like? Is it heterosexual or homosexual? Might this gaze be used to disrupt a male's capacity to suppress the feminine and other forms of difference?[32] Several of Madonna's videos place looking relations at their center and either mock the fantasy of dominance and unity at the core of the male gaze or look back at the camera in such a way as to question the idea that only men can dominate by looking. While a shot of Madonna's eyes gazing at the viewer is a feature of many of her videos (like "Borderline" and "Express Yourself"), "Lucky Star," one of Madonna's first videos (February 28,

1984), and "Open Your Heart" (July 17, 1986) are particularly illuminating for a discussion of gender and filmic looking relations.

In the opening frame of "Lucky Star," we see a black-and-white close-up of Madonna's face. Then, Madonna slowly removes a pair of sunglasses and gazes directly at the camera. The video ends with the same shot, but now Madonna puts the glasses back on. The way the video is framed gives the viewer the sense that Madonna is the bearer of the look and that she will be in control of how the camera looks at her. Although, as usual, the lyrics suggest a woman fully dependent on her lover for happiness, the way the video is shot supports Madonna's by-now-famous claims that she is in control.

Unlike most of Madonna's videos, "Lucky Star" does not tell a story; there is no narrative in either the song or the video. Instead, what we see is Madonna and two dancers, all dressed in black, dancing on a completely white background. There are several close-ups that would suggest a fetishistic camera gaze set to reassure a male viewer. Yet each time Madonna is seen in close-up, she makes it clear that she knows she's being watched and disrupts the process of fetishization by facetiously winking or opening her mouth and moving her tongue in a mock lascivious way. The camera is not catching her unawares; Madonna's ironic and comedic talents are apparent from the beginning of her career.

What a male-held camera usually deems erotic is what men find erotic, such as shots of women's legs or breasts. In "Lucky Star," however, the part of Madonna's body most prominently featured is her belly button. And, as it happens, Madonna was quite taken with her belly button at the time "Lucky Star" was made:

> The most erogenous part of my body is my belly button. I have the most perfect belly button—an inny, and there's no fluff in it. When I stick a finger in my belly button I feel a nerve in the centre of my body shoot up my spine. If 100 belly buttons were lined up against a wall I would definitely pick out which one was mine.[33]

The quote confirms Madonna's control over what the camera shoots; what she wants seen is what *she* finds erotic. Academic critic John Fiske, whose essays on Madonna include audience response, finds that young girls feel Madonna gives them permission to enjoy their bodies, to take pleasure in what they like about themselves rather than what men like.[34] Indeed, my students, who were twelve to fourteen when "Lucky Star" came out, recall practicing Madonna's dance steps in their rooms with their female friends, then performing them at parties; in their words, the performance was not for the benefit of boys but was a pleasureful experience of autoerotism and female friendship.

Thus, although "Lucky Star" may at first glance seem made for a male fetishistic gaze, Madonna takes control of what is to be looked at and how it is to be looked at. In doing this, she opens a space for a female look that is not masochistic and not male-identified and which has nothing to do with reassurance about body integrity. On the contrary, the female gaze permitted by this video is one that takes pleasure in parts of the body not coded erotic by the culture and one that, in practice, brings women together for a mutual pleasure that excludes men.

As in "Lucky Star," looking relations are an explicit theme of Madonna's ironic video about adults-only peep shows, "Open Your Heart." Although the song has nothing to do with the peep show, it too is about male-female looking relations—specifically, about a lover who is too self-absorbed to notice Madonna as she burns with desire. The video opens with a shot of a cardboard woman, slowly revealed to be adorning the marquis of the adult theater. The woman has light bulbs at her breasts, and her wide-open legs straddle the box office. A sleepy old man, probably the owner, is in the box office as a young boy tries to buy a ticket. The boy, opening and closing one eye after the other, looks at the various posters of naked women, whose breasts, in a touch of puritan hypocrisy, are blacked out. As he notices the poster of Madonna, that night's star, there is a fade to the inside of the theater. Inside, the first shot is of two men dressed in navy whites, holding hands, leaning on each other, and staring blankly. Then we see Madonna, who is in the middle of a stage, seated on a chair and wearing a black corset with gold tassels on her nipples, black gloves, black fishnet stockings, and black wig. One of Madonna's first moves is to remove her wig and reveal her bleached-blond hair, a move that reminds us that we are in a world of artifice behind which may lie only another world of artifice.

The video continues with shots of the several men who sit in rooms behind glass windows that flank the stage. There are old men, young men, fat men, men in polyester, sophisticated men, a man obsessively taking notes, a man with a camera who takes a picture of Madonna, a black man who looks decidedly like Prince. Madonna is the sexual object of their gaze, and at first glance it may seem that the video contains a traditional view of woman, shot for the enjoyment of a male viewer. Yet a black shade, which blocks their view of Madonna when their time runs out, goes down when the men do not expect it, suggesting that they are not really in control of what they see. The men are in fact made to look rather silly throughout, which would discourage a male viewer's identification with them. Meanwhile, Madonna sings, absolutely oblivious to the men who watch her, focused instead straight ahead at the camera. There is nothing about this video that would be reassuring to a male spectator.

The video is structured around images of looking and not looking, as is the song. Madonna's lyrics are ironically juxtaposed to the visuals, as she sings, "If you gave me half a chance you'd see / My desire burning inside of me / But you choose to look the other way." "Is it you're afraid to look in my eyes," and, later in the song, "I follow you around but you can't see / You're too wrapped up in yourself to notice / So you choose to look the other way." As she sings of the man she cares about, who chooses to look the other way, the men to whom she is oblivious look directly but impotently at her.

Toward the end of the video, we see the young boy dancing in front of a mirror, still barred from the theater. The next shots are of each of the men in their booths, now erotically out of control and made to look ridiculous as they bang their heads, play fetishistically with cloth, smoke a cigarette; Madonna remains oblivious. Then Madonna emerges from the theater, dressed in the same clothes worn by the boy (a Charlie Chaplinesque gray suit with baggy pants, black porkpie hat, black patent shoes, and white socks). She kisses the boy and they go off down the road dancing together and having fun. The old man comes running after them, yelling at Madonna to come back because they still need her; Madonna ignores him, because she's finally having fun. As usual in a Madonna video, the underdog gets the girl because the underdog is just more fun to be with. The boy does not get to peep at Madonna's less dressed body, but he does not seem to care; the real erotics are in the dancing. The two take off in a setting that mixes elements of *The Wizard of Oz* and the end of *Modern Times* with those of De Chirico's dark surrealist paintings.

The narrative begins in a way reminiscent of Mulvey's dire warning that "sadism demands a story." Yet the narrative ends not with the destruction of the sexy female, the female that arouses but does not reassure the male, but rather with her escape from the scene of her oppression just at the moment when the men are out of control. While the lyrics again are most traditional, with the phallic refrain, "Open your heart to me, baby / I hold the lock and you hold the key," the visuals show Madonna oblivious to the male gaze that feeds her and finally escaping it altogether. A viewer might identify with Madonna, or with the young boy, who could in fact be the person in the song who feels unnoticed but worthy of love, but there is little chance that any viewer, male or female, would identify with the adult males in the video. To identify with Madonna or the boy is not to take one's place in the power structure; rather, it is to identify with the world of play, a world opposite to the "adults-only" world of the theater. This is in fact one of the few places in Madonna's work where power is refused.

We have been discussing ways that Madonna's work challenges traditional views of sexuality and gender identity. Since gender play is central to Madonna's work, she has evoked a lot of commentary by feminist academics and journalists. These critics seem compelled to take a stand on whether or not we can see Madonna's art as part of a feminist enterprise. As noted above, a dominant strand of academic feminism is Lacanian, and Lacanian feminists greatly value disruptions of unity and therefore greatly value Madonna. Musicologist Susan McClary has gone so far as to claim that Madonna's music itself challenges the whole history of Western narrative music by refusing to bolster a masculine identity based on suppressing anything that it perceives as other.[35]

Non-Lacanian feminists have also been very positive about Madonna, although many of them have reported that reconciling their feminism with their liking for Madonna has been a struggle, as reflected in Sheryl Garratt's title "How I Learned to Stop Worrying and Love Madonna."[36] Judith Williamson, a left-wing feminist writer, writes against a "simplistic feminism" that, in criticizing Madonna's "brash sexual image is inadequate to explain why millions of women and girls . . . imitate and adore her." In a moment reminiscent of Gilligan's research with girls, Williamson continues: "For she retains all the bravado and exhibitionism that most girls start off with, or feel inside, until the onset of 'womanhood' knocks it out of them."[37]

The feminism of which Williamson is critical is a contemporary puritan strand that confuses the enjoyment of sexuality with sexual objectification. Thus, Shelagh Young writes in "Feminism and the Politics of Power" that older feminists may be out of touch with a generation raised to be sensitive to exploitive images.[38] If younger feminists enjoy *Cosmopolitan* and Madonna, it is not because they are misguided, blind to their own oppression, but because they read differently, because they are "streetwise,"[39] and because they are in the process of constructing their own feminism. Younger feminists are perhaps freer to enjoy their bodies than older feminists have been. The danger of a unitary view of feminism is the same danger we exposed in the discussion of gender identity: when one group of feminists tries to speak in the royal "we" about women, several other groups of feminists are excluded.

Madonna's enjoyment of her sexuality provides a healthy corrective to those feminisms that place a woman's relational and nurturant capacities at the center of her personhood. This is the line taken, too, by Camille Paglia, an art critic rivaled only by Madonna in her ability to self-promote. Setting back the date rape movement twenty years in her startlingly ignorant assertion that "no" has always been a part of the "alluring courtship ritual of sex and seduction," Paglia also claims to know what real feminists and real men really are, and she declares Madonna a real feminist.[40]

I make no such assertions here, for feminism, in my view, is as multiple as femininity. As I have suggested along the way, however, my own discomfort with unequivocally claiming Madonna for my version of feminism has to do with her adherence to power hierarchies. In scrambling to claim Madonna for feminism, many commentators overlook (or, in Paglia's case, celebrate) the dynamics of dominance and submission that emerge in nearly every song, video, performance, and interview. While Madonna disrupts traditional power relations by challenging conventional notions of identity and asserting women's power, she rarely questions the conservative cultural assumption that someone has to be on top and someone on the bottom. So whether she is singing about being down on her knees, dismissing the Egyptian slaves from her boudoir, or reversing looking relations such that men instead of women are humiliated, Madonna reveals in her work a worldview based in inequality, one in which only one person of any pair is a subject and the other an object, one in which Madonna likes to think of herself as "in control" and on top.[41] Thus, Madonna gets to exercise many facets of identity, but the others with whom she is involved do not. This goes not only for male-female relations; in the Blond Ambition Tour, power inequalities among women emerge when Madonna mockingly (or not?) shoves around her black backup singers, yelling "I'm the boss."

My criticism is not intended to invalidate the claims that I have made for Madonna in this essay; it is intended to temper the black-and-white approach of many of those who write about her and to provoke thought about what it is about her and her power that attracts many women and makes some of her male critics so angry. Madonna is radical, and her radicalism lies in the fact that she constantly questions cultural assumptions of femininity and masculinity and continues to construct for herself her own version of femininity. This project and the way it has stimulated her fans to do the same marks Madonna's contribution to contemporary crises in identity and to feminism.

▶ Notes

1. Jane Flax, *Thinking Fragments: Psychoanalysis, Feminism, and Postmodernism in the Contemporary West* (Berkeley, Los Angeles, Oxford: University of California Press, 1990), p. 44.

2. See, for example, Elinor Langer, "The American Neo-Nazi Movement Today," *The Nation* (July 16–23, 1990).

3. Judith Williamson, "Woman is an Island. Femininity and Colonization," in Tania Modleski, ed., *Studies in Entertainment: Critical Approaches to Mass Culture* (Bloomington and Indianapolis: Indiana University Press, 1986), pp. 99–118.

4. Christopher Lasch at times seems to blame women, along with experts, for a variety of social ills, such as disruptions in the family. See his *The Culture of Narcissism: American Life in An Age of Diminishing Expectations* (New York: W.W. Norton, 1979) and *Haven in a Heartless World. The Family Besieged* (New York: Basic Books, 1977).

5. Mike Barnicle, "Madonna's Peep Show," *The Boston Globe*, June 7, 1990.

6. See, for example, Kate Millett, *Sexual Politics* (New York: Doubleday, 1970), or Shulamith Firestone, *The Dialectic of Sex: The Case for Feminist Revolution* (New York: Bantam, 1971).

7. See, for example, Juliet Mitchell, *Psychoanalysis and Feminism: Freud, Reich, Laing, and Women* (New York: Pantheon, 1974).

8. Freud has several papers on the construction of gender. These include *Three Essays on the Theory of Sexuality* (1905), S.E., vol. 7; "Some Psychical Consequences of the Anatomical Distinction Between the Sexes" (1925), S.E., vol. 19; "Femininity" (1933), S.E., vol. 22; "The Dissolution of the Oedipus Complex" (1924), S.E., vol. 19; "Female Sexuality" (1931), S.E., vol. 21. S.E. is an abbreviation for the standard edition of the *Complete Psychological Works of Sigmund Freud*, James Strachey, ed. and trans. (London: The Hogarth Press, 1953–74).

9. See Jacqueline Rose's introduction to Jacques Lacan, *Feminine Sexuality*, Juliet Mitchell and Jacqueline Rose, eds. (New York: Norton, 1983).

10. Luce Irigaray, *Speculum of the Other Woman* (1974), trans. Gillian C. Gill (Ithaca: Cornell University Press, 1985), and *This Sex Which is Not One* (1977), trans. Catherine Porter (Ithaca: Cornell University Press, 1985).

11. See Kaja Silverman's discussion of gender, fashion, and psychology in "Fragments of a Fashionable Discourse," in Modleski, ed., *Studies in Entertainment*, pp. 139–52.

12. Carol Gilligan, *In a Different Voice* (Cambridge, Mass.: Harvard University Press, 1982).

13. Nancy Chodorow, *The Reproduction of Mothering: Psychoanalysis and the Sociology of Gender* (Berkeley: University of California Press, 1978).

14. See Jean Baker Miller, "The Development of Women's Sense of Self," *Work in Progress*. (Wellesley, Mass.: Stone Center for Developmental Services and Studies, 1984).

15. Carol Gilligan, Nona P. Lyons, and Trudy J. Hanmer, eds., *Making Connections* (Cambridge, Mass.: Harvard University Press, 1990).

16. Marjorie Garber argues that Madonna's cross-dressing represents a move to open a third gender space and thus question the certainties of gender ascription. While I agree with much of Garber's argument against gender rigidities, I feel, at the same time, that such an argument takes something away from what Madonna does for women; my sense is that Madonna restores ambiguity to gender but does so from the embodied perspective of a woman. Because of this, she makes women, not men, feel more powerful. See Marjorie Garber, "Fetish Envy," *October* 54 (Fall 1990), pp. 45–55, and *Vested Interests: Cross-Dressing and Cultural Anxiety* (New York: Routledge, 1991).

17. As E. Ann Kaplan notes, in the video itself, Keith Carradine is hardly the poor boy Madonna takes him to be, which further confuses the issue of whether she is a material girl. See *Rocking Around the Clock: Music Television, Postmodernism, and Consumer Culture* (New York: Routledge, 1989), pp. 89–142. See also pages 39–46 in this book.

18. *National Times*, August 23–29, 1985, p. 9, cited in John Fiske, "Madonna," in his *Reading the Popular* (Boston: Unwin Hyman, 1989), p. 103. My argument here is greatly indebted to Fiske's insights in both "Madonna," pp. 95–113, and "Romancing the Rock," pp. 115–32. See also pages 58–75 in this book.

19. See Teresa de Lauretis, Introduction and Chapter 1 of *Alice Doesn't: Feminism, Semiotics, Cinema* (Bloomington: Indiana University Press, 1984), pp. 1–36.

20. See Fiske, "Madonna." A proponent of British cultural studies, Fiske sees Madonna as a warrior in the cultural struggle over who controls meaning.

21. Here I am recapitulating Alison Light's insights in her study of Du Maurier's *Rebecca*; see " 'Returning to Manderley'—Romance Fiction, Female Sexuality and Class," *Feminist Review* 16 (Summer 1984), pp. 7–25.

22. For an in-depth study on how primatologists have drawn the lines between humans and animals, see Donna Haraway's *Primate Visions* (New York: Routledge, 1989).

23. Madonna, in *Madonna: Behind the American Dream*, *BBC Omnibus Series*, first broadcast in Great Britain on December 7, 1990.

24. Marjorie Garber notes the pun Madonna makes by wearing a double-breasted suit in the Music Video Awards version; see Garber's "Fetish Envy," p. 56.

25. Madonna, in *Madonna: Behind the American Dream*.

26. At the end of the video a title appears that directly alludes to the Lang film: "Without the heart there can be no understanding between the hand and the mind." According to an interview in *Vanity Fair*, she ran into trouble with David Mamet in his *Speed-the-Plow* when she interpreted her role in this same redeeming angel vein; Mamet had seen the figure as evil. See Kevin Sessums, "White Heat," *Vanity Fair* (April 1990), p. 210.

27. Garber, "Fetish Envy," pp. 55–56.

28. Robert May, "Concerning a Psychoanalytic View of Maleness," *The Psychoanalytic Review* 73/4 (Winter 1986), pp. 175–193.

29. Ellen Goodman, "Another Image in the Madonna Rolodex," *The Boston Globe*, December 6, 1990. See also pages 164–166 in this book.

30. Sessums, "White Heat," p. 214.

31. Laura Mulvey, "Visual Pleasure and Narrative Cinema," *Screen* 16/3 (Autumn 1975), pp. 6–18.

32. See, for example Lorraine Gamman and Margaret Marshment, eds., *The Female Gaze: Women as Viewers of Popular Culture* (Seattle: Real Comet Press, 1989) and a recent edition of the feminist film journal *Camera Obscura* on "The Spectatrix," 20/21 (May–September 1989).

33. *Madonna: Close up and Personal*. London: Rock Photo Publications, 1985. Cited in Fiske, "Madonna," p. 100.

34. Fiske, "Madonna," pp. 95–113.

35. Susan McClary, "Living to Tell: Madonna's Resurrection of the Fleshly," *Genders* 7 (Spring 1990), pp. 1–21. See also pages 101–127 in this book.

36. Sheryl Garratt, "How I Learned to Stop Worrying and Love Madonna," *Women's Review* 5 (March 1986), pp. 12–13.

37. Judith Williamson, "The Making of a Material Girl," *New Socialist* (October 1985), pp. 46–47.

38. Shelagh Young, "Feminism and the Politics of Power: Whose Gaze is it Anyway?" in Gamman and Marshment, eds., *The Female Gaze*, pp. 173–88.

39. Janice Winship, "A Girl Needs to Get Street Wise: Magazines for the 1980's," *Feminist Review* 21 (Winter 1985), p. 46.

40. Camille Paglia, "Madonna—Finally, a Real Feminist," *The New York Times*, December 14, 1990, p. A39. See also pages 167–169 in this book.

41. One of the more interesting revelations in *Truth or Dare* is how complicated the issue is of who is in control and on top of things in both her professional and her private life.

WRITERS: CHARLIE KADAU AND JOE RAIOLA

▶ From *Rolling Stone* Polls, 1990

ARTIST OF THE YEAR

1. Sinéad O'Connor
2. *Madonna*

BEST SINGLE

1. "Vogue," Madonna

BEST FEMALE SINGER

1. Sinéad O'Connor
2. *Madonna*

WORST FEMALE SINGER

1. Sinéad O'Connor
2. *Madonna*

BEST VIDEO

1. "Vogue," Madonna

WORST VIDEO

1. "Cherry Pie," Warrant
2. "Step by Step," New Kids on the Block
3. "Nothing Compares 2 U," Sinéad O'Connor
4. *"Vogue," Madonna*

BEST TOUR

1. Madonna

WORST TOUR

1. New Kids on the Block
2. *Madonna*

BEST-DRESSED FEMALE

1. Madonna

SEXIEST FEMALE

1. Madonna

Critics' Poll

BEST VIDEO

"Justify My Love," Madonna

BEST TOUR

Madonna

HYPE OF THE YEAR

The "Justify My Love" Controversy

(from *Roman Numeral Two: An Altogether New Book of Top Ten Lists*)

Top Ten Revelations in the New Madonna Movie *Truth or Dare*

by David Letterman

and the *Late Night with David Letterman* writers

10. Was kicked out of *Up with People* as a teenager for grabbing herself during halftime show

9. We think that maybe she sometimes dyes her hair

8. She invented the auto air freshener

7. Inner-ear problems mean she has to wear special iron shoes for balance

6. Fire marshal once closed down her bedroom for overcrowding

5. Metal brassiere handy for opening long-neck Buds

4. Opening act on the Blond Ambition Tour: Buddy Hackett

3. Warren Beatty is only four foot ten

2. She's actually a painfully shy recluse who will do anything to avoid media attention

1. She once slept with Nancy Reagan

(from *The Village Voice*)

Madonnathinking Madonnabout Madonnamusic

by Robert Christgau

est I get off on the wrong foot, let me emphasize up top that there's never been a celebrity like Madonna. And though it doesn't suit my thesis, let me add that a movie, *Truth or Dare*, is what put her over the top. Formally, I mean. Because there can no longer be much doubt that Madonna now regards celebrity itself as her art, or that she plies it with such gut instinct and manipulative savvy that all past and present practitioners—all those Swedish nightingales and sultans of swat and little tramps and cleopatras and blond bomb-shells and rebels without a cause and king pelvises and fab fours and billion-dollar thrillers and, though here one pauses, Teflon presidents— seem like stumbling naifs by comparison. In early 1990 the disappoint-ing sales of the *Like a Prayer* album (still a mere triple platinum, well behind *Like a Virgin* and *True Blue*) made some wonder whether she'd played out her string. Now her capacity for self-renewal seems virtually infinite, and even if the bubble bursts, this century will not see her like again. I'm being ironic, sure—she deserves nothing less. But only a little, because I'm a convert. Madonna has rendered me a postmodernist in spite of myself, one of the burgeoning claque of marginal, generally left-leaning intellectuals for whom she has come to embody nothing less than mass culture itself.

For cultural conservatives, Madonna's invasion of discourse is a not altogether unexpected outrage—the dire future José Ortega y Gasset warned their forebears about. And consider this: *even they know who she is*. What once would have been undifferentiated ignorance and hostility is now inescapable familiarity—the rare highbrow who's never heard

Madonna sing or seen her perform or read her talk or mused about her multimedia mastery has almost certainly expended gray matter on her anyway. Her prestige is so pervasive that sometimes it irritates the middlebrow peons on the star beat who function as Madonnathink's worker bees. Most of them know her oeuvre better than your average highbrow, of course, but few are at home with it, and their punditry has been of radically mixed quality. Journalists become so cynical about the media that all but the most fawning or fair-minded flatter their own acumen by assuming the worst. So pro, con, or neither, a lot of what they write about her is pretentious, shallow, or both. And to step right into it, I'll note that many of the exceptions to come my way have been by rock critics: thank you Barry Walters, Joyce Millman, James Hunter, Gina Arnold, Dishmaster Don Shewey, and poor Steve Anderson, who was hit by a class action suit from this newspaper's sexual liberation posse for suggesting that there was more gym than boudoir in the way she pumped her crotch.

The most fascinating exegeses, however, originate in the outlying districts of academia, where a network of younger acolytes trade bibliographical references and videotape while hep elders publish and teach. Although I've heard snickers about Harvard's Madonna course, a *Boston Globe* tie-in by the prof, clinical psychologist and women's studies lecturer Lynne Layton, seemed fairly sane to me. Granted, Layton isn't altogether rah-rah—"role reversals don't seem to me to be what feminists have fought for these last 20 years," and so forth. But I say such homely points are legitimate, because I still think Madonna—along with the rest of this universe of signs we call the world—is subject to criticism, not just in the cultural theory sense nor even the *explication de texte* sense, but in the if-you-can't-say-something-good-about-a-person-don't-say-anything-at-all sense. Really, star fans—dissing Madonna isn't square by definition. She's great, but that doesn't make her perfect, and as tendentious as it may be to speculate about how her mixed messages might affect her multifarious audience, it's nevertheless empowering, so to speak, to resist the gravitational pull of her thereness and adjudge this bit fabulous and that bit lame and the one over there provocative yet problematic. Credible though its notion of choice may be, "Papa Don't Preach" remains an antiabortion song for most who hear it—preferable as such to Graham Parker's "You Can't Be Too Strong," but not to the Sex Pistols' "Bodies."

Such essential distinctions are foreign to most Madonna scholars, who despite their purported oppositionality are forever slipping over the borderline between postmodernist meta-analysis and positivist passivity. Reflecting the not unhealthy rise of sociology and perceptual psychology in the formerly "humanistic" arena of left aesthetics, their Madonnathink tends to be about mass culture itself—usually not mass culture as it is experienced, though that is the noble aim, but mass culture as a site of theory. Much of it feels translated—only the younger acolytes convey anything approaching the intimacy that comes naturally to millions of fans—and sometimes you get the feeling that their subject's incomparable fame relieves interpreters of the need to truck with lesser cynosures. In short, Madonna is honored less as an artist than as a cultural force. And this has to make you wonder. It's true enough that such concepts as "artist," "author," and "genius" carry the ideological baggage of bourgeois meritocracy. But though her scribes may downplay her agency with the most democratic of motives, as intellectuals they hold on to their own, no matter 'ow 'umbly they strive to serve the people. Madonna gains their approbation not on her own terms, which most certainly include "art" and "power," but on their own. One might even suspect that they love her not for all the things she is, but because it's fun to stick a bleached blonde in your thesis advisor's face.

John Fiske's terms are those of an audience/consumer advocate—he believes receptors make their own popular culture, defined as "the culture of the subordinate who resent their subordination." So in *Reading the Popular*, he charters Madonna's wannabes—and also, yes, Madonna—as groundbreaking *bricoleurs*. E. Ann Kaplan's special interest is the construction of the subject. So in *Rocking Around the Clock* she slices open the "Material Girl" video like a surgeon, albeit one who doesn't know the difference between a car and a pickup truck or a producer and a director. There's definitely an ivory-tower taint to such analyses and other more journalbound arcana. It's not as if ordinary folks who'd thought a little about the most famous person in the world didn't already have a grip on some of this stuff—ideas do exist before they're put into writing by Ph.D.'s. But there's also a more fundamental problem: the unremittingly visual focus. What is mass culture as academic postmodernism conceives it? Mass culture isn't something you read, and it certainly isn't something you hear. It's something you see. Basically, it's television.

I don't mean to suggest that Madonna isn't a creature of MTV, or that the tube isn't as mass as culture gets. But it isn't TV per se that generates our icons. What television personality is as omnipresent as Madonna, or even Michael Jackson? Bill Cosby, maybe? Walter Cronkite? Bart Simpson? Forget about it. Hollywood itself hasn't produced a full-fledged idol since Marilyn, in whose reflected glory Madonna was long assumed to bask. Instead, superstardom has become conspicuously coextensive with rock 'n' roll. I'm not sure why this is, but rather than privileging music's mythic magic, I'm inclined to suspect it's because icons are a special if far from exclusive domain of the young, with time on their hands and identity problems wracking their very souls. Nevertheless, you have to figure that the specifics of Madonna's music contribute in no small part to her total triumph, and therefore merit exegetical scrutiny. But popular culture theorist Fiske demurs: "The pleasures of music are remarkably resistant to analysis," he notes preemptively, and anyway, "critics are disparaging" about her music (which they aren't, and as if that would stop him). And Kaplan, a film scholar who turned MTV expert doing the couch potato with her teenaged daughter, relies on Nik Cohn's wonderful but notoriously inaccurate *Rock From the Beginning* and an obscure 1973 survey by the dreadful, long-departed *Times* stringer Mike Jahn to lead her to the foreordained conclusion that "rock music" is, er, postmodern. Or is that dead?

Well, surprise—either it's neither or it's plenty else besides. As polymorphously absorptive as the universe of signs may be, it doesn't obviate the usages of art and craft, be they narrative thrills or good beats you can hum along to—it coexists with them, another layer of available symbolic experience. If Fiske has every right to juxtapose chapters on malls, videogames, and TV news to one on Madonna, she's nevertheless not *merely* a phenomenon, an all-purpose "text"—she's also a *producer* of musical texts, texts that reconfigure her thereness as they reward and confound traditional modes of aesthetic reception. By comparing Madonna to other women singers, breaking down pop's collaborative processes, and arguing that MTV is good for rock and roll, multiculturalist Lisa Lewis's eye-oriented *Gender Politics and MTV* respects this inconvenient complication. But even Lewis says she "found very little in the way of useful models" for integrating "musical analysis" into "textual analyses of videos," betraying the critical limitations of a feminist fan who can't believe it isn't sexist to hate Pat Benatar—and who can't conceive why Madonna's music might be not just valid, but better than Pat Benatar's.

In *Feminine Endings*, rogue musicologist Susan McClary chides Fiske and Kaplan, both of whom she dwarfs as stylist and critic. Then she sets about righting their omissions with a lengthy musical analysis (for slower students, video illustrations are provided) of "Live to Tell," "Open Your Heart," and "Like a Prayer"—the climactic exhibit in McClary's argument that tonal music's compulsive return to home key fuels a powerfully subliminal male supremacist narrative. This is audacious work, both in itself and in its challenge to the blindered snobbishness of academic musicology, which ignores pop as a matter of scholarly principle. That Madonna professes to have no idea what McClary is talking about doesn't diminish its truth value. But because McClary comes out of academic musicology, she too ignores crucial stuff. Having established that Madonna refuses the sort of melodic resolutions that define "masculine cadential control" in the two Whitesnake songs she parses, she gives no indication that she's examined less macho pop—I'd suggest Paula Abdul before Pat Benatar—for similar structures. And those "musical affiliations . . . with African-American music" must stand out more when Monteverdi and Tchaikovsky are your daily bread. On the bell curve of a music that owes r&b bigtime all the way to Whitesnake, Madonna is fiftieth percentile—a trailblazer in a raceless dance music with discernible roots in postpunk and Eurodisco who's also on flirting terms with such whitebread subgenres as Vegas schlock, show tune, and housewife ballad. The real racial provocations she reserves for live shows—and also, of course, videos.

Among intellectuals whose interest in rock 'n' roll shriveled up with hippie and/or punk, Madonna's music is pigeonholed as disposable when its virtues are acknowledged at all. This meshes neatly with Fiske: "Madonna is only the intertextual circulation of her meanings and pleasures; she is neither a text nor a person, but a set of meanings in process." It's just in a culture so late to recognize the contingency of art and the creativity of the audience. And it's fair enough treatment for a celebrity-first whose speciality is the single—who designs music to get played on the radio/TV and then disappear. In this market system, the album is how pop music attains relative permanence—still contingent, but stable in itself, which celebrity can never be—and except for the debut,

Madonna's best-selling albums have been patchy. But her compilations—the 1987 *You Can Dance* remixes and, especially, 1990's *Immaculate Collection*—are stunning, and as likely to remain stunning as *Blonde on Blonde* or *"Live" at the Apollo*. Their corny cool, postfeminist confidence, pleasure-centered electronic pulse, and knowing tightrope dance along the cusp of the acceptable capture a sensibility as well as an age.

But they're music, not just "culture." Listen to the singles collection, which dips to mortal only two or three cuts in seventeen, and then watch the impressive but less consistent video comp of the same name, and notice how differently Madonna approaches the two forms, achieving the open-endedness postmodernists crave with diametrically opposite tactics. Except for the surreally wondrous "Cherish," which comes by its ambiguity subtly (and which nobody writes about), her videos are baroque, cluttered, multileveled riots of overdetermination. Even the kitchen-sink "Like a Prayer" single, on the other hand, is schlock done clean, and the minimalist discipline of most of her hits reflects a tour in SoHo frequently elided by those who celebrate her Detroit roots. (It was actually "metro" Detroit, in a family her claque started IDing as "Italian" when "working-class" wouldn't cut it any more.) I could be wrong—after a decade of junk expressionism, her videos have their own aesthetic pedigree—but I suspect that the music, with its spaces that cry out to be filled, will endure longer than the garish videos, if the Test of Time still turns you on. I don't want to make too much of how arty she is, or in any way deny her radical interpretability, especially since the artist in her aims for panschlock universality and deserves credit for getting there. But it's worth emphasizing that, not just for her but for her audience, Madonna's songs give up "vulgar" and rarefied pleasure simultaneously—and that Fiske to the contrary, it's cynical, condescending, inaccurate, and perversely philistine to declare the rarefied an exclusively "bourgeois" realm.

Among its numerous aesthetic coups, *Truth or Dare* confounds candor as a category for public people. Instead of waiting for her own Memphis Mafia to spill the beans, Madonna commissioned Alek Keshishian to act as her authorized Albert Goldman, and at times she appears alarmingly cruel, phony, and manipulative. At some level she clearly *wanted* to humanize and perhaps even debunk herself, yet as the most self-aware celebrity in history, she knew it was impossible—that every self-revelation would only reinforce a myth she spends half her career shaping and the other half hanging on to for dear life. It would be dumb to feel sorry for her, but equally dumb not to recognize that her power masks pain and carries burdens. If celebrity itself is her true art, music—and, yes, video too—is her refuge. For both her and many of the fans who adore her, it will remain, nostalgia for some and continuing revelation for others, long after her celebrity has become a bore, escaped her control, or both.

(from *The New Yorker*)

Vicarious Thrills (A Play in One Scene)

by Hal Rubenstein

PLACE: Elevator, 711 Fifth Avenue (home of Columbia and Tri-Star Pictures).

TIME: A recent Thursday, 8 P.M.

SCENE: A pretty woman is already on board, listening to Prince's "Graffiti Bridge" on headphones. She sings along, Jean Hagen–style. On eleven, her equally attractive but Walkman-less friend gets on. The wired-for-sound woman speaks over the tape, which remains on during the subsequent dialogue.

PRETTY WOMAN (*singing to herself*): "Nothing comes from talkers but sound . . ." (*Speaking, as friend enters*): You still here?

EQUALLY ATTRACTIVE FRIEND: I couldn't leave till I heard from my friend in Cannes. She saw *everything*.

PRETTY WOMAN: So did they really meet?

FRIEND: Yeah. You can't believe what she said to Sean—"Nice to see you"!

PRETTY WOMAN: She's really matured.

FRIEND: I think she's found herself.

PRETTY WOMAN: I better find *my*self one SM with J [*translation: straight man with job*] at your party or you're gonna hear about it.

FRIEND: Show off them implants. No oxford cloth.

PRETTY WOMAN: They're almost healed.

FRIEND: In the nick of beach time.

PRETTY WOMAN: Sunscreen number four, here I come. What time should I get there?

FRIEND: My brother's friends are coming at ten, so primp accordingly.

PRETTY WOMAN: I'll be there at nine, lock myself in your bathroom for an hour, and emerge like Botticelli's Venus.

FRIEND: From the toilet.

PRETTY WOMAN: Nice. Just call me the Blond Ambition Tour, Part 2.

FRIEND: Bob says his friend Chris looks like Sean.

PRETTY WOMAN: Eight-thirty, I'll be there at eight-thirty. Gotta go. Late for my waxing.

FRIEND: No patterns, now. Don't want to scare the natives.

PRETTY WOMAN (*exits singing*): "But the world still goes around and 'round."

(from *The Progressive*)

Politics in a Post-Feminist Age

by Ruth Conniff

I keep hearing lately that Madonna is a feminist, a great role model for women. I'm perpetually interested in the problem of defining modern feminism, so I went to see Madonna's new movie, *Truth or Dare*. I found her outrageous and funny from the opening scenes, and refreshingly, aggressively sexy. After about an hour, though, I began to get restless. Watching this beautiful young woman gyrate and preen, call people "pussy" and "bitch," change her clothes, and have her makeup done becomes tiresome after a while.

It reminded me of a speech I heard last year at Yale. The editor of *Self* magazine, addressing a group of students interested in journalism, announced that we were graduating into a "post-feminist age." Women are free to celebrate their femininity again, she said. The struggle is over. As a result, magazine models look sexier and more curvaceous than ever.

That makes Madonna a good model for *Self*, anyway. But what Madonna has to say to the rest of us—women in general—is still more a fashion statement than a political message. And therein lies a crucial difference.

The difference between fashion and politics is evident in "women's magazines" like *Self* as soon as you turn to the masthead. Women editors and sub-editors dominate the top half of the page. But on the bottom line there is always a man's name. While women work for notoriously low pay, posing for photographs and writing redundant copy about beauty and trends, the publishers and CEOs listed in small print are raking in big bucks.

The personnel department at Condé Nast Publications put it to me this way: "We're looking for someone who can type sixty words a minute, and who knows what's hot and what's not." Women are still consumers and employees of fashion. We do not control the market.

Madonna's case, of course, is a little trickier. She is a woman who collects the profits when she sells herself. But for most women, the benefits do not trickle down. Madonna communicates the same old cultural messages we've always received, about the importance of youth and beauty and sex appeal. As she herself says, "Money makes you beautiful." But while Madonna gets richer and more beautiful, the rest of us make sixty-five cents for every dollar a man earns, and a record number of our children live in poverty. Still, we keep buying the same repackaged images and beauty products, vainly hoping that they will improve our lives.

Distinguishing between fashion and politics is an urgent task right now not only for women, but for everyone in our consumer culture. It is particularly important for the current generation of young people, who are supposedly defining the politics of the 1990s and beyond.

Bret Easton Ellis, author of *American Psycho* and another pop star of dubious political depth, calls us the "twentysomething" generation. He describes us this way: "Some have adopted the counterculture idealism rooted in vague childhood memories; some claim the materialistic mentality of the 1980s; others are stuck in the middle of this mess. Most of us frequent both sides of the spectrum in any given week. . . . Our style is assimilation, our attitude reaction."

Our generation has no values, according to Ellis. Our task is to pick our way through the thicket of images and messages, and select a style and attitude of our own. Politics melt into posture.

Madonna is the perfect symbol for Ellis and his nihilistic twentysomethings. On film, she admits she is not a great singer or dancer. "But that doesn't matter," she says. "I want to push people's buttons. I want to be provocative. I want to be political." Madonna's politics, it turns out, amounts to asserting her right to masturbate on stage—a brilliant metaphor for the vacuous mentality Ellis both embodies and describes.

This vacuousness shows its sinister side in *Truth or Dare* when Madonna finds out that her makeup artist—a shy, overweight young woman—has been drugged and raped during the concert tour. In a shocking scene, we hear how she woke up in her hotel room, naked and bleeding. Madonna's response is to giggle. "She must have told someone she was on the tour and they wanted to fuck with her," is her only comment. Then the film is back on track, recording the antics of its glamorous cast, and the miserable makeup woman has retreated again into the background.

Surely, even in our "post-feminist age," we can do better than this. There must be a more helpful approach to the social realities of the 1990s than apathy and masturbation—some deeper political analysis, some concern for real people and issues.

Enter Dinesh D'Souza and the rest of the PC alarmists, who serve up an entirely different version of kids today and what's wrong with 'em. The trouble is, they say, students are so fanatically fixed in their radical beliefs that they are crushing free thought.

On close inspection, D'Souza's views turn out to be remarkably similar to Ellis's, and just as bleak. Both men portray their peers as stupid and narcissistic. While Ellis's twentysomethings are bubbleheaded slaves to fashion, D'Souza's strident activists are brainless goosesteppers. They are not sincerely concerned about social justice, they are just posturing, casting themselves as victims to follow a fad.

What Ellis and D'Souza—and Madonna, too, for that matter—ignore are the real social injustices in this country that are worth getting worked up about.

After the economic orgy of the 1980s, universities, along with the rest of the nation, are in a political crisis. Many of us who recently came of age share a paralyzing suspicion that vague "counterculture idealism" is, as Ellis indicates, inadequate. At the same time, we are confronted by stark problems—festering racism and misogyny, increasing class stratification, violence and desperate poverty in our cities, and the erosion of our fundamental constitutional rights. How do we begin to address all this?

The feeling of tension and cynicism that exists among young people is caused by more than frustration over choosing an appropriate style. It arises from a sense that we are powerless to bring about concrete political change. If we are fragmented and reactive, it is because we feel besieged by empty hype. We don't trust the appeal to "universal values" made by right-wingers like D'Souza and privileged academics who claim to have no political motives. But we need to establish some common values from which to critique our society and change it.

Instead, we are still shopping in the fashion market manipulated by politicians and pop stars, all of whom, we are perfectly aware, are selling us a bill of goods.

We need a better role model than Madonna. We need a sense that we can do something more productive for society than getting and spending.

We have no choice but to start resolving this crisis now. The door slammed shut behind my graduating class, the class of 1990, as my peers chased after the last of the glut of glittery jobs on Wall Street. This year, seniors papered their dorm rooms with rejection letters from the same firms. Now is as good a time as any to start considering alternatives and rethinking our values.

Madonna and Sandra: Like We Care

by Deb Schwartz

I **speak to you** now not only as an usher at the AmFAR benefit premiere of *Truth or Dare* but as a star of that very film. (You remember me from shots of the New York Gay and Lesbian Pride March: short, brunette, marching down Fifth Avenue behind a Queer Nation banner shouting "We're here, we're queer, get used to it"—call it a cameo, okay, call it a bit part, fine.) Yes, I share reel time with that salon blonde, that romancer of Vichy bottles. So why didn't you even say hello, Madonna, at the postscreening party? Was it my outfit? You crossed the dance floor, moving from one private room to another, only your pale hands and wrists visible above the circle of burly security guards. You carried an enormous bowl of popcorn high above the crowd, and after all I did for you, you offered me not a single kernel. Yet another example of Madonna's cold-blooded attitude toward lesbians: she takes what she wants from us and then gives nothing back. *Quelle tragédie.* Like I care.

Many lesbians adore Madonna. They wear black bras and rosaries as they bump and grind in lesbian clubs, they paint her on triptychs, they erect altars to her in their bedrooms. These were the ones going wild over anything pointing to the existence of something between Madonna and Sandra Bernhard.

It's easy to identify with Madonna, and thousands do. The polymorphous quality of her sexual address allows for a number of different points of identification—come on in, plenty of room, because in the universe of Madonna's body "It makes no difference if you're black or white / If you're a boy or a girl."

While distinctions of race and gender "make a difference" in the real world on many levels, Madonna creates and inhabits places where such distinctions are erased, and identification with a variety of bodies, black, white, boy, girl, gay, straight, is easily accomplished. In her "Justify My Love" video, Madonna presents a number of different polymorphous desires, and the objects of these desires are positioned equally in terms of appeal and availability—the array of gender and sexual differences is presented as flavor varieties of the same product.

But she arouses queer desire, as opposed to identification, because most of the sexual poses she works are nonheterosexual. Madonna's fetishes aren't hetero-centered: she wants the church, her daddy, clothing, her gay-boy dancers, success, little boys and girls, her own body. A number of these desires can only be read by fellow perverts: Madonna's affections toward the little boy in the "Open Your Heart" video and the little boy (or girl?) in "Cherish" are read as pedophilia only by those with similar erotic imaginings. But her autoeroticism plainly marks her as a pervert. Madonna cannot keep her hands off herself: she constantly strokes her limbs and face, grabs her crotch, or masturbates onstage. When she jills off, she foregrounds a sexual activity displaced by heterosexuality, engages in an act that is directed not at pleasing men but at pleasing herself. Her deviance here is her erotic relationship to a same-sex body, even if it is her own. Recall the media's titillation: the ooh-such-a-naughty-girl responses to her crotch-grab photos. Here is a girl burning up for no one's love but her own.

Not all lesbians get off when Madonna does. Many loathe her, think she has sold lesbians out: she teasingly suggests her lesbian pro-clivities in her videos, performances, and interviews but never comes out as a lesbian, never makes a pitch for the viability of lesbianism. (Possible headline to sate this crowd's appetite might read "Madonna to Barbara Walters: 'I think lesbians are really just the greatest.'") Some like her music and don't give a damn about her persona. Still more (oh, the mélange of voices clamoring to be heard) think she can't even fashion a danceable song.

From time to time I'm tempted to say, things in the world of girly girls must be in pretty sorry shape if lesbians can get all hot and bothered (either in adoration or in anger) over Madonna. Really, can't we do better? Can't we argue over the pros and cons of one of our own, a woman in the media mainstream who unapologetically announces that she has sex with women? After teasing the media for months with her relationship with Sandra Bernhard and its romantic overtones, Madonna never stepped forward and laid it on the line: "Look, I'm a big dyke, okay? Can we move on?" or "No, honestly, being so repressed and all, I could just never, well, you know, with a woman." Instead, she maintained a flip, mocking stance toward her inquisitors, contradicted herself, and then denied the allegations while Sandra confirmed them.

Madonna's coyness infuriated a lot of lesbians who felt that she was throwing away a precious and long-awaited opportunity to achieve lesbian visibility in the media mainstream. Looky, America, not just any Jane X getting it on with Suzy Q, but your chosen daughters: successful girls, girls who wrap their scantily clad bodies in the Stars and Stripes. Here we have a massively sexy, gorgeous, internationally famous blond pop star boinking a massively sexy, gorgeous famous redhead comedian. Just as Linda Evangelista and Christy Turlington are not models but supermodels, these two could have been not just lesbians, but megalesbians. Never mind those androgynously coiffed pop stars who lesbians "know" go their way though they never mention s-e-x or much less g-e-n-d-e-r in their songs addressed to the neutered "you." (A country-western crooner and a T-shirted folk guitarist come to mind.) Here was a girl who foregrounded and commodified her deviant desires: perversions with pop culture currency! If you're going to do it, do it right.

Madonna did not deliver (by coming out) on the visibility issue. But was this such a shock? Madonna—in all other ways so sincere and consistent in her self-presentation and so forthright in discussions of her private life? I don't think so. Maybe this is Madonna's true take on lesbianism: maybe she is lezbophobic and unwilling to put herself on the line in the name of gender and sexual liberation. But why would Madonna, queen manipulatrix of images and identity, she who is supremely aware of the malleability of fact and fiction, be suddenly moved to quit her fabulous game and spill her "true feelings"? Madonna, who makes her own news, and therefore wrests control from reporters and interviewers, has a history of toying with a press that hopes to toy with her. Did anyone walk out of *Truth or Dare* and breathe a sigh of relief: "Ah, yes, thank goodness for documentaries, now I feel I truly know Madonna"? It would have been out of character for her to suddenly regard the press as a neutral transcriber of truth when she had spent so much time romping through it, kicking up sand in the playground of image and information she had made her own.

It seems odd, therefore, that lesbians, whose very existence has long been obscured, slandered, or rendered invisible in the media, would now put faith in its institutions to perform liberatory acts and believe that the trinity of newsprint, video, and talk show will set us free.

The anger that rose up in response to Madonna's silence or equivocation in the press may have had more to do with the betrayal effected in an abandonment of a media opportunity than a reaction to her deeper sentiments regarding lesbianism. Yet Madonna's response can be perceived as a betrayal only if you believe in the inherent legitimizing effect of an appearance in the media. The media, fundamental builder and keeper of the closet, will, when it finds it advantageous, trumpet its noble obligation to provide the public with information. But the media has never been a public servant and has always been fickle in its decisions to expose or bury juicy tidbits of public figures' private lives. Recall, if you will, revelations of the names of rape victims and rapists, and prostitutes and johns, while you attempt to locate a consistent journalistic commitment to exposure.

Madonna, in a real change of pace, did it her way. If she were interested in the notion of stable and coherent identities, she would join the ranks of outers. But this conception of sexuality has nothing to do with sex, and Madonna is engaged in the generation of eroticism.

Coming out is an exercise in abstraction, an announcement of subjectivity, and does nothing to foreground the reality of sexual practices between women (or men). There is no guarantee that the straight person who says "Whatever makes you happy, honey," when you say "I'm a lesbian" will not flip his wig when he sees your hand on your lover's knee.

Madonna and Sandra subverted the fallacy that acceptance of an abstract declaration of one's sexual identity will insure an acceptance of one's sexual practices. They did this by substituting flirting for outing. Instead of investing in the concept of a stable identity (that is, sitting with hands folded in laps, dimes between knees, and calmly stating "That's right, Mr. Letterman, we're lesbians"), they made lesbian sexual practice visible. They engaged in a more radical form of visibility that underscored their interest in the practice of sex rather than the formation of identity.

Thanks to Elizabeth Freeman for valuable critiques and suggestions.—D.S.

madonna: plantation mistress or soul sister?

by bell hooks

White female "stars" like Madonna, Sandra Bernhard, and many others publicly name their interest in, and appropriation of, black culture as yet another sign of their radical chic. Intimacy with that "nasty" blackness good white girls stay away from is the closeness they seek. To white and other nonblack consumers this gives them a special flavor, an added spice. After all, it is a very recent historical phenomenon for any white girl to be able to get some mileage out of flaunting her fascination and envy of blackness. The thing about envy is that it is always ready to destroy, erase, take over, and consume the desired object. And that's exactly what Madonna attempts to do when she appropriates and commodifies aspects of black culture. Needless to say, this kind of fascination is a threat. It endangers. Perhaps that is why so many of the "grown" black women I spoke with about Madonna felt that they had no interest in her as a cultural icon, said things like "The bitch can't even sing." It was only among young black females that I could find die-hard Madonna fans. Though I often admire and, yes, at times even envy Madonna because she has created a cultural space where she can invent and reinvent herself and receive public affirmation and material reward, I do not consider myself a Madonna fan.

Once I read an interview with Madonna where she talked about her envy of black culture, where she even stated that she had wanted to be black as a child. It is a sign of white privilege to be able to "see" blackness and black culture from a standpoint where only the rich culture of opposition black people have created in resistance marks and defines us. Such a perspective enables one to ignore the way white supremacist domination and the hurt it inflicts via oppression, exploitation, and ongoing assault in everyday life wounds and pains. White folks who do not see black pain never really understand the complexity of black pleasure. And it is no wonder then that when they attempt to imitate the *joie de vivre* that they see as the "essence" of soul, of blackness, that their cultural productions may have an air of sham and falseness that may titillate and even move white audiences yet leave many black folks cold.

Needless to say, if Madonna had to depend on masses of black women to maintain her status as cultural icon, she would have been dethroned some time ago. Many of the black women I spoke with expressed intense disgust and hatred of Madonna. Most did not respond to my cautious attempts to suggest that underlying those negative feelings might lurk feelings of envy, and dare I say it, desire. No black woman I talked to declared that she wanted to "be Madonna." Yet we have only to look at the number of black women entertainers (Tina Turner, Aretha Franklin, Donna Summer, Vanessa Williams, Yo-Yo et al.) who gain greater crossover recognition when they demonstrate that they too, like Madonna, have a healthy dose of "blond ambition," to know that their careers have been influenced by Madonna's choices and strategies.

For masses of black women, the political reality that underlies Madonna's and our recognition that this is a society where "blondes" not only "have more fun" but where they are more likely to succeed in any endeavor is white supremacy and racism. We cannot see Madonna's change in hair color as being merely a question of aesthetic choice. I agree with Julie Burchill in *Girls on Film* when she reminds us: "What does it say about racial purity that the best blondes have all been brunettes (Harlow, Monroe, Bardot)? I think it says that we are not as white as we think. I think it says that Pure is a Bore." But I know that it is the expressed desire of the nonblond other for those characteristics that are seen as the quintessential markers of racial aesthetic superiority that perpetuate and uphold white supremacy. In this sense Madonna has much in common with the many black women who suffer from internalized racism and are forever terrorized by a standard of beauty they feel they can never truly embody.

Like many black women who have stood outside the culture's fascination with the blond beauty, only able to reach it through imitation and artifice, Madonna often recalls that she was a working-class white girl who saw herself as ugly, as outside the mainstream beauty standard. And indeed what some of us like about her is the way she deconstructs the myth of "natural" white girl beauty by exposing the extent to which it can be and usually is artificially constructed and maintained. She mocks the conventional racist-defined beauty ideal even as she rigorously strives to embody it. Given her obsession with exposing the reality that the ideal female beauty in this society can be attained by artifice and social construction, it should come as no surprise that many of her fans are gay men, and that a majority of nonwhite men, particularly black men, are among that group. Jennie Livingston's film *Paris Is Burning* suggests that many black gay men, especially queens/divas, are, like Madonna, equally driven by "blond ambition." Madonna never lets her audience forget that whatever "look" she acquires is attained by hard work—"it ain't natural." And as Burchill comments in her chapter "Homosexuals' Girls":

> I have a friend who drives a cab and looks like a Marlboro Man but at night is the second best Jean Harlow I have ever seen. He summed up the kind of film star he adores, brutally and brilliantly, when he said, "I like actresses who look as if they've spent hours putting themselves together—and even then they don't look right."

Certainly not even die-hard Madonna fans ever insist that her beauty is not attained by skillful artifice. And indeed a major point of the documentary film *Truth or Dare* was to demonstrate the amount of work that goes into the construction of her image.

Yet when the chips are down, the image Madonna most exploits is that of the quintessential "white girl." To maintain that image she must always position herself as an outsider in relation to black culture. And it is that position of outsider that enables her to colonize and appropriate black experience for her own opportunistic ends even as she attempts to mask her acts of racist aggression as affirmation. No other group sees that as clearly as black females in this society. For we have always known that the socially constructed image of innocent white womanhood relies on the continued production of the racist/sexist sexual myth that black women are not innocent and can never be. Since we are coded always as "fallen" women in the racist cultural iconography, we can never, like Madonna, publicly "work" the image of ourselves as innocent females daring to be bad. Mainstream culture always reads the black female body as sign of sexual experience. In part, many black women who are disgusted by Madonna's flaunting of sexual experience are enraged because the very image of sexual agency that she is able to project and affirm with material gain has been precisely what this society has used to justify its continued assault on the black female body. The vast majority of black women in the United States are more concerned with projecting images of respectability than with the idea of female sexual agency. Those of us who are concerned with black female sexual agency and transgression often do not feel we have the "freedom" to act in rebellious ways in regard to sexuality without being punished. We have only to contrast the life story of Tina Turner with that of Madonna to see the different connotations "wild" sexual agency has when it is asserted by a black female. Being represented publicly as an active sexual being has only recently enabled Turner to gain control over her life and career. For years the public image of aggressive sexual agency Turner projected belied the degree to which she was sexually abused and exploited privately. (She was also materially exploited.) Madonna's career could not be all that it is if there were no Tina Turner, and yet unlike her cohort Sandra Bernhard, Madonna never articulates the cultural debt she owes to black females.

In her most recent appropriations of blackness, Madonna almost always imitates phallic black masculinity. Although I have read many articles that talk about her aping of masculine pose, none of them talk about her appropriating these codes from specifically black male experience. In his *Playboy* profile, "Playgirl of the Western World," Michael Kelly describes Madonna's crotch-grabbing as "an eloquent visual put-down of male phallic pride," pointing out that she worked with choreographer Vince Paterson to perfect the gesture. Yet even though Kelly tells readers that Madonna was consciously imitating Michael Jackson, he does not contextualize his interpretation of the gesture to include this act of appropriation from black male culture. And in that specific context the groin-grabbing gesture is an assertion of pride and phallic domination that usually takes place in an all-male context. Madonna's imitation of this gesture could just as easily be read as an expression of envy.

Throughout much of her autobiographical cultural narrative as it is unveiled in interviews runs a thread of expressed desire to possess the power she perceives men having: Madonna may hate the phallus, but she longs to possess its power. She is always first and foremost in competition with men to see who has the biggest penis. She longs to assert phallic power, and like every other group in this white supremacist society, she clearly sees black men as embodying a quality of maleness that eludes white men. Hence, they are often the group of men she most seeks to imitate, taunting white males with her own version of "black masculinity." When it comes to entertainment rivals, Madonna clearly perceives black male stars like Prince and Michael Jackson to be the standard against which she must measure herself and which she ultimately hopes to transcend.

Fascinated by yet envious of black style, Madonna appropriates black culture in ways that mock and undermine, making her presentation one that upstages. This is most evident in the video "Like a Prayer." Though I have read numerous articles that discuss public outrage over this video, none focuses on the issue of race. No article calls attention to the fact that Madonna flaunts her sexual agency by suggesting that she is breaking the ties that bind her as a white girl to white patriarchy and establishing ties instead with black men. She, however, and not black men, does the choosing. And the message is directed at white men, suggesting that they label black men rapists only for fear that white girls will choose black partners over them. Cultural critics commenting on the video do not seem at all interested in exploring the reasons Madonna chooses a black cultural backdrop for this video, that is, a black church and religious experience. Clearly, however, it is this backdrop that adds to the video's controversy. Brooke Masters writes in "Madonna: Yuppie Goddess":

> Most descriptions of the controversial video focus on its Catholic imagery: Madonna kisses a black saint, and develops Christ-like markings on her hands. However, the video is also a feminist fairy tale. Sleeping Beauty and Snow White waited for their princes to come along, Madonna finds her own man and wakes him up.

Notice that this writer completely overlooks the issues of race and gender. That Madonna's chosen prince was a black man is in part what makes the representation potentially shocking and provocative to a white supremacist audience. Yet critics concentrate solely on whether she is violating taboos regarding religion and representation.

In the United States, Catholicism is most often seen as a religion that has few black followers or none at all, and Madonna's video certainly perpetuates this stereotype with its juxtaposition of images of black, non-Catholic representations with the image of a black saint. Given the importance of religious experience and liberation theology in black life, Madonna's use of this imagery seemed particularly offensive. For she made black characters act in complicity with her as she aggressively flaunted her critique of Catholic manners, her attack on organized religion. Yet no black voices that I know of came forward in print calling attention to the fact that the realm of the sacred that is mocked in this clip is black religious experience and that this appropriative "use" of that experience was offensive to many black folk. Looking at the video with a group of students in my class, "The Politics of Sexuality," where we critically analyze the way race and representations of blackness are used to sell products, we discussed the manner in which black people in the video are caricatures reflecting stereotypes. They appear grotesque. For example, the only role black females have in this video is to catch (that is, rescue) the "angelic" Madonna when she is "falling." This is just a contemporary recasting of the black female as Mammy. Made to serve as supportive backdrop for Madonna's drama, black characters in "Like a Prayer" remind one of those early Hollywood depictions of singing black slaves in the great plantation movies or those Shirley Temple films where Bojangles was trotted out to dance with Miss Shirley and spice up her act. Audiences were not supposed to be enamored of Bojangles; they were supposed to see just what a special little old white girl Shirley really was. In her own way, Madonna is a modern-day Shirley Temple. Certainly her expressed affinity with black culture enhances her value.

Eager to see *Truth or Dare* because it promised to focus on Madonna's transgressive sexual persona (which I find interesting), I was too angered by the spectacle of her domination over, not white men (certainly not over Warren Beatty or Alek Keshishian), but people of color and working-class women, to appreciate those aspects of the film I might have enjoyed. In *Truth or Dare*, Madonna clearly reveals that she can only think of exerting power along very traditional white supremacist capitalist patriarchal lines. That she made people who were dependent on her for their immediate livelihood submit to her will was neither charming nor seductive to me or the other black folks that I spoke with who saw this film. And we thought it tragically ironic that Madonna would choose as her dance partner a black male with dyed blond hair. Perhaps had he appeared less like a white-identified black male consumed by "blond ambition," he might have upstaged her. Instead he was positioned as a mirror, into which Madonna and her audience could look and see only a reflection of herself and the idealization of "whiteness" she embodies. Madonna used her power to ensure that he and the other nonwhite women and men who worked for her, as well as some white subordinates, would all serve as the backdrop to her white-girl-makes-good drama. Joking about the film with other black folks, we commented that Madonna must have searched long and hard to find a black female who was not a good dancer, one who would not deflect attention away from her. And it is telling that when the film does briefly reflect something other than a positive image of Madonna, the camera highlights the rage this black female dancer had been suppressing, which surfaces when the "subordinates" have time off and are "relaxing."

As with most Madonna videos, when critics talk about this film they tend to ignore race. Yet no viewer can look at this film and not think about race and representation without engaging in forms of denial. After choosing a cast of characters from marginal groups—nonwhite folks, heterosexual and gay, and gay white folks—Madonna publicly describes them as "emotional cripples." And of course in the context of the film this description seems borne out by the way they allow her to dominate, exploit, and humiliate them. Those Madonna fans who are determined to see her as politically progressive might ask themselves why it is she so completely endorses those racist/sexist/classist stereotypes that almost always attempt to portray marginal groups as "defective." Let's face it, by doing this Madonna is not breaking with the white supremacist, patriarchal status quo; she is endorsing and perpetuating it.

Some of us do not find it hip or cute for Madonna to brag that she has a "fascistic side," so well documented in the film. Well, we did not see any of her cute little fascism in action when it was Warren Beatty calling her out in the film. There the image of Madonna was the little woman who grins and bears it. No, her "somebody's got to be in charge side," as she so names it, was most expressed in her interaction with those representatives from marginal groups who are most often victimized by the powerful. Why is it there is little or no discussion of

Madonna as racist or sexist in her relation to other women? Would audiences be charmed by some rich white male entertainer telling us that he must "play father" and oversee the actions of the less powerful, especially women and men of color? So why did so many people find Madonna's assertion that she dominates the film's interracial cast of gay and heterosexual folks because they are crippled and she "like[s] to play mother"—cute? This was not a display of feminist power, this was the same old phallic nonsense with white pussy at the center. And many of us watching were simply not moved—we were outraged.

Perhaps it is a sign of a collective feeling of powerlessness that the many viewers of this film who were disturbed by the display of racism, sexism, and heterosexism (yes, it's possible to hire gay people, support AIDS projects, and still be biased in the direction of phallic patriarchal heterosexuality) in *Truth or Dare* have said so little. Sometimes it is difficult to find words to make a critique when we find ourselves attracted by some aspect of a performer's act and disturbed by others, or when a performer shows more interest in promoting progressive social causes than is customary. We may see that performer as above critique. Or we may feel our critique will in no way affect the worship of her/him as a cultural icon.

To say nothing, however, is to be complicit with the very forces of domination that make "blond ambition" necessary to Madonna's success. Tragically, all that is transgressive and potentially empowering to feminist women and men about Madonna's work may be undermined by all that it contains that is reactionary, in no way unconventional or new. And it is often the conservative elements in her work converging with the status quo that have a more powerful impact. For example: Given the rampant homophobia in this society and the concomitant heterosexist/voyeuristic obsession with gay lifestyles, to what extent does Madonna progressively seek to challenge this if she insists on primarily representing gays as in some way emotionally handicapped or defective? When Madonna responds to the critique that she exploits gay men by cavalierly stating "What does exploitation mean? . . . In a revolution, some people have to get hurt. To get people to change, you have to turn the table over. Some dishes get broken," I can only say this don't sound like liberation to me. Perhaps when Madonna explores those memories of her white working-class childhood in a troubled family context in a way that enables her to understand intimately the politics of exploitation, of domination and submission, she will have a deeper connection with oppositional black culture. If and when this radical critical self-interrogation takes place, she will have gained the power to create new and different cultural productions, work that will be truly transgressive—acts of resistance that transform rather than simply seduce.

(from *Christianity and Crisis*)

Being "Real," Using "Real"

by Kathleen Talvacchia

I refuse to be intimidated by reality anymore. After all, what is reality anyway? Nothin' but a collective hunch. My space chums think reality was once a primitive method of crowd control that got out of hand.

—Trudy, in Jane Wagner's *The Search for Signs of Intelligent Life in The Universe*

Liberation theologians have taught us that a person's location within a society's power structure affects how that person interprets what is real and what is true. In the United States, theology done from the perspective of those who have traditionally lacked power and suffered social oppression—the poor, African Americans, women, homosexuals, Native Americans, and Asians, to name a few—not only changes the way we do theology, but creates a new set of criteria for theological truth.

The epigraph above highlights two important features of the "real": Reality is a social construction and notions of what is real function as a tool of social control. These two ideas operate at the heart of two current documentary films, Jennie Livingston's *Paris Is Burning* and Alek Keshishian's *Truth or Dare*. Both films attempt to get "behind the scenes" and show us a world in which appearances are deceiving, not to be taken fully at face value.

Yet the "deception" functions very differently in each film. For Madonna (the subject of *Truth or Dare*), blurring our perception of common gender role definition allows her to comment and critique a social system of which she is essentially a part. For the characters profiled in *Paris Is Burning*, blurring our perception of gender roles allows them commentary and critique within the system, but it is a system that excludes them on many levels.

Truth or Dare is a "documentary" insofar as it chronicles the life and times of Madonna and her crew on her Blond Ambition Tour. The film consists of grainy black-and-white film of life "behind the scenes," interspersed with color footage of the actual song and dance numbers. But Madonna and her entourage are so hyper-aware of the camera that all semblance of cinema vérité disappears into a seemingly manipulative attempt continually to reinvent Madonna's image. Who is the real Madonna? Electrifying entertainer, savvy businesswoman, sexual siren, demanding bitch, nurturing mother, feminist—all of them? She intends that we can never be sure. All celebrities thrive on being able to shock, tease, and fascinate their fans with a constant stream of acts designed to keep them in the public eye. Madonna has made it into her art-form.

What about the politics involved in such antics? Clearly Madonna wants (by her own admission) to "press buttons" and provoke us to rethink socially accepted understandings of female behavior. Mixing masculine and feminine gender characteristics and reversing traditional gender roles, she is able to react against a sexually repressive society that "educates" women into rigid gender roles which inhibit their freedom and foster passivity in social relations, including sex.

In the song "Express Yourself," for example, Madonna appears in a blue pin-striped man's suit. But the crotch has been cut out, as well as the chest, both revealing pink undergarments. Pink garter straps hang out from underneath the suit to complete the androgynous look. The song speaks of the need to express oneself sexually, and while the look may be androgynous, many of Madonna's actions (crotch-grabbing, pelvic thrusts) are stereotypically male. The implication is that sexual power can be the realm of women also. A norm which defines "real women" as sexually passive, waiting for the man to initiate, is turned on its head with the image of a female in a man's pants with a woman's undergarment from crotch to chest assertively seeking sexual gratification.

"Like a Virgin" provides another example of gender blending that challenges passive female reality. Madonna gyrates on a red satin bed with a male consort on either side waiting to fulfill her sexual desires. As the song nears completion she decides that she wants neither man, and in one of the most controversial actions of her show she simulates masturbation and orgasm. Clearly, the image of a shy and innocent virgin is replaced by that of a powerfully sexual woman who decides how and who will fulfill her physical needs.

Madonna's efforts to play with reality so as to expand and thereby transform it serve as useful social critique of a rigid system. However, the critique is blunted by the safety in which she can poke and prod entrenched systems of gender oppression. Madonna's numbers imply that to be liberated all a woman need do is act "like a man," and this she proposes safely ensconced in a visibly heterosexual lifestyle. The consequences of "acting like a man" would be greatly changed if she were a lesbian. Does Martina Navratilova meet with acceptance from the mainstream because she is as powerful as a man in her tennis game? Does Audre Lorde gain acceptance from the mainstream because she is as verbally powerful as a man? Madonna can get away with it because she is still safely heterosexual and white. Also, her wealth insulates her from many of the consequences of her androgyny. She travels with bodyguards and most likely does not need to ride the subway at three A.M. to get home after a show.

Yes, Madonna has a "politics"; she clearly has an agenda she wants to advocate about the oppressiveness of traditional gender role stereotyping. But her politics shows no social analysis of the patriarchal structure that creates rigid gender roles and behaviors. She may be pushing against the walls of gender oppression, but the walls are the walls of a patriarchal construct that she does not "appear" to see. A good example of this occurs in a scene where she meets her father after her show in hometown Detroit. She shyly tells him that she has to change out of her costume and retreats to her inner dressing room where she proceeds, with great fanfare, to expose her bare breasts to the camera. Side by side the viewer faces Madonna as "good girl," modest before her father, and as sexual rebel, shocking and defying established norms. Such contradictions are part and parcel of patriarchy's "good girl/bad girl" dichotomy.

▶ How Close to Reality?

The one oppression that Madonna reacts to—gender oppression—is strangely absent from the people who are the subject of Jennie

Livingston's extraordinary *Paris Is Burning*. Livingston introduces us to the world of black homosexual men who participate in an activity called "vogueing." A cross between runway modeling and formal dancing, vogueing involves creating a character, male or female, and presenting that character at "balls"—organized competition among "houses." One receives points from the judges for the ability to carry off the most authentic representation of a particular acceptable social type—both visually, through clothes and walk, and as a whole attitude. In voguers' own words, houses are essentially gay street gangs that compete with each other in organized vogueing balls.

For these men, some of whom are transsexuals, reality as it is defined by those with power in the society is very much about social control. During the opening frames of the movie, one of the characters states that his father told him at an early age that he had three strikes against him—being black, male, and gay—and that because of this he would need to live with more strength than he ever thought he might be able to have. This awareness of social oppression permeates the film.

For example, old-time drag queen Dorian Corey describes balls as fantasies that allow you to live realities denied you because of prejudice and discrimination. As Corey speaks, the viewer watches two voguers dressed impeccably as businessmen. To be a Wall Street executive, states Corey, demands formal schooling, the level of financial stability that schooling assumes, and heterosexuality. At one time it also demanded being white and male. However, in the balls all of those distinctions disappear; the distance between what you aspire to and what you are shrinks to the level of how "real" you can be in your presentation of a Wall Street executive. As voguer Pepper Labeija states earlier, "The ball is as close to reality as we are going to get."

The central value becomes "realness," and all of the competition, both formal and informal, is judged by the ability to be as real as possible. Corey explains that realness is the ability to "blend" or "pass" the trained or untrained eye, that is, to be virtually undetectable in looking as much as possible like your straight counterpart. Realness is not about satire of social roles; it is about actually being able to be that role. Beyond the balls, realness is important as a method of survival in a society hostile to homosexuals. Gender realness, then, is the ability to move through mainstream society undetectable as a drag queen or transsexual so that, as Corey states, you can get home at night without getting beat up.

The issue of survival emerges as a key distinction between the two movies. Madonna's attempts to stretch reality and confront our notion of it occur in a social system that for the most part includes her. It is true that as a woman and as an Italian American she experiences oppression, and she clearly acts out of resistance to those oppressions. But she is not nearly so disenfranchised as the marginalized people seen in *Paris Is Burning*. As a heterosexual white woman, the roles she takes on are seen to be just that, roles. And while they may be controversial or frightening to mainstream society, beneath it all Madonna is essentially a heterosexual woman, and not, as in *Paris Is Burning*, a gay man emulating a straight woman. Balls and vogueing get at the core of our ideological rigidity about masculine and feminine gender roles assigned to biological males and females. Even though we may not like it, gender role reversal is easier to stomach in the form of pop theater than on the streets of New York City.

On the other hand, although the voguers possess an incisive social analysis about racial, economic, and sexual orientation oppression, they are remarkably silent on the rigidity of the gender roles they so carefully create for themselves. For example, while teaching young women at a modeling agency, voguer Willie Ninja comments that by learning how to model women can have equal rights but can continue to get what they need from men by using their feminine wiles; after all, "they won't get it if they act like a man." Just as with Madonna, these men are pushing against the wall of oppression, but are still within a patriarchal construct. Pepper Labeija shows the most sensitivity to gender oppression when he states that he has never been a woman; rather, he has been a man emulating a woman, and so he does not know exactly what it is like being a female. For those who wish to get a sex change and live as a woman, he reminds them that it may be tough living as a gay man, but it is equally tough living as a woman.

For these gay men survival in part involves keeping a certain balance between the realness of what they could be and the realness of the limitations they face in a world permeated with oppression. For Madonna, no real perspective is needed between what is possible and what really is. Wealth, fame, heterosexuality, and whiteness shield Madonna from the threats marginalization brings.

In the end we are left with two thoroughly enjoyable challenges to standard notions of reality. We may feel encouraged, like Trudy, to "refuse to be intimidated by reality anymore."

(from *The New Yorker*)

by Roz Chast

(from *The National Review*)

Single Sex and the Girl

Meet Madonna, scourge of the Pharisees, defender of artistic integrity, exposer of Christian uncharity.

by Joseph Sobran

In one scene in *Truth or Dare*—a documentary, of sorts, of her "Blond Ambition" concert tour—Madonna phones her father to ask if he's coming to see her perform. He says he understands her act is pretty "racy" and inquires as to whether she'll "tone it down" for him and the family. No, she answers; she won't "compromise my artistic integrity."

A few minutes later, we see that uncompromised artistic integrity as she lies on a bed onstage. The stage is dark, except for the bed. Standing beside her are two black male dancers wearing weird conical brassieres. As she sings "Like a Virgin," she vigorously massages her crotch, moaning and arching her back spasmodically. There's more, but you get the basic idea. The huge crowd goes wild.

Madonna is a genius at getting attention. Everything she does gets attention—her records, her videos, her movies, her marriage, her divorce, her amours (including a joke that she'd had a lesbian relationship with the comedienne Sandra Bernhard). When she showed up at the Cannes Film Festival with her hair dyed a new color, her face appeared on the front page of the New York *Daily News*. She has been on the cover of every magazine except *National Geographic*.

How does she do it? As she admits, she's not a great singer, a great dancer, or even—at least in repose—a great looker. She can't act. Yet she has the most flamboyantly theatrical personality since . . . well, who was the last one? Bette Davis? Joan Crawford? Tallulah Bankhead?

Some people have what I can only call contagious vanity. You may even dislike them, but you can't take your eyes off them. Madonna is like that. In a country where people want to be liked (maybe even more ardently than they want to be loved), she dares you to hate her.

"Madonna is the true feminist," writes Camille Paglia, herself a sort of antifeminist feminist. "She exposes the puritanism and suffocating ideology of American feminism . . . Madonna has taught young women to be fully female and sexual while still exercising total control over their lives. She shows girls how to be attractive, sensual, energetic, ambitious, aggressive, and funny—all at the same time."

▶ Kink and Danger

She's undeniably magnetic, but it's a calculating magnetism, a carefully constructed aura of kink and danger. If she seems to be shattering conventions, she's also there to pick up the pieces. One of her steamier videos, "Like a Prayer," shows her in a Catholic church adoring a statue of a black saint, who comes to life and kisses her passionately. She receives the stigmata, and there are burning crosses and things, and . . . well, again, you get the idea: a deliberate fusion of such themes as sex, race, and religion. These elements are combined in surreal montage, and the effect is eerie, shocking, Weimar decadent.

An even more explicit video, "Justify My Love," did succeed in outraging people, and even easygoing MTV refused to play it. "The video is pornographic," Miss Paglia writes. "It's decadent. And it's fabulous. MTV was right to ban it." But she chides Madonna for copping out on *Nightline* by pleading "her love of children, her social activism, and her condom endorsements." If you want to shock people, go ahead and shock 'em. But don't blame them for *being* shocked.

The trouble is that Madonna wants to have it both ways. (One problem in writing about her is that everything tends to sound like a double-entendre.) She clearly knows what she's doing, but wants to pretend she doesn't. Her calculation is shown in one sequence in *Truth or Dare* when her tour arrives in Toronto and she is told that the police are prepared to arrest her if she does the masturbation bit. She asks what the penalty is. She learns she'll probably just be booked, fined, and released. This, to her, is a cheap price to pay for the international front-page publicity she stands to get, so she goes ahead with it. The cops back down and do nothing. Never has the structure of incentives been so favorable to artistic martyrdom.

A similar event occurs in Italy, where she finds on her arrival that the Vatican has denounced her in advance. She holds a press conference and says that as an Italian-American she resents this prejudicial treatment. Hers is no "conventional" rock act, but "a total theatrical experience." The note of pique sounds sincere enough, but she also knows that in her terms the Vatican has done her a favor. Madonna has a keen sense of whom it's profitable to offend and whom it isn't. She surrounds herself with blacks and homosexuals. She is heavy into AIDS education: "Next to Hitler, AIDS is the worst thing to happen in the twentieth century," she told *Vanity Fair* recently—a good, conventional, and convenient view to hold in her line of work. And when the Simon Wiesenthal Center in Los Angeles attacked her for including the phrase "synagogue of Satan" (from the Book of Revelation) in one of her songs, she apologized.

In the film, one of her dancers worries that his scene of simulated sex with her will hurt his career. "In this country it works the other way around," she answers. "The more notorious you are, the more you are going to work! Don't you guys understand that?" Indeed. Nothing is more conventional than the daring. In *Truth or Dare*, she talks nonstop raunch, bares her breasts, gets into bed with a naked dancer and whoops about the size of his organ (it's all right, he's gay), and much, much more.

▶ The Good Christian

Raised a Catholic by devout parents (her mother died when she was six), Madonna's target of choice is Catholicism. Her concert and video performances abound in crucifixes, dancers dressed as priests fondling her, and so forth. It's exciting. It's outrageous. It sells. Naturally, much of her following consists of lapsed Catholics, typified by the columnist Pete Hamill, who calls her "a good Christian." You can write a Hamill column with your eyes closed: Jesus preferred Mary Magdalene to the Pharisees, drove the money-changers out of the Temple, hated prigs—a lot like Pete Hamill, come to think of it. This sort of approval (terribly smug, in its own way) implies that because Jesus forgave unchastity, he didn't regard it as a sin. Not only is this a non sequitur, it overlooks some very stern words in the Gospels, sterner, in fact, than anything in Saint Paul, the favorite scapegoat of lapsed Christians who want to insist that it's only the *Church* they object to—nothing against Jesus, you understand.

Charity is of course the supreme Christian virtue, and those who fail in chastity often insist that they make up for it in charity. But there is more than one way of being uncharitable, and self-serving solicitude for today's accredited victims—"compassion," for short—doesn't necessarily cover a multitude of sins. In *Truth or Dare* we learn that Madonna leads her troupe in prayer before every performance. But the tone of her prayer is imperious and stagy. The viewer wonders if praying with the boss—or rather standing there submissively while *she* prays—is part of the job description of dancer. The question acquires a special urgency when the prayer turns into a chewing-out of some of those in the circle. She stops just short of demanding divine retribution against those who have offended her.

Madonna is even less charitable toward the Church itself. "I've always known that Catholicism is a completely sexist, repressed, sin- and punishment-based religion," she told an interviewer for *Us* magazine. She was even blunter to *Vanity Fair*: "I think it's disgusting. I think it's hypocritical. And it's unloving. It's not what God and Christianity are all about." Nearly every interview she gives includes bitter remarks about the Church and its "rules." It's the only subject, apart from herself, she regularly talks about.

But her father is still a faithful Catholic, and in *Truth or Dare* we see her fretting at the idea of his seeing her perform "Like a Virgin." In fact she *does* "tone it down" when he's in the audience, and she hales him onto the stage to be introduced to the crowd. He seems a mild fellow, confusedly proud of his famous daughter. Her anxiety about being seen by him *in flagrante* is puzzling: she seems bent on offending everyone who believes in the things he believes in, but not *him*. Why this exemption? If she hates the faith she was raised in, why doesn't she blame the man who raised her?

"She doesn't want to live off-camera," jokes Warren Beatty, her beau at the time of the filming. "Why would you bother to say something if it's off-camera?" Because Madonna finds everything about Madonna absolutely fascinating, that's why. Imagine a film in which it's left to Warren Beatty to sound the note of common sense.

"I find myself drawn to emotional cripples," Madonna says, explaining the odd assortment of characters she surrounds herself with. "I like to play mother." Oh. We see her visiting her own mother's grave (for the first time); naturally, she dresses in black for the occasion, brings a camera crew along, and lies down to kiss the tombstone. We see her backstage, complaining about a mike failure to a hapless technician. We see her dining with friends. We see her shopping in Paris. We see her meeting an old school chum, who she tells us once did something naughty to her at a pajama party. (The school chum, now a mother of five, denies it when informed of it; she looks shocked by this ambush, having named a daughter Madonna.) We see her telling someone or another that her mission is to be "provocative" and "political." We see, in fact, two hours of this carefully staged "spontaneity," and two hours trapped in a dark room with *that* ego feels like a week.

▶ The Real Madonna

Talking to *Vanity Fair*, Madonna gets defensive: "People will say, 'She knows the camera is on, she's just acting.' But even if I *am* acting, there's a truth in my acting . . . You could watch it and say, I still don't know Madonna, and *good*. Because you will never know the real me. Ever." You mean there's *more*?

Well, if we never know the real Madonna, we won't have Madonna to blame for it. She talks about herself volubly, incessantly; she poses for photo stills dressed up as Marilyn Monroe and other sexpots. It's as if her privacy might unfairly deprive us of something. Or rather, as if she wanted to *become* all the fascinating women of the past, and reveal their mysteries to us. Instead she creates the disconcerting impression that all the mystery may have been bogus; maybe those women *were* like her: self-absorbed little bores who talked in clichés about "art" and "truth," when they weren't talking about themselves. One would rather not know.

As for "truth," Madonna isn't interested in any that may inconvenience her. It never crosses her mind that there may be more to Catholicism than her spiteful parody of it, which is of an order of glibness that would embarrass Phil Donahue. For her there is no fundamental order in life, only arbitrary "rules." Do whatcha want, as long as you practice "safe sex," that mirage of those who think selfishness and sensuality can be calculating and civic-minded even at the peak of ardor. It isn't just that she's hopelessly banal whenever she tries to share an insight. It's that she has reached that pitch of egomania at which celebrity supposes itself oracular. That's when you say things like "Power is a great aphrodisiac," and you think it sounds impressive. (We may note in passing that the Me Decade is now entering its third decade.)

And as for "art," well, philosophers differ. But it's widely believed by wise people that art and ego sit uneasily together. The true artist, even if his ego is as muscular as Beethoven's, creates something outside himself. Art is not "self-expression" in the sense that its focus of interest lies in its creator; rather, it is self-contained. Its value doesn't depend on our knowledge of the artist. *Hamlet* is a great play no matter who wrote it. *Parsifal* is a great opera even if Wagner did compose it.

But for Madonna, art is defined by the censors: it's whatever they don't like. So someone who gets the censors howling must be an artist.

Silly, but a lot of people agree with her, and they buy tickets. Madonna offers something new under the sun: vicarious self-absorption. It takes a special kind of imagination to identify with a solipsist.

Madonna just doesn't glory in herself: she glories in her *self.* And *Truth or Dare* suggests a novel ambition: to make the self, even in its private moments, an object of universal attention. Who was the love of your life? someone asks her. "Sean," she murmurs, meaning her ex-husband, Sean Penn (of whom it was once said that he had slugged every photographer except Karsh of Ottawa). Sean, she explains, was madly jealous and domineering, but "at least he paid attention." Better hostile attention than none at all.

Like most pop music, Madonna's songs are about love. But love is the subject about which she shows no understanding at all. She is the perfect expression of an age that has reduced the erotic to the sensual: the gratification of the self rather than the yearning for union with another. "Lovers" become interchangeable and succeed each other quickly, each being merely instrumental to the self and its cravings. Real love is like art: it demands the subordination of the ego. Kinky, exciting, shocking: these are the attributes of love as she conceives it. It would make no sense to tell her that sodomy is at best a stunted and misdirected form of eros, since heterosexual love, as she exemplifies it, has the same character. The purpose of this love is neither permanent union nor procreation, but pleasure and ego-enhancement. For her, in fact, the erotic isn't all that different from the autoerotic, except that there happens to be another person present.

But the word *autoerotic* is self-contradictory. Being in love with yourself isn't love. And having sex with yourself hardly qualifies as sex. The Victorians thought masturbation led to blindness. If they'd said moral blindness, they might have had a point. At least Madonna seems to intimate a connection. "Masturbation," Woody Allen has said, "is having sex with someone you love." When we watch Madonna doing "Like a Virgin," clutching her private parts (if they can be called private anymore), simulating ecstatic convulsions, we're seeing her having sex, as it were, with someone she loves, all right—maybe the only one she *can* love.

(from *The National Review*)

Immaterial Girl

by John Simon

Madonna is a young woman of no special distinction: she does not sing or dance or act or write songs especially well, and though, dolled up, she can look sexy on stage or screen, seeing her at a party confirmed my suspicion that natural endowments had little to do with any of it. Business acumen and hype had a big part in it, though, starting with her dropping her surname and calling herself plain Madonna, a name eliciting reverence and awe among all Christians. Also among art lovers, to whom the great Renaissance depictions of the Virgin, and even such secular Madonnas as Lisa and Lucrezia, are objects of aesthetic veneration. There is, further, the titillation of the forbidden, of sacrilege: here is a Madonna you can see in the seminude and imagine having sex with. That, surely, is the message of her concerts, videos, and album covers, of the censorship battles her appearances have aroused.

Don't get me wrong: Madonna is not entirely without talent, but as you watch *Truth or Dare*, you conclude that this talent scarcely exceeds that of, say, an average band singer of the Big Band era, or one of those Hollywood starlets who, after a few minor roles, disappeared into marriage, drug addiction, or suicide. But there is that quality more important than serious talent: fanatical belief in oneself. There can be no doubt that the foremost practitioner of this latter-day Mariolatry is Madonna herself.

To Madonna's credit be it said that in the young prodigy Alek Keshishian, she has found a filmmaker with the right sensibility and aptitude to be her photohistorian, and that she evidently permitted him to film, besides various performances, plenty of backstage and private activity, some of it rather frank. But it is the privilege of celebrity—at least as it is conceived nowadays—to be its own morality: hype makes right. Impudence passes for candor; exhibitionism, for honesty.

The excerpts from the concerts are shown in color; the rest is black and white. Quite so: for Madonna, the show *is* life, in life's own colors; whereas life is something monochromatic, stylized. The crowds—in America, Europe, Japan—eat her up. The curious thing, though, is to see how small Madonna (a small person to begin with) appears to the average fan not seated at the front of one of those giant stadiums or auditoriums. But, then, TV and MTV have miniaturized the human frame: television size is the normal format of celebrity. As long, that is, as the sound and the fury are there full blast. Madonna's cavortings on stage are relentless, and even more so is the amplified music. I imagine that, by a kind of synaesthesia, explosive sound makes the crowd *see* big.

Throughout, we watch Madonna planning, plotting, command-ing, cajoling, praising, rebuking, threatening (the Canadian police are no match for *her*!)—in short, proving herself an above-average comman-dant and wheeler-dealer. For those she does business with, Madonna is a tyrant. For her numerous personnel—performers, technicians, staff—she is everything from Big Sister to brood hen, from understand-ing Mom to sassy dominatrix. And, with magnificent megalomania (or comic self-delusion), she is always the Artist fighting for the freedom of self-expression in her Art. Only when she has to play Detroit, with her father in the audience, does she show anxiety. But though Papa does voice—actually, only murmur—a demurrer, his daughter's success, fame, and wealth (whose beneficiary, like his ne'er-do-well of a son, Madonna's loutish brother, he is) compel him to join in worshipping at the shrine. The old-style patriarch is putty in the hands of the revision-ist goddess.

Madonna's shrewdness is evidenced also in her choice of singers and dancers. The women are carefully chosen to be ethnic and less attractive than she is; the men, likewise, are mostly ethnics and, it would seem, homosexuals. This leaves her both an equal-opportunity employer and unequaled in pulchritude and power. Particularly revela-tory is a protosexual flirtation she conducts with a physically well endowed but emotionally weak black male dancer; this relationship is the prototype of her domination and is of considerable clinical interest.

There is no full-fledged sexuality in the movie, but near the end, in a game of truth or dare, Madonna is asked to show her technique with men, and performs fellatio on an empty bottle. She acquits herself with a mixture of arrogant aplomb and ludicrous pathos. I was reminded of her lengthy and inept performance at last year's Academy Awards ceremony when, doing an act over which she didn't have the control she exercises over her concerts, she was "dying" before millions of viewers from Los Angeles to Timbuktu. In vaudeville days, she would have earned the hook ten times over; here and now she was going to brazen it out, and did. The formula is not so much truth or dare as die and dare, dare anyway. A mouth that won't take no for an answer can coax an orgasm even out of an inert piece of glass.

But to prove to us what a good person she is underneath, *Truth or Dare* also affords us the touching spectacle of Madonna prostrate on her mother's grave, pouring her heart out to Mom. And always, always she carries on about her Art. If patriotism, as Dr. Johnson observed, is the last refuge of a scoundrel, may not Art (with a capital A) be the last refuge of a no-talent?

(from *Sports Illustrated*)

Immaterial Guy

by Leigh Montville

The woman is so busy. She has the movie and the music and the traveling and the press conferences and the openings and the dancing and the money and the houses and the workouts and . . . the phone rings. How can she remember every little thing that happens to her?

"Madonna!"

"Who is this?"

"How's my Material Girl?"

"Who is this?"

"You know who this is. Your favorite rightfielder. . . ."

"Rightfielder?"

"Mr. Forty-Forty."

"I don't go out with anyone over forty. Except Warren Beatty. Who is this?"

"Jose."

"Oh say what?"

"Jose. J-O-S-E. Jose."

"I don't know any Jose."

"Jose. We had dinner. Jose. . . . This is a hint. Jose Can . . ."

"Cannes?"

"Jose Can . . ."

"I didn't meet any Jose in Cannes. Not that I can remember."

"Jose Canseco. A photographer from the *New York Post* took my picture when I left your apartment building. All the papers wrote about it. I'm the baseball player. I was showing you how I hit for power. I rolled up that copy of *Vogue* in your living room. I swung the copy of *Vogue* and hit the little balled-up piece of paper you threw to me. It bounced off the big window overlooking Central Park. A shot."

"I'm sorry. I don't remember."

"I was joking with you. I told you the only color for your hair that you haven't tried is white. I said you should dye your hair white and you'd look like Sparky Anderson."

"Sparky who?"

"I told you that, being close to you, I hadn't felt so excited since I faced Roger Clemens and he was throwing heat at me on the black. Which is the truth, by the way."

"Heat on the black."

"Jose. You have to remember."

"I don't know any Jose."

"I told you that when you came to Miami I'd take you out in my car. I fill it with special rocket fuel. We'll do two hundred miles an hour around the curves, playing your music as loud as we can."

"I don't go out with race car drivers. That's a rule that I have. The foreign ones don't speak English, and the American ones all wear caps advertising chewing tobacco. Not my style."

"I'm not a race car driver. I'm a baseball player."

"The only baseball player I know is Kevin Costner, and he's a dweeb."

"No, I'm a real baseball player. I play for the A's."

"The Haze? It sounds like a rock group. Was that Jimi Hendrix's group?"

"The Oakland A's. We were world champions two years ago. We would have won last year, too, except I was hurt."

"I don't know much about baseball."

"I told you that we could be the Couple of the '90s, bigger than Jane Fonda and Ted Turner. We would be the modern Joe DiMaggio and Marilyn Monroe."

"A lot of people have told me that I look like Marilyn. Before I stopped bleaching my hair, of course. . . ."

I told you that you looked like Marilyn. You do."

"Well, at least that's better than that Sparky What's-His-Name."

"I told you that when I got back to New York maybe we could go out to this sports bar I know and drink some beers and watch some games on television and maybe play a little Pop-a-Shot. I get coupons for being on those dugout interview shows during rain delays."

"Dugout interviews? Is that like the *National Enquirer*? I don't do those anymore. Those people have dug out more stuff about my life than I want dug out. The helicopters at my wedding to Sean were the worst. What a scene."

"No, no, the dugout is a place. In baseball. You sit in the dugout and some man points a microphone in your face, and then afterwards you get the coupons for the free meals and stuff at the sports bar."

"I don't do sports bars, thank you."

"Well, it doesn't have to be a sports bar. We can do the clubs. I have money. We can do the clubs. I'll pay."

"I don't do clubs with people I don't know."

"You do know me! I'm Jose! I'm Jose Canseco! Little kids stand in line for hours and pay for my autograph. Grown men copy down my words about all subjects and put them in the newspapers. I'm rich. I'm famous. I'm absolutely now."

"And your name is Jose?"

"Jose."

Pause.

"Michael Jackson, if you call me one more time with these tricks of yours, I'm never going to talk to you again. You're such a kidder. I fell for it the time you called and said you were Lauren Bacall. I fell for it the time you said you were Nancy Reagan. I'm not falling now. No way, Jose."

"But. . . ."

"Ciao, Michael. Better luck next time."

Bzzzzzzzzzz.

The Madometer

(from *Time Out*)

by Dominic Wells

	Prince	Marilyn Monroe	Pet Shop Boys
Over-underwear	Sang in black undies and G-strings when Madonna was still in a pinafore		Chris Lowe strips to his boxer shorts on stage
Fitness Freak			
Sexually Outrageous			On-stage eroticism and do they know their name refers to a peculiar practice involving rodents?
Ego		Despite legendary tantrums, her fragile sense of self-worth was her greatest enemy	
Religion	Play 'Darling Nikki' backwards, and it says: 'Hello, how are you/ Fine, your God knows that the Lord is coming soon'	Tried Judaism after marrying Arthur Miller, but when served matzo balls asked 'Is that the only part of the matzo you eat?'	Lashings of Catholic guilt – cf 'It's A Sin'
Hair-hopping	*Almost* made beards fashionable		For the moustaches and amazing quiffs in their show
Acting Ability			
Swearing			
Comments	As his high score demonstrates, Prince is the male Madonna. Though he can still outdo her in outrageousness, built-in redundancy has resulted in Prince running out of steam in the '90s; whatever happened to 'Graffiti Bridge'? Total: 19½.	The original Madonna prototype; still has enormous power long after the final breakdown. Responsible for new safety features, such as an anti-drugs lock, being fitted in later models. Nowadays, however, she fails in too many categories to be a credible rival. Total: 13.	Run on Duracell; as much longevity as Madonna herself. Only recently became wannabes with their new live show, featuring angels, dancing clerics, simulated wanking and some fab costumes. Total: 10.

	Cyndi Lauper	The Virgin Mary	Madonna
Over-underwear			
Fitness Freak			
Sexually Outrageous		For the Immaculate Conception. Since Christ and the Holy Ghost are one, she was made pregnant by her own son before his birth	
Ego			Surprisingly insecure; very generous to her dancers
Religion	Ex-convent school girl, but thought the nuns 'were like robots'		
Hair-hopping	Started to dye her hair at 12	Changes her hair in every portrait, though the halo remains the same	
Acting Ability	'Vibes' flopped, and the omens don't look great for 'Off And Running'	Joseph believed her	Not bad in 'Desperately Seeking Susan'
Swearing		Big on blasphemy. As in: 'Jesus Christ, come and get your dinner'	Broadcast live from Wembley: 'On the subject of "Fuck", I'd like to say that "Fuck" is not a bad word. "Fuck" is a good word.'
Comments	A slightly earlier model of Madonna, but from the same mould, Cyndi Lauper has always seemed more intelligent and more spontaneous than the rival she now tries to emulate — perhaps that's why she's been left so far behind. Total: 16.	They don't make 'em like they used to. Madonna's namesake and inspiration is still rockin' after 2,000 years. They fell out with each other, however, when the Vatican declared that in the Middle Ages the singer would have been burnt as a witch. Total: 14.	In the end, there's only one Madonna. She may have shared the '80s with Michael Jackson and Prince, and the likes of MC Hammer may sell more records, but so far in the '90s there's no one to touch her for star appeal and stubborn staying power. A miracle of engineering. Total: 21.

(from *Oracle*)

Wild Child

by Janey Stubbs

"**E**xpress Yourself**"** is the title of one of Madonna's massive international hits, and she has become one of the highest-paid entertainers ever, by doing exactly that. Self-expression is a fundamental need for the Sun in Leo person, who must let their light shine out like the Sun. But although apparently brimming with confidence, few Leos feel secure enough just to be themselves and this can give rise to a voracious appetite for attention and admiration. How can they really be sure they are important if people don't keep telling them they are? Warren Beatty, one of Madonna's ex-lovers, has said that she wants to live only when she is in front of the camera.

With Madonna's Sun in Leo, but buried in the depths of the Twelfth House, there is a fundamental struggle to find an identity. People with the Sun in the Twelfth House tend to have a shaky identity and a poor self-image, but with the Sun in Leo there is a natural tendency to seek validation through the eyes of others. This particular placement carries the seeds of great insecurity. With Leo's need for recognition and the Twelfth House fear of being invisible, Madonna is likely to feel that she only exists when she has an audience. She has therefore set out to make herself as visible as possible, and she does this in true Leo style by exaggerating and dramatizing everything she does, so that she has now become famous not so much for her ability as a singer but for the force of her personality. In this way, her public and private life have become one. Her new film, *Truth or Dare*, is a perfect example of this. In the film, her concert performances take second place to her offstage life, which is the real show, so that even a visit to a throat specialist becomes a scene for our amusement and entertainment.

Madonna displays all the fire and passion that are characteristic of

Leo. She has made a drama out of her life and cast herself in the starring role. Everything she does, and says, is designed to make the maximum impact. Her stage act is fiery, energetic, and raunchy. This is Leo at its most rampant.

Madonna's fiery nature is accentuated by a wide square from Mars to the Sun, which adds aggression and attack. She is someone who must have what she wants and goes all out to get it. With Mars in the earthy, sensuous Sign of Taurus, it is not surprising that she uses her sexuality to achieve her aims, and with Mars in the Ninth House she has made a religion out of sex! In a perfect description of this Ninth House Mars in Taurus, she has said that passion, sexuality, and religion are all one to her. Indeed, this juxtaposition of religion and sex infuses everything she does. Brought up in a strict Catholic home, she has said that when she was young she wanted to be a nun, but didn't like the idea of not having sex!

Her stage show is a mixture of sexual imagery and religious symbolism that inevitably causes controversy, and with Mars also square to Uranus she is going to want to shock. This aspect magnifies the willfulness and individualism of the Leo Sun square Mars. It shows a belief in her absolute right to do exactly as she pleases, no matter what the consequences. She is going to feel more alive and vital when she is being provocative and will therefore tend to set out to deliberately antagonize others. She needs the reassurance of an extreme reaction to prove to herself that she is making herself felt. Of course, this behavior attracts a great deal of aggression, and she is at the receiving end of a lot of anger—people want to attack her.

This aspect also describes the somewhat sadomasochistic sexual imagery she likes to convey, both in her performance and in her songs, such as "Hanky Panky," in which she expresses pleasure in being treated roughly and being spanked. This, of course, arouses a lot of anger in other women who feel that it fosters the idea that women really like to be abused by men. But Madonna thrives on controversy and will not compromise. A Mars–Uranus aspect shows an inflexible will and a desire to do her own thing at all costs.

Turning to her Ascendant, we can see that a lot of energy is concentrated there, with the Moon, Mercury, and Pluto all rising. This is the mark of someone who throws herself into life with great emotional and intellectual intensity. The force of this energy really shows in her powerful and magnetic personality. People either love her or loathe her—few are indifferent.

Having these three planets and the Ascendant in Virgo shows the tremendous care and attention to detail that goes into her appearance. She works fantastically hard at perfecting the image she wants to project and spends several hours a day working on her physical fitness.

The earthiness of Virgo also shows in her very solid physical presence and her unsubtle sensuality in which very little is left to the imagination. With Mercury conjunct Pluto, sex has become something of an obsession to her, and she constantly talks about it—seeing it as her mission to transform others' attitude to sex. With Mercury–Pluto she tends to be brutally frank, and with this combination rising she meets the world with a disturbing perceptiveness and bluntness. Although she is reluctant to give interviews and very seldom does so, it seems as though every word she speaks makes an impact and receives world-wide media attention.

With Mercury–Pluto there is a desire to uncover and communicate what is hidden and taboo and a fascination with the darker side of life—something that she has exploited to the full.

Madonna says that she enjoys irony and that people take what she says too seriously, but Mercury–Pluto is hard to take lightly and she seems to throw down a gauntlet with everything she says. With the Moon also rising, there is a vulnerable side to Madonna which must be hurt by all the criticism, even though she, herself, has provoked it. A person with the Moon on the Ascendant meets life with feeling nature unprotected and exposed, and she makes no secret of her feelings— letting the whole world know that she is still in love with Sean Penn and how painful it is for her now that he and his present girlfriend have just had a baby.

▶ Emotional Rejection

The Moon is square to Saturn, which is an extremely difficult aspect. People with this combination have usually experienced some sort of emotional rejection as children, which makes it very difficult for them to trust their feelings or believe that others really care for them. This builds up a pattern of defensiveness that causes them to constantly hurt themselves by rejecting others to protect themselves from being rejected. Madonna has said that her family are all emotional cripples, which is an apt description of this aspect. In addition, her mother died when she was only six years old, which, as she says, changed her forever. It was after this that she became ambitious, and this reflects the Moon–Saturn need to become entirely self-reliant and to depend on no one. There is also a feeling that love and affection have to be earned by pleasing others. It is not surprising then, that Madonna has turned herself into a fantasy of what she believes men want—using her femininity to earn what she needs from life. But although this has succeeded on a material level, it still leaves the possibility of personal happiness as far away as ever.

▶ Glamour and Drama

The fantasy aspect is also emphasized by a Venus–Neptune square. Venus in Leo is very dramatic and colorful, and with it in aspect to both Jupiter and Neptune in the Second House, Madonna is able to use her glamour and seductiveness to earn a fortune beyond most people's wildest dreams. With these two planets in the Second House, she spends prodigiously—her proposed expenses for her stay in Cannes for the film festival amounted to around £16,000 a day!

This combination reveals an extremely romantic side to Madonna. There is a longing for the perfect love that is way beyond the ordinary, and this leaves a restless yearning that is almost impossible to satisfy. But it is very creative and drives her on to express herself in a way that taps into the unfulfilled longing and romantic dreams of a mass audience. It is also reflective of her enormous popularity and suggests that she will be using her magic to captivate vast numbers of people for a very long time to come.

Birth Chart Data: *Madonna*

Date: Saturday 16th August 1958
Time: 7.0 0
Zone: 5.0 W
Latitude: 43 36 N
Longitude: 83 54 W

ASPECTS

MC	sextile	Venus
Sun	sextile	Jupiter
Moon	square	Saturn
Venus	square	Neptune
Neptune	sextile	Pluto
MC	square	Pluto
Sun	trine	Saturn
Mercury	sextile	Neptune
Mars	square	Uranus
Node	sextile	Sun
Ascendant	conjunct	Mercury
Moon	conjunct	Mercury
Mercury	conjunct	Pluto
Node	conjunct	Jupiter
Sun	square	Mars
Moon	trine	Mars
Venus	square	Jupiter
Saturn	trine	Uranus

Name		Degrees	Minutes	Sign	House
☉	Sun	23°	7'	Leo	(Twelfth)
☽	Moon	11°	30'	Virgo	(First)
☿	Mercury	5°	39'	Virgo (R)	(Twelfth)
♀	Venus	0°	32'	Leo	(Eleventh)
♂	Mars	15°	24'	Taurus	(Ninth)
♃	Jupiter	26°	24'	Libra	(Second)
♄	Saturn	19°	8'	Sagittarius(R)	(Fourth)
♅	Uranus	12°	42'	Leo	(Twelfth)
♆	Neptune	2°	18'	Scorpio	(Second)
♇	Pluto	1°	43'	Virgo	(Twelfth)
☊	Node	25°	20'	Libra (R)	(Second)
	MC		2° 32'	Gemini	
	Ascendant		7° 17'	Virgo	

The Merrill Markoe Interview

by Merrill Markoe

Recently I began to worry about the fact that I was the only columnist in America who had not written about Madonna. Then her movie came out, followed by more interviews and articles, and I grew concerned that there was just nothing left to be said about her. All this was *before* the big two-part piece in *Rolling Stone* where Madonna sat down with Carrie Fisher and they discussed every remaining thing that both of them had neglected to mention in the multitude of lengthy in-depth interviews each of them had given previously. Now I was truly frightened. But what could I do? It *is* a California state law that *everyone* with access to a publisher *must* turn in at least *one* piece about Madonna by the end of this fiscal year. So with time running out, I invited my friend Elayne Boosler over to help me reflect on the Madonna–Carrie Fisher confab. She arrived with a bottle of champagne and her dog Petey, who immediately developed a perverse attraction to my dog Lewis that never let up for one second of the five hours we all hung out.

BOOSLER: Well, they begin the article by mentioning that they both go to the same shrink. You tried to get me to go to your shrink for many years.

MARKOE: I actually *did* go to one of your shrinks once. Between us we've seen quite a few shrinks. I don't know if either of us went to their shrink.

E B: They mention that they're both competing to be the best or worst patient their shrink has. I'm guessing they've achieved that. They want to impress their shrink. I want to impress my dry cleaner.

M M: What can you do to impress your dry cleaner?

E B: I bring in extremely clean clothing. I get it cleaned first.

M M: See, I go the opposite way. I try for really spectacular stains. To give the impression I lead a fast, dangerous life. You have to be the best customer or the worst customer.

E B: I'm the best.

M M: I'm the worst.

E B: My dry cleaner is the only person I gave my picture to because he meets me at airports with clean clothes when I'm on tour. But I think he should put up pictures of doctors, lawyers, Ralph Nader, guys who know quality. Who would take the recommendation of a comedian?

M M: Oddly enough, Carrie and Madonna don't even touch on this subject.

E B: I bet their shrink does their cleaning. They probably pay five hundred dollars an hour. For that I think you also get your pants pressed.

M M: Now they get to the fact that they've both been married and divorced.

E B: We haven't.

M M: We all have famous exes. But I don't think we want to talk about that.

E B: Madonna's nickname is tattooed on Sean Penn's toe. Have you ever had a man tattoo your nickname anywhere?

M M: Well, they all *wanted* to but I always talked them down. Do you even have a nickname?

E B: No. I had one guy who called me Pumpkin. I said, "Do you call all your girlfriends Pumpkin?" He said, "Just the last six." I don't think Jews *have* nicknames.

M M: Carrie Fisher is a mixed breed but I guess you don't need a nickname when your name is Carrie. It would have to be longer and more formal. Like Carlisle.

E B: I never thought of Eddie Fisher as Jewish because he married a woman who was wearing so much makeup and who was going to get fat later. Actually, that *is* very Jewish.

M M: You mean Elizabeth Taylor? I think my father would have left my mother for Elizabeth Taylor. So we have that in common. I would like to note at this point that your dog Petey has been having what I'll refer to as air-sex with my dog Lewis pretty much nonstop.

E B: And now he's having it with himself. He's the only guy who takes "Go fuck yourself" so literally. I remember when I was a kid there was a picture of Elizabeth Taylor on the cover of *Life* magazine on her fortieth or fiftieth birthday. How old is she now? Ninety?

E B: Just under eighty. She's seventy-eight.

E B: She supposedly had just come out of the shower and was wearing no makeup, so we know how long this took. Five hours of six makeup artists going, "It'll be very natural."

M M: And then they get the sandblaster out.

E B: She was wearing just two purple towels. One on her head, and one on her breasts. . . .

M M: And just a hint of anesthetic behind each ear to dull the pain from the surgery.

E B: They were actually doing a live liposuction on her during the picture. They had live men sucking the fat out of her and my father says, "Look at this! The most beautyful woman in the world! She's forty or fifty and she doesn't need to wear a stitch of makeup." I was two years old and I said, "You idiot. You think this woman has no makeup on?" Now we get to the part where they learn they have Warren in common.

M M: Did you fuck Warren?

E B: Oh, sure. Who hasn't?

M M: It's a city ordinance. I wanted to be his best patient.

E B: Carrie says, "I was seventeen and making *Shampoo*." That probably means she was twenty-five.

M M: She made shampoo? From scratch? That's very young to know how to make shampoo. I've made toothpaste with baking soda but I wonder where she learned to make shampoo?

E B: She didn't make it herself. She made it with Warren Beatty.

M M: Bad reality. Good anecdote. They say that a lot in here.

E B: It's a very writerly thing to say.

M M: Do you get many anecdotes out of bad reality?

E B: No. I work mainly with okay reality and try to make it really interesting.

M M: Me, too. I don't like to talk about bad reality. It's too painful. I think the weirdness of everyday bland reality is my specialty. Now here they talk about how they both have hostility toward men.

E B: We don't. We just let them step on us but then we try and trip them on their way out.

M M: And later we talk about them. I guess I never thought of Madonna as being hostile toward men.

E B: Well, do you put your tits in a pencil sharpener when you go to work?

M M: Madonna says she likes to shock but not offend.

E B: I like to shop but not offend.

M M: I think she shocks and offends. I keep trying to like her, but she keeps pissing me off.

E B: Well, here Carrie Fisher points out that she uses a lot of crass language. Like in her movie talking about being finger fucked by a girl from her high school.

M M: Why do you suppose she wants everyone to know that about her? This is what I always call "the curse of too much information." Why would anyone want everyone to know all this really personal stuff about them?

E B: I think it's about feeling desperate. Some people don't exist unless someone is looking. The other reason is you're trying to get a mortgage. Then they have to know everything. Including who you finger fucked. Maybe she was buying a house.

▶ Part 2

M M: I'm just going to designate this part 2, if that's okay.

E B: Fine.

M M: My point is that both of us use our lives in our work, but we both edit and censor heavily.

E B: This guy who made Madonna's film observed her every day for seven months. I have my picture taken, and in two minutes I'm saying, "Hurry. Hurry." Well! Here Madonna uses the word *assuage*. I'm extremely impressed. It almost makes up for the crude stuff. Although she may have said "assauge." This we don't know. My guess is she said "assauge."

M M: She also says "epiglottis" somewhere in there.

E B: She does not!

M M: I guess she's not a dumb girl.

E B: I guess you didn't see that *Nightline* interview. You know, if we only had a video cam the dogs could be on Bob Saget's show and we could win like a million dollars and not have to do any of this. Petey! Enough!

M M: I can't believe they aren't worn out yet.

E B: Why can't we find guys like this? I sat next to Madonna at a Laura Nyro concert and she was further from her stage persona than anyone I've ever seen. She looked so different it was unbelievable.

M M: Did Madonna know who you were?

E B: No. But McDonald's knows who I am. It says here that Madonna went to a seder and got drunk because she was out of her element. We would get drunk because we were with our families.

M M: Too far into our element.

E B: You know, now on Passover people who used to leave a chair for Elijah leave a chair for Madonna. They figure it's the same odds.

M M: The odds would be better if they left two chairs. Elijah might show up sooner if he thought he'd be sitting next to Madonna. Have you ever met Carrie Fisher?

E B: No. But I once sang a duet with Eddie Fisher. On *The Perry Como Show.* [*She begins to sing*] "Oh! My Papa! / To me he was so wonderful!"

M M: It's nice watching dogs hump to that song. I feel I finally understand it.

E B [*singing*]: "Oh! My Papa! / To me he was so grand."

M M: Gees, what a weird song that was. Like a funeral dirge.

E B: Have you ever heard "My Yiddishe Mama"? Talk about a bad song. [*She sings*] "My Yiddishe Mama / I miss her more than ever now / My Yiddishe Mama / I long to kiss that furrowed brow."

M M: The dogs are really banging away to this one.

E B: That's how it's used these days. To get animals to mate faster on farms.

M M: I think Jews stopped writing songs like these once therapy was invented. In fact, I think songs like these are *why* therapy was invented. Madonna says when she first heard the word *penis* she was horrified.

E B: I was wondering lately what chance women have for happiness when you consider that two-thirds of the word *happiness* is *penis*?

M M: I think, before we close, we should take a little time to discuss blow jobs, since that, for me, was the most startling and amazing part of the Carrie Fisher and Madonna discussion. Where Madonna came out against them. Do you have anything to say about them?

E B: No.

M M: Well, with that I think we've covered everything. At least I pray we have.

(from *Newsday*)

On Madonna Books

by Liz Smith

J. **Randy Taraborrelli,** the author who is the scourge of Miss Diana Ross and Mr. Michael Jackson, has, as you may already know, targeted his next subject (or victim, depending on one's viewpoint?)—Madonna. But here are the details: Taraborrelli has signed a spectacular six-figure deal with Putnam, and he expects *Madonna* to be published in the spring of 1993.

Taraborrelli appears to be approaching this star with even more determination than he brought to bear on Ross and Jackson. He told us, "Some of my sources are scared to death to talk to me. They've all signed 'nondisclosure contracts' that make Diana Ross's look like child's play. According to Madonna's, if you work for her, you can't talk to people like me until fifty years after termination of employment. But that hasn't stopped me from getting people to talk." (Madonna's press rep, Liz Rosenberg, while admitting that some Madonna employees have signed such documents, laughed and said, "Personally, I've never even seen such a thing. We're really scared . . . NOT!" And if anybody knows where all the bustier-clothed skeletons are, it's Liz.)

"She is an extremely powerful woman, as you know," continued Taraborrelli. "Remember the part in *Truth or Dare* when she slams the door in the face of the cameraman and says, 'You can't come in here, this is business'? Well, I go in there and behind that closed door, because now her business is my business!"

Hmmmm, well that's Randy's opinion. I'm sure the Big M feels justified in thinking her business is her business. But this comes with the territory, and no matter what Taraborrelli uncovers, it's unlikely to have a detrimental effect on her career. In fact, the only problem is that by the time this book is published, Madonna's career and life and persona may be such as to render it obsolete.

And while we are on the subject of "tell-all" books, their authors and subjects, I have now read the two current Madonna bios, Douglas Thompson's *Madonna Revealed* and Christopher Andersen's *Madonna Unauthorized*. So what's all the shouting about?

Thompson's book is little more than a cut-and-paste job, Andersen's is well researched and well written—it's a fascinating work, though naturally full of stuff that Madonna herself would prefer to ignore. But neither book tells us anything about Madonna we haven't already (1) heard from her own lips, (2) assumed, (3) read somewhere else. I mean, is it any big surprise to read that Madonna is considered to be manipulative, ruthless, and highly sexed?

What struck me about both books was the final twist given to Madonna's personality—summing her up as a confused woman obsessed with Marilyn Monroe and clearly heading for a Monroe-like finale. How absurd.

I won't pretend to know what drives Madonna, or what her personal demons are, but I do find it strange that these male authors have attempted to portray her as the stereotypical "woman out of control heading for a big disaster." Madonna has, from time to time, emulated Marilyn's "look"—but this hardly means she identifies with her or is "fated" to have a tragic life. After all, Madonna has just as often emulated Marlene Dietrich, Louise Brooks, and Clara Bow. Her heroes are women such as the late Martha Graham and artist Frida Kahlo.

But is it more satisfactory to view Madonna, a powerful woman who hasn't always "played nice," as a tragic figure? Funny, you seldom see the ruthless big men of Hollywood—actors, producers, or studio heads—portrayed the same way.

It's the old double standard. And even for the strong, willful, successful likes of Madonna, it is still applied.

Madonna Tongue n' Chic' Sandwich

A triple decker of tongue and chicken on a toasted bialy

Madonna and Me

by Elizabeth Tippens

I**t began innocently enough**, as they say, a lone Madonna postcard stuck to my refrigerator with a muffin magnet. But over the course of the next several months I'd succeeded in plastering my entire refrigerator with pictures of Madonna. So much has been made of Madonna's self-reinvention that the fact of it may not seem worth pondering; she's blond and then she's not blond, zaftig then Amazonian, waifish then glamorous. And yet when I lined up row after row of postcards and magazine cut-outs, this mosaic of images gripped my imagination. Just as Madonna herself exists as something of a Rorschach test, unsettling some and exciting others, my Madonna refrigerator served as a nightmarish composite of inkblots that jostled my psyche each time I reached for a diet Coke.

I would often stand and stare at the photographs, my eye traveling from paparazzi shots of bodyguarded jogs through Central Park, or paint-the-town girldates with Sandra Bernhard, to wooden studio stills from *Dick Tracy*, to the bohemian thriftshop invention of *Desperately Seeking Susan*, and back again to the sculpted athlete in fishnet stockings and the legendary bustier. I stood and stared, for too long sometimes. Had I erected a shrine? Or, like a good detective, was I waiting for my compiled evidence to show me something that no single piece could deliver? What was I looking at in all these incarnations of the same woman? What was I looking for?

I was not always the fan I am today. My interest in Madonna crept up on me. I remember seeing the "Lucky Star" video for the first time and thinking that this girl looked a lot like a lot of girls you saw around New York at the time. With her black lingerie, fingerless gloves, and giant hair ribbons, she was altogether feminine, but with funk. Madonna possessed a waif's endearing charm and a street kid's savvy. She reminded me of girls I'd waited tables with on Columbus Avenue or actresses I knew in Chelsea or Hell's Kitchen, where I lived at the time. I liked her dance moves; people weren't dancing much then (this was post-disco and pre-MTV), and I liked the way she'd taken a street look onto television. There was the excitement of recognition as I thought, I know this girl. But there remained the issue of talent: she really could not sing. Well, the talent question nagged at me. And yet, what I perceived to be the absence of talent fascinated me. New York is filled with people who are fun to look at, and here was one of them lolling in front of the camera. But why this girl and not some other girl? What I thought of as the arbitrary nature of her rise bothered me. Was her name picked out of a hat? I'd moved to New York to be an actress, and though I'd very recently left acting to write fiction (exchanging one *un*sure thing for another), I thought about this kind of thing a lot. Who makes it? How? And why? Would I?

Madonna moved to New York at nineteen, and I at twenty-one. We'd both had some college, Madonna one semester as a dance major at the University of Michigan, and I one year at Carnegie-Mellon University's professional training program for actors. Like Madonna, I suspected that college would have little to do with any future success or failure: New York was all that mattered. To get there I returned to my home town of Washington Grove, Maryland, where I drove my father's car into Washington, D.C., each night to wait on tables. When I'd saved almost two thousand dollars, my best friend Dick and I loaded up a U-haul truck and headed north. Dick's mother had said to simply follow the signs that read NEW YORK.

Dick had gone to Carnegie-Mellon too, but we'd met and become friends a few years before that when he was the only member of our summer theater production of *West Side Story* to refuse to smear dirt on his pants. Dick was tall, blond, and handsome, elegant, bitchy, and openly gay, at least as openly gay as you can be when you're eighteen years old and living in your parents' house in the Maryland suburbs. It wasn't so much that I approved or disapproved of his stand against dirtying a nice pair of his own pants, it was the audacity of the stand itself that intrigued me, the idea that at eighteen you could have such a highly developed persona as to know exactly what suited you or did not suit you. Dick had an image. He also had an entire cast and crew of this little theater company in Maryland believing he was *somebody*. And he wasn't even playing a leading role! Along with his precocious sense of self, he had great warmth and was a rapt and curious listener. And in spite of traits that might have seemed obnoxious in someone less witty, less self-aware, most everybody was crazy about him. His "image" was not without large doses of irony, and, to dislike Dick was to risk not being in on the joke.

Dick and I clicked and stayed clicked. In the spirit of a Jacqueline Susann heroine, we were dying to move to New York to be actors or singers or celebrities or just any regular person with evening clothes who got invited to a glamorous dinner party. We had some vague, embryonic ideas about doing something truly artistic, something spawned from who we were, something original and very special. It was hard to picture exactly what, and most times to imagine "it" was to conjure a blur. But we were oddly like-minded on this vague and crucial subject. Here was the best friend I'd been looking for my whole life, somebody in whom I could confide my true aspirations, and who would encourage me to dream. I clung to Dick for dear life, without even realizing until years later that it was for dear life that he clung to me too. So, unlike Madonna, who arrived in New York with thirty-seven dollars in her purse and not one friend, I had Dick, or rather we had each other. I was not entirely alone, although being new to a strange city, I certainly felt that way most of the time.

In its way, New York supports the journey of an artist. Here, you can arrive without portfolio and take yourself seriously. As Madonna must have been in her early days, I am one of those people whose sense of themselves is all tied up with the City of New York. I simply find it inspiring, as she must have. New York has always been *the* magic word, conjuring nothing less than endless possibilities. Only in New York could Madonna have uncovered something as unique as Madonna, and only in New York, I believed, would I uncover what was unique in me. And yet, the New York experience is far from a painless one. Pitted against the best and the brightest, the most ambitious and beautiful, one is allowed no comforting delusions. New York has a way of fragmenting a young person, of obliterating the identity hard-won in adolescence, of confirming your worst fears that you are nobody very special. In New York, even Dick no longer seemed to know if his pants should be dirty or clean. Immediately I fell into a depression.

During those first years in New York, I auditioned sporadically, modeled nude for a famous sculptor, sang a repertoire of offbeat standards at Village nightclubs, and took my acting classes. But mostly I waited tables at trendy restaurants on Columbus Avenue, where I felt singled out for being blond, young, uninterested in cocaine and alcohol, unfashionably heavy, shy, serious, Southern, and just about anything else that when held up for comparison against almost anyone seemed all wrong. I remember sleeping very late into the afternoon and then taking long baths before work. By the end of the night I'd be covered with grime and smelling like smoke, but I liked to start out clean. I'd slip slowly under water, feeling my long hair splayed out like a fan as I floated there, submerged. I wished I could have stayed in the bathtub forever.

At work I could not figure out how to be like the other girls. I admired the lean and hungry look of these gaunt girls in black, and began starving myself, eating only hard-boiled eggs and drinking ten glasses of water a day. But the outer layer of female fat persisted, as it still does, in staying put, stubbornly protecting my bones, muscles, and internal organs. When I was too dizzy to get up off the bed, I began eating again.

I also undertook to transform my fine straight hair. I got a long curly perm that made me feel more like someone fun, and bleached my hair several shades lighter than its natural color. I didn't look much like myself anymore, and that was just fine. At some point, though, my fluffy hair began to feel like someone else's hair, like a wig, and I wanted my own hair back again.

All of this was ten years ago now, and I can see these incarnations of myself beginning to line up like snapshots on some imaginary refrigerator. I see myself trying to look like someone fun and doing things that seem so forced and unnaturally extroverted, so inorganic to who I am, that I can't imagine what I was trying to prove, except maybe that I was utterly fearless. Really I was numb.

As casting directors and agents turned me away for being "just not right" or too fill-in-the-blank, and as the experience of acting in an Off-Off-Broadway play failed to make me feel much of anything, I found myself turning inward, which is where I began to feel the reemergence of creative drive. The writer in me, which had never appeared before, sprang forth suddenly and joyfully, and within a matter of a few years I began to publish my short stories in *Cosmopolitan* and *Mademoiselle*. Here was the "it" Dick and I had spent night after night pondering.

I often think of Madonna as the extrovert's extrovert. Here is a woman whose psyche is shaped so contrarily to mine that I see her as the most extreme example of what I could have been like, had I been an extrovert instead of an introvert; she's the sublime fantasy of my ultimate alter ego. Maybe I think she behaves as I'd behave if being among people energized rather than depleted me, if being looked at made me feel like dancing instead of making me want to hide. And maybe that is why I get such a kick out of Madonna even as I sometimes find her show-offy antics embarrassingly immature.

Carl Jung said of extroverts, "[This type] is never to be found in the world of accepted reality-values, but he has a keen nose for anything new and in the making. Because he is always seeking out new possibilities stable conditions suffocate him." And, "He brings his vision to life, he presents it convincingly and with dramatic fire, he embodies it. . . . But he is not play acting, it is a kind of fate." Change the "he" to "she," and you could be talking about Madonna. Jung also says that this type, the "intuitive extrovert," often ends up a business tycoon. (*Forbes* once listed Madonna as a growth industry!) I identified with Madonna, her drive, and her unapologetic desire to make something of herself, though on her, the extrovert, it just *looked* so different. So, in spite of the difference between Madonna and me, when I say that I knew this girl, or girls like her, I also mean that I recognized myself in her, and by the time I saw her dancing around in that "Lucky Star" video, I knew that just by being young and trying to make it in New York, she'd already been through some of the things I'd been through too: the loneliness, the dismantling of an identity, and the search for the best possible self.

Jung writes of "a kind of fate." Who succeeds? And how? Why? Would I? I still thought about those things when I first realized that Madonna would be more than a flash in the pan, more than the pop princess of the moment. I remember sitting in a doctor's office reading a *Time* cover story about Madonna. Yes, the article said, Madonna was her real name. I remember being stunned by this new information. It made me think of something Laurence Olivier had said about his own name, that if he'd been born with the English name Lawrence Oliver, instead of the more dashing (and French) Laurence Olivier, his whole life would have been completely different. Destiny! I love things like that.

It was around this time that Madonna's famous "Boy Toy" belt buckle came under fire, pretty much from everyone. I didn't know what Madonna meant by flaunting the "Boy Toy" buckle, but I knew she meant *something*. Perhaps it was meant to be playful, a wink at the mentality that really thought of women in those terms. In any case, as with Dick and his choice that his hoodlum's pants should remain clean, I admired Madonna's self-definition, the irony in sendups like her "Material Girl," and of course her general audacity, her maverick's unwillingness to play by the rules.

My interest in Madonna was by now building steadily. Could she sing? Well, she was getting better, but it was becoming clear to me that singing was hardly the point of Madonna. Was she a feminist, or not? Hard to say. In fact, I was beginning to identify with the mixed messages she was sending the world on that count. The eighties were a rather confusing time to become a woman, what with the New Traditionalists breathing down our necks and reports everywhere that there simply were not enough men to go around. For my part, I worked like the devil to advance my own writing career, but I also allowed my rich, older boyfriend to contribute substantially to my financial support, and I made ends meet by writing copy for the likes of *Lingerie World* and *Penthouse*. Was I a feminist? Could any woman afford to be? Feminism had by now become a dirty word, and a point of confusion for the MTV generation.

When Madonna arrived in New York for her Virgin Tour, the news was full of reports of young fans, "wannabes," dressing up like Madonna and hanging around Madison Square Garden, where she was scheduled to perform. Here she was, returning to the city that spawned her, a "wannabe" who had triumphantly become. In the spirit of fun, of female bonding, of Destiny, I tied a big pink Madonna bow in my hair. A fan was born.

I have been a true-blue, die-hard fan three times in my life. When I was a little girl I worshipped Shirley Temple, during my adolescence James Taylor moved me beyond words, and of course Madonna has been the subject of my grown-up fancy. Luckily for me, a local television channel broadcast *Shirley Temple Theater* every Sunday at eleven

A.M. During my childhood I found her 1930s Depression-resistant cheerfulness irresistible. The fact that most of her movie characters were in show business allowed for lots of showy song-and-dance numbers, fuel for my fantasies that I would one day be a star.

When I was fourteen I fell in love with James Taylor. In him I found a figure who could represent the creativity and drama particular to adolescence, its turbulence and despair. Pop culture of the seventies saw a lack of inspiring role models for the Thinking Girl. It was the era of TV angels who jiggled and bounced and were commanded by the anonymous voice of male authority. Perhaps these trite and one-dimensional offerings were the reason that as an adolescent I chose a man to most admire. Men, it seemed to me, were permitted more complexity and even some welcome contradictions. I wish Madonna had been around to influence me and my friends. (I do think we were looking for her.) Her outspokenness and enjoyment of her own sexuality offer images of empowerment to teenage girls. At a time when many may be leaning toward defining themselves by how others see them, instead of by their own passions and talents, Madonna gives girls an exuberant alternative.

Yes, had Madonna been around when I was a teenager, I'm sure she would have received my resounding approval. How could any teenager not love a woman who often shocks for the sheer adolescent thrill of it?

Perhaps my interest in Madonna is best viewed within the context of my interest in celebrities in general. I have absolutely always cared who did what and with whom. Each week at the newsstand I eye the latest issue of *People* and ask myself, Do I really care? Invariably, I do. Unfortunately, my boyfriend David shares this closeted addiction (it makes us oddly but nicely compatible) and has been known to try to appropriate my brand-new unread issues. We once fought bitterly over who would get to devour the latest *People* first. After a laughable tug-of-war, we ended up cutting the thing in half with scissors. Unlike the mother in the story of Solomon, neither one of us was willing to be unselfish. Now mutilated, truly it was trash, but trash we were apparently unwilling to be without our half of.

I love a good celebrity sighting, too, which on an average day in New York has put me face to face with the likes of Woody Allen,

Mikhail Baryshnikov, Robert De Niro, and even Madonna herself. (I once saw her with Sean Penn at the Love drugstore on Seventieth and Broadway. What did they buy? Bubble gum.) And then, if you care about such things, there are the opportunities for celebrity interaction. One of the most charming conversations of my life took place at a party where I was introduced to director Mike Nichols. Coincidentally, I'd had a dream about him a few nights before and was enchanted to find myself actually looking into his face. Here is how it went:

MIKE: You look familiar. Haven't we met before?

ME: Yes, in fact. I had a dream about you.

MIKE: Ah, that's it then.

Could you live on that forever, or what?

Perhaps because I enjoy it so, I have never felt that my relentless interest in famous people was the waste of time it is supposed to be, although I'm not sure what I hope to learn by following their lives, chronicling their careers, or bumping into them in pharmacies. Maybe I hope their lives will answer some large life question that I hadn't even thought to ask. Or maybe, as all writers are, I am just nosy. I want the news, the scoop, the dirt. I want to know how people live—their pettiness, their weaknesses, their dark, private Hells, and okay, their triumphs, too.

For a while I kept a list on my wall of famous people with back problems. I have my own back problem, the pain of which often lands me flat on my back, unable to work. Somehow JFK, Elizabeth Taylor, Mario Cuomo, Philip Roth, Linda Blair, David Letterman, Errol Flynn (he lay around on the floor all the time like I do), Betty Ford, and James Drury (that guy on *The Virginian*) all triumphed over their back pain and managed to do things with their lives. Well, I have to tell you, sometimes they did give me hope.

How does a person find his path in life? How does *who* you are affect what happens to you? From a psychological perspective I am fascinated by biography. And then there is the business of Destiny: all things being equal, how is it that some achieve greatness while others pump gas? I am especially drawn toward reading about people in the arts, since there is no prescribed way to become an artist. Each artist must be a pioneer, bushwacking his way down an untrod path, while remaining misunderstood in out-of-context situations that don't take his talent into account. I love reading about artists' misunderstood childhoods, or the shit jobs they worked at before their talents were recognized and appreciated. It's Cinderella, the wronged sibling, who is really the special one. How satisfying.

And how *un*satisfying it is to read about some lazy beauty lying on the beach who gets snapped up and made a movie star by some famous director. I know a now-successful movie and TV actor who used to hang around a Hell's Kitchen bike shop smoking pot all day. Maddeningly, ambition is not always the determining factor. There you go: one thing I've learned about life by following the stars. It's a life truth all right, not that it does anybody any good to know it.

I can't get with the Royal Family at all, even Diana. I like the more egalitarian nature of American celebrity. I like the idea that anyone with brains, talent, or guts can rise from humble beginnings to make it in America. That's the kind of rags-to-riches philosophy I clung to when, as an eccentric child in a small town, I dreamed of becoming an actress or a singer or anyone who lived in New York City and had long fingernails and at least one black cocktail dress. It was possible to become "That Girl." In America, even without royal blood you could become a queen. But, as in a fairy tale, you must first suffer terrible injustices. You must be tested. The arts have long been the province of those with nothing to lose; how low you are willing to go (Madonna ate out of garbage cans and flopped in unheated New York apartments) may actually be a measure of how wildly successful you can also envision yourself.

I am as interested in what Madonna represents to others as I am in what she means to me personally. In fact, part of her appeal to me is the way she turns images of femininity on their ear, shocking and unsettling many, dispelling traditional notions of women as one thing or another, virgins or whores, waifs or millionaires, mothers or lovers. As early as *Desperately Seeking Susan*, film critic Pauline Kael recognized Madonna's power to present simultaneous and conflicting images of womanhood when she called Madonna a "trampy, indolent goddess." Not only has Madonna invented herself (in the time-honored American tradition), but she has continually refused to be forever anybody's girl. I am comparing her here to Paula Abdul, who with her hit single, "Forever

Your Girl," simply wants to please. I recently read a *New York Times* account of the preparations for Abdul's Under My Spell Tour, in which she was assured by friends and fans that her concert would be "warmer" and "friendlier" than *some other people's concerts.* Warm and friendly? Where is the point of view in warm and friendly? Unlike Madonna, Paula Abdul, and countless other female stars, present themselves as men's warm and friendly fantasies, never thinking to create a fantasy of their own. How revolutionary then, that in her music, her videos, and her stage show Madonna presents herself from her own point of view, a woman's point of view, and one in which notions of being a virgin or a whore don't even necessarily exist, or better still, may co-exist.

In early 1989, Madonna released her *Like a Prayer* album, and I began talking about Madonna in therapy, in response to some dreams I'd been having about her.

"The name alone!" my therapist, Rosalind, exclaimed. Rosalind was gifted, the kind of therapist who views psychotherapy more as a calling than as a career choice. A beautiful woman with blue eyes and silver hair, she'd worked her way through school as the Hertz girl. (Only in New York!)

"Yeah," I said, "the name!"

We saw Madonna's emergence in my subconscious as a positive influence. As Rosalind pointed out, the Virgin Mary, the traditional Madonna, was defined by, and even achieved fame through, her role as a wife and a mother. On the other hand, this new Madonna was *not* defined by her relationships to others. Her fame was her own! So right there, just by calling herself Madonna and dressing and behaving as anything other than chaste, she was likely to cause a psychic stir.

Here is one of the dreams I remember from that time: I am on my way to a stage somewhere to perform in a play with Madonna. On the way I decide that my throat is sore and that I want some hot tea. I stop in a donut shop (Madonna once worked in a Dunkin' Donuts in midtown Manhattan) and order the tea. The tea is warm and soothing, but I suddenly find I am late for the play. I rush out of the donut shop and find my way through a maze, to the backstage area of the theater, where I am supposed to perform. But I am too late. The show is over and Madonna is gone.

So what's it mean?

Rosalind, a Jungian, saw the stage as representing my life, and the cup of warm tea as a way in which I held myself back from life. She pointed out a tendency of mine to stop and try to comfort myself instead of getting on with what I needed to do. But the comfort backfires. It only deters me from my goals.

At the time of this dream I was trying to untangle myself from a troubling and doomed relationship with a much older man named Lew, who, after seven years, had proven himself to be unsatisfying as a partner for a variety of reasons. And yet I continued to rely on him for support, both financial and emotional. The dream told me that as long as I continued to run to this man for comfort, I would never get on with my life. Now remember, in the dream, Madonna was waiting for me there on the stage of life.

Here was an image of a woman who was utterly independent, defining herself on her own terms. I'd met Lew when I was twenty-two and not yet finished experimenting with unsuitable hairdos. Then, I was willing to collaborate with the world on the subject of who I was, and Lew, older and wiser, a savvy, charming New York know-it-all, an indisputable success in life as a record producer and real estate developer, was more than happy to add his two cents. But as I pushed thirty this collaboration seemed increasingly inappropriate. I was ready to define myself, by myself. I'd outgrown Lew's images of me as, well, *young* mainly, and also dependent. I no longer had what certain men look for in a much younger woman: an unguarded heart.

The dream is about the dreamer. As an aspect of my own psyche, Madonna could be of use to me now, a helper. It was around this time that I created my Madonna refrigerator collage, a little shrine where I could stand and meditate on the contradictions inherent in being a woman, on the power I might possess to transform and transform again and still be me, and also on the possibilities for future selves that lay ahead. I was listening when Madonna sang: "Don't go for second best, baby. . . ." I managed to break it off with Lew. For good.

The Madonna collage is now dismantled, and nothing hangs on my refrigerator except a Lynda Barry cartoon clipped from *The Village Voice* and my chiropractor's new schedule. I took the whole thing down a while ago when I began to feel that I was turning into a woman in stretch pants who is forced to build an addition to her house in order to accommodate her Elvis memorabilia, or the urban, Madonna-crazed equivalent of her anyway. In other words, I'm over my obsession with Madonna.

Now that the obsession has subsided, am I still a fan?

In the ten years I've lived in New York, I've tried on more than a few potential identities and have shed the ones that did not fit. If your life is your greatest work of art, then the search for the best possible self is ongoing. But I do feel as though the most painful part of that search is behind me now. I have a relationship and a career that suit me—no small achievement—and, as I continue to publish my writing, accomplishments enough to claim some measure of worldly success. So who needs Madonna?

Dick called me one afternoon with top-secret news. He's appearing in an Off-Broadway musical called *Pageant*, a spoof of beauty contests in which six men dressed as women vie for the title of "Miss Glamoress." *Pageant* is the biggest Off-Broadway hit in the last ten years and has attracted a number of celebrities to its audience. In the first few months of the show Dick, now a minor celebrity himself, called me almost every morning with news of another famous person's attendance the night before. Joan Rivers came, as did Joan Collins, Steve Martin, Paul Simon, all those top models like Linda Evangelista, Mikhail Baryshnikov, Geena Davis, and many more.

I was sworn and double sworn to secrecy before Dick told me that Madonna would be coming to the show.

I'll admit it, I got excited.

"But I'm not kidding about not telling anyone," he warned. "If it's leaked to the press, she swears she won't show."

I asked Dick to get me a ticket, as close to Madonna's table as possible.

I had seen Madonna on several occasions, once on Broadway in David Mamet's play, *Speed-the-Plow*, once at the Meadowlands on her Blond Ambition Tour, and that time at the Love drugstore, and there was another incident of close proximity when Fifty-seventh Street was backed up with traffic and unruly crowds because Madonna was spotted getting her hair done. But the night I saw her at *Pageant* surely represented some kind of pinnacle in the career of this Madonna fan. Indeed, I was seated about ten feet away from Madonna's table, and as I watched Madonna watch Dick perform the comic monologue that *The New York*

Times called "screamingly funny," as I watched her giggle and bat her eyelashes, I thought of us as a kind of triangle brought together by nothing less significant than stellar convergence. The stars (the real kind) had aligned to bring Dick and Madonna and me together. Destiny. Oh, I know, this kind of thinking, taking the lives of the famous personally, is precisely what must scare the bejesus out of the famous, and what must cause Madonna's giant of a bodyguard to hover ever close to his charge. But still, we regular people can't help ourselves, as we look to make order out of the chaos of life.

After the show, as Madonna was making a quick exit, I made a beeline for her table. There, in front of her empty seat, I found her unfinished bottle of Evian water. I grabbed it.

I am not a fickle person. I do not exchange loyalty to one star for another. Just last month I saw James Taylor in concert for the tenth time, and I'd go pretty far out of my way to see Shirley Temple. All right, I wouldn't go as far as Prague (for those not following her career, Shirley Temple Black is the U.S. Ambassador to Czechoslovakia), but still, I'm known to head straight for *The Little Princess* when I'm sick or depressed. The intensity of individual obsessions may subside, as I move from one fascination to another, but once a fan, always a fan. Madonna will always make me smile as she tweaks the world and turns brass to charm.

And the water bottle? I still have it, tucked away in a kitchen cabinet, where it is of absolutely no use to anyone. And yes, it is still partly filled. With holy water? Of course not. So why don't I just throw it away?

Madonna Postage Stamps
from the island of St. Vincent

▶ From *Rolling Stone* Polls, 1991

BEST FEMALE SINGER

1. Mariah Carey
2. Bonnie Raitt
3. Siouxsie Sioux
4. *Madonna*

WORST FEMALE SINGER

1. Paula Abdul
2. Mariah Carey
3. *Madonna*

SEXIEST FEMALE ARTIST

1. Mariah Carey
2. Paula Abdul
3. *Madonna*

BEST-DRESSED FEMALE ARTIST

1. *Madonna*

Madonna Interview

MADONNA: I wanted to be a big star. I wanted to dance. I wanted to sing. I wanted to be famous, I wanted everybody to love me.

FORREST SAWYER (*voice-over*): For the first time, Madonna, her latest video, and the controversy surrounding it.

ANNOUNCER: This is ABC News *Nightline*. Reporting from New York, Forrest Sawyer.

F S: It has become virtually a seasonal affair. The weather changes, and there is a new Madonna controversy. This one is a video that MTV, the popular cable music video channel, refused to air. Instantly, a storm of questions arose. Is this a kind of censorship? Has Madonna finally gone too far? We'll look for some answers when I talk with Madonna in just a few minutes, and we will see—in its entirety—the video that has caused all this noise.

But first, the controversy itself, with correspondent Ken Kashiwahara.

KEN KASHIWAHARA, ABC NEWS (*voice over*): Nudity, suggestions of bisexuality, sadomasochism, multiple partners. Finally, MTV decided Madonna had gone too far. Her latest video, "Justify My Love," was banned.

Now, for the first time, the channel has decided to take a pass on a clip by pop music's hottest star.

For six years, this star has turned shock into success, consistently pushing the outer limits of the outrageous, of what is permissible and what is not. Madonna has attracted millions of fans around the world and offended many in the mainstream.

"Like a Prayer," for example, was criticized by religious groups as blasphemy, and because of this video, Pepsi-Cola canceled a Madonna TV commercial, despite having paid her $5 million.

M (*NBC, Tonight*): I wouldn't have turned out the way I was if I didn't have all those old-fashioned values to rebel against.

KK (*voice-over*): Madonna's career has been fashioned by her vision of sexuality, from her gyrations to her dress. Madonna underwear, worn as outerwear, became a fashion craze. Even her serious endeavors tend to be sexually suggestive—Madonna urging get out the vote.

M ("*Rock the Vote*"): And if you don't vote, you're going to get a spanking.

KK (*voice-over*): While MTV has banned "Justify My Love," the pay TV channel Jukebox has decided to show it.

ANDREW ORGEL VIDEO JUKEBOX NETWORK: We're not a censor, and we don't—you know, we don't position ourselves as a censor. I think we're very sensitive, though, to our audience.

KK (*voice-over*): So whether she is deliberately provocative and in bad taste, or performing within the limits of artistic expression, Madonna continues to carve a career out of controversy. This is Ken Kashiwahara for *Nightline*.

FS: And now the video. Obviously, we are broadcasting it late at night, and we expect that only adults are watching. You should know this video includes graphic portrayals of sexuality and nudity.

("*Justify My Love*" *video/music*)

FS: And, when we come back, Madonna.
    (*Commercial break*)

FS: She is certainly controversial, but she is also certainly popular. Madonna's first four albums sold 48 million copies, and *Forbes* magazine calls her the top-earning female entertainer this year. Madonna joins us from Los Angeles.

Am I correct in assuming that if an artist wants an album or a record to be very popular, you need to have airplay, or usually you need to have airplay on MTV?

M: Well, it's a very important marketing tool for an artist, yes.

FS: So should I assume, then, that you went through the ordinary process, that is to say that you, with MTV in mind, put together your video and simply submitted it to their standards committee, thinking it would get the clearance that it always has?

M: Yes, I did.

FS: Well, you know that—or at least your record company knows that nudity is banned by MTV, they're not going to allow any—

M: Well, let—I'm not so sure about that, because when I did my "Vogue" video, there's a shot of me where you can—I'm wearing a see-through dress and you can clearly see my breasts. Now, they told me that they wanted me to take that out, but I said I wouldn't, and they played it anyways. So I thought that once again I was going to be able to bend the rules a little bit.

FS: Well, you certainly were bending the rules a lot more than you had in the past, or did you feel that you were well within the bounds that you had bent?

M: Well, I guess half of me thought that I was going to get away with it and that I was going to be able to convince them, and the other half thought, well, no, you know, with the wave of censorship being, you know—and the conservatism that is, you know, sort of sweeping over the nation, I thought that it was going to be—there was going to be a problem.

FS: Well, when you say you thought you could get away with it, am I right, have you sort of pushed the envelope a little bit with each one? With every video you've tried some new things, if only to be experimenting for your own reasons?

M: Well, I think that's what art is all about, experimenting, but it is an expression, it is my artistic expression, and for me a video is the filmic expression of the song, you know, a visual that describes what the song is about. And you've got to listen to the words of the song, you know. It's about a woman who's talking to her lover, and she's saying "Tell me your dreams, am I in them? Tell me your fears, are you scared? Tell me your stories, I'm not afraid of who you are." And so, you know, we're dealing with sexual fannies [*sic*]—fantasies, and being truthful and honest with our partner, you know. And these feelings exist. And I'm just dealing with the truth here in my video.

FS: Well, let me tell you why I asked that, because there are a lot of people in the industry who have said, "Look, this is one of the best self-marketers in the business, we have never really seen anything like it, and she knows how to push right to that edge." And this was a win-win for you. If they put the video on, you would get that kind of play, and if they didn't, you'd still make some money. It was all, in a sense, a kind of publicity stunt.

M: Well, it may seem like it was a publicity stunt, and actually, I was very lucky, but I must say, I did not plan on selling this video. I just went in there to shoot it, and I said: "You know what? I'm not going to think about whether it's going to get played or not, I'm not going to—I'm just going to do it. This is what—this is how I truly feel about this song, this is how I want to express myself."

And when we gave it to MTV, we—you know, we asked them if they would play it. They came back a while later and they said no. I said, "Is there one scene or another that you specifically object to?" And they said, "No, it's the whole tone." So we didn't really even have a chance to try to make it viewable. They didn't—they rejected it completely.

And so then I had to think, you know, with my manager, what next? What should we do? And we decided, hell, you know, let's sell it, let's sell it like a video single, it's never been done before. And you know, the controversy just happened, it wasn't planned. But, you know—

FS: But in the end you're going to wind up making even more money than you would have.

M: Yeah, so lucky me.

FS: But the question that I think a lot of people are concerned about is, you say you go into the studio—

M: Yeah.

FS: —and you want to illustrate this song, and you're doing it in the way that you want.

M: Yeah.

FS: But they see a kind of trend, where you are pushing the limits of sexuality, in this case, you have nudity and you have bisexuality and you have, apparently, group sex. And they're thinking that maybe you're—

M: I'm pushing—

FS: —pardon me?

M: —what are you saying? You're saying I'm pushing the limits of sexuality?

FS: No.

M: Because I'm not—

FS: You're pushing the limits of what's permissible.

M: —okay.

FS: That you're carrying it a little further each time. And I guess what people are asking, then, is where is that line? Where do you finally say, "Okay, this is far enough"?

M: Well, that's a good question, but then, I would like to address the whole issue of censorship on television. Where do we draw the line in general? I mean, if MTV—

FS: Well, you can't go that far—yeah, first you have to tell me where you draw the line.

M: —well, okay, I draw the line in terms of what I think is viewable on television. I draw the line where—with violence and humiliation and degradation, okay? And I don't think any of these issues are evident in my video. That's where I draw the line. That's what I don't want to see, you know.

FS: Then I guess that—then, one woman's art is another woman's pornography. I'm thinking of the "Express Yourself" video.

M: Mm-hmm.

FS: I mean, there are images of you chained, there are images of you crawling under a table—

M: Yes, but I am chained—

FS: —and there are a lot of people upset by that.

M: —yes, yes. Okay, I have chained myself, though, okay? No—there wasn't a man that put that chain on me. I did it myself. I was chained to my desires. I crawled under my own table, you know. There wasn't a man standing there making me do it. I do everything by my own volition. I'm in charge, okay. Degradation is when somebody else is making you do something against your wishes, okay?

FS: So is—I understand. Is the expression, then, of sexuality so long as it's two consenting adults—

M: Absolutely.

FS: —any form of sexuality all right on television?

M: Well, then I would like—okay, first I'd like to say I don't believe in censorship of any kind, but then I would like to say that I believe in labeling, so that I would believe in some kind of, you know, warning label or some kind of label that would say to adults, you know, after a certain hour we're allowed to, you know, play these kind of adult theme videos, you know.

But then, okay, so I've dealt with sexuality, but I also think that we should also have categories for other issues that I think are not necessarily good for ten-year-olds to watch, okay. I mean, I think MTV should have their, you know, their violence hour, and I think they should have their degradation-to-women hour, and then we could have an hour where we deal with adult sexual themes. But, you know, if we're going to have censorship, let's not be hypocrites about this. Let's not have double standards, you know.

I mean, why is it okay for ten-year-olds to see, you know, someone's body being ripped to shreds or Sam Kinison spitting on Jessica Hahn? Why aren't we going to deal with these issues? Why is that okay? Why do parents not have a problem with that, but why do they have a problem with two adult—you know, two consenting adults displaying affection for each other, regardless of their sex?

FS: Madonna, you've raised about thirty important questions and I think we ought to get at those when we come back.

M: Well, I only have a few minutes, so—

FS: We're going to come right back after we pay some bills here, and we'll explore those questions in just a moment.
(*Commercial break*)

FS: Madonna, I wonder if you were being facetious a moment ago. You said despite your concerns about violence and degradation to women, maybe MTV should consider having an hour for violence, and an hour that displays degradation to women, despite the fact that it's broadcast right into people's homes where their children can see it.

M: Well, I'm saying we already have these videos that display degradation to women and violence, that are played twenty-four hours a day. But yet they don't want to have a video playing that deals with sex between two consenting adults. So I'm saying, you know, where do we draw the line? Why is this good for a ten-year-old to watch, and why is it—and I guess I was being sarcastic, you know, to say: Look, give me a chance, you know, let me have my slot. Give me a warning label. Warn parents so it doesn't take them by surprise, so that they have a chance to take their child away from television, but also warn them about violence, and warn them about, you know, scenes in videos that depict degradation to women.

FS: But you know—

M: I think that—

FS: —you know how very hard it is for a parent to control the child having access to TV, and they sit there and they watch MTV all day long.

M: Yes.

FS: Now, would you—if you were in that parent's position and it was your ten-year-old, your eleven-year-old, would you not be worried about their seeing this kind of stuff?

M: Well, personally, I wouldn't be worried about it, and this is why. Because I think that sexuality is something that Americans would really rather just sweep up under the rug, and I think that if my video provokes an open discussion, you know—maybe kids will go and ask their parents these questions, you know. If it provokes an open discussion about sex with their parents, I think this is a really good thing, okay—

FS: But, Madonna, you have to help me here. When a ten-year-old sees you chained to the bed or sees your boyfriend bound up, and another woman comes by while you're there—

M: No, don't get—

FS: —maybe you know that that's a fantasy, and you know that other people are able to deal with all kinds of sexuality, but a ten-year-old's going to get awfully confused here.

M: Good. Then let them get confused and let them go ask their parents about it, and let their parents, you know, explain to them that it is a sexual fantasy and that these things exist in life, like they see violence, okay? It exists in life. It's not a pretty picture, necessarily, you know, it's a frightening thing. But it's a reality. Why are we willing to deal with the realities of violence and sexism, and why aren't we willing to deal with sexuality? Why?

I mean, the networks won't even play ads on TV that are about condoms, about birth control, about practicing safe sex. We're pretending like we don't have a lot of teenagers that are having sex in the world right now. What—why are we, you know, why are we subjecting ourselves to this kind of ignorance?

FS: Look, I'll tell you what their answer is going to be, to you. They're going to say: "You know what, we really are concerned about these issues, and we really are concerned that our children understand them, but quite frankly, it is our job to instruct our children"—

M: Really?

FS: —"and we don't want you on television—in the kinds of ways that you're on television—giving those images to our children. Thanks, anyway."

M: Well, guess what? They're not doing their job. Because the teenage pregnancies in this country have reached, you know, a highest high. I mean, we have sophomores in high school who are having their second babies already, okay. And the rate of AIDS is raising in the heterosexual community at a really frightening rate, okay. So why is that? These parents are not doing their jobs, you know.

FS: There is the question, and I guess this is what you're trying to tell me, that you're balancing between an artist's need for self-expression—

M: Yes.

FS: —an artist's need to explore any kind of issue—and that certainly includes sexuality—and the responsibility that comes along with the kind of prominence that you have, and the fact that you're a role model for people. And I guess you have to wrestle with that, don't you?

M: The fact that I'm a role model, I have to wrestle with that?

FS: Well, that there is a responsibility that comes along—

M: Okay.

FS: —with your position.

M: Okay. You know what? I feel that I am behaving in a very responsible way. If you say I have a responsibility as a mainstream artist, whatever, I feel that I am being responsible, because I am—see, as I said at the beginning of the interview, I'm talking about some—the video is displaying people being honest to each other about their sexuality. They're not alienating anyone, they're not degrading anyone. It's about honesty, it's about the celebration of sex. There is nothing wrong with that, okay, and my respon—that is my responsibility. And I'm also very responsible because I do deal with sexuality a lot in my shows and in my music, you know. I promote safe sex whenever I can. I put literature in my albums about birth control and using condoms. I am responsible.

FS: But my point really goes back to that other question, and I'm not suggesting that you're not, I'm just saying that you have to ask yourself, or do you not, the question, when you go into the studio, or when you put on your show, you want to be able to explore these kinds of things because that's what art is.

M: Right.

FS: But at the same time, you have to reflect on what's going to be responsible. So then, do you say, "Where do I draw the line?" Or does it keep going further and further?

M: But I—as I said to you before, I am being responsible. You know. Where I draw the line is what I said. I don't believe in gratuitous violence and I don't believe in degradation, you know, the degradation of any human being, okay. And I would never promote those things in any of my art, and I don't.

FS: You've taken some heat, I know, and you would like to have a chance to talk about it, from some women who feel that maybe you're not expressing the values that they want feminism to express, for—all the way from way back when you wore the belt buckle that said "Boy Toy" to the "Material Girl" video, which they feel reflects old values of women, even if it was satirical to express yourself. Do you have an answer to them?

M: To the feminists—feminists' point of view?

FS: Who raise that kind of question—

M: Well, I would like to point out that they're missing a couple of things, because, you know, I may be dressing like the typical bimbo, whatever, but I'm in charge. You know. I'm in charge of my fantasies. I put myself in these situations with men, you know, and everybody knows, you know, in terms of my image in the public, people don't think of me as a person who's not in charge of my career or my life, okay. And isn't that what feminism is all about, you know, equality for men and women? And aren't I in charge of my life, doing the things I want to do? Making my own decisions?

FS: I don't think anybody would question whether you're in charge of your own life. I do have a last question for you. What is the next sort of thing that we could be looking forward to? Do you have it in mind already?

M: What is—you mean—you want me to promote one of my products, my own products?

FS: No, no, no, no.

M: My up-and-coming button-pushing products?

FS: No, no, no, no, that's not the point. The point is, if you—will you continue to explore sexuality in the fashion that you have?

M: Absolutely.

FS: Will you try to carry it a little further in a way that—

M: I—well, I don't know. I can't predict what I'm going to feel artistically. I don't think anyone can. But it is a very important issue to me, and I'm sure I will be dealing with it more in the future.

FS: I have no doubt about it. You were kind to talk to us tonight, Madonna. Thank you very, very much.

M: Thank you for listening to me.

FS: When we come back, we are going to look at some of the latest stories out of the story that we've been following for these many weeks, the Persian Gulf.
(*Commercial break*)

FS: Here is the latest on the Persian Gulf. The five permanent members of the Security Council are prepared to offer Saddam Hussein a guarantee of immunity from attack if he withdraws completely from Kuwait and releases all hostages. *The Guardian* of London reports that Vice President Quayle has confirmed the United States would guarantee that Saddam Hussein could return power if he fulfills the UN resolutions.

And adding insult to injury, Iraq is sending Great Britain a six-figure bill for holding several dozen British hostages in a Baghdad hotel.

That's our report for tonight. I'm Forrest Sawyer in New York. And for all of us here at ABC News, good night.

Madonna Vide/Disc/Film/Etc.— ography

▶ Music Videos

Long-Form

Madonna. Warner Music Video, 1984. (includes promotional clips for "Burning Up," "Borderline," "Lucky Star," and "Like a Virgin")

Madonna Live: The Virgin Tour. Warner Music Video, 1985.

Madonna Ciao Italia: Live From Italy. Warner Reprise Video, 1988.

The Immaculate Collection. Warner Reprise Video, 1990.

Promotional Clips (Conceptual)

"Burning Up" (Mary Lambert, dir.), 1983.

"Lucky Star" (Arthur Pierson, dir.), 1984.

"Borderline" (Mary Lambert, dir.), 1984.

"Like a Virgin" (Mary Lambert, dir.), 1984.

"Material Girl" (Mary Lambert, dir.), 1985.

"Crazy for You" [*VisionQuest* promo], 1985.

"Gambler" [*VisionQuest* promo], 1985.

"Into the Groove" [*Desperately Seeking Susan* promo], 1985.

"Live to Tell" [*At Close Range* promo], 1986.

"Papa Don't Preach" (James Foley, dir.), 1986.

"True Blue" [two versions], 1986.

"Open Your Heart" (Jean-Baptiste Mondrino, dir.), 1986.

"La Isla Bonita" (Mary Lambert, dir.), 1987.

"Who's That Girl?" [*Who's That Girl* promo], 1987.

"Like a Prayer" (Mary Lambert, dir.), 1989.

"Express Yourself" (David Fincher, dir.), 1989.

"Cherish" (Herb Ritts, dir.), 1989.

"Oh Father" (David Fincher, dir.), 1989.

"Vogue" (David Fincher, dir.), 1990.

"Justify My Love" (Jean-Baptiste Mondrino, dir.) [sold as first-ever "video single"], 1990.

MTV Performances

"Like a Virgin," 1984 Video Music Awards

"Express Yourself," 1989 Video Music Awards

"Vogue," 1990 Video Music Awards

Endorsement

"Make a Wish" [two-minute Pepsi commerical, broadcast worldwide March 2, 1989]

Public Service Announcement

"Vote!" for "Rock the Vote" campaign [broadcast October 22– November 6, 1990]

▶ Records and Compact Discs

Albums

Madonna (Reggie Lucas, John "Jellybean" Benitez, Mark Kamins, prods.). Sire, 1983.

Like a Virgin (Nile Rodgers, prod.). Sire, 1984.

True Blue (Madonna, Patrick Leonard, Stephen Bray, prods.). Sire, 1986.

You Can Dance [collected remixes] (Madonna, Stephen Bray, Jellybean Benitez, Mark Kamins, Reggie Lucas, Nile Rodgers, Patrick Leonard, prods.). Sire, 1987.

Like a Prayer (Madonna, Patrick Leonard, Stephen Bray, Prince, prods.). Sire, 1989.

I'm Breathless: Music from and Inspired by Dick Tracy (Madonna, Patrick

Leonard, Bill Bottrell, Kevin Gilbert, Shep Pettibone, prods.). Sire, 1990.

The Immaculate Collection [hits]. Sire, 1990.

Singles (all on Sire Records except where noted)

"Everybody," 1982.

"Burning Up," 1982.

"Holiday," 1983.

"Lucky Star," 1984.

"Borderline," 1984.

"Like a Virgin," 1984.

"Material Girl," 1985.

"Crazy for You" (Geffen), 1985.

"Angel" / "Into the Groove," 1985.

"Dress You Up," 1985.

"Live to Tell," 1986.

"Papa Don't Preach," 1986.

"True Blue," 1986.

"Open Your Heart," 1986.

"La Isla Bonita," 1987.

"Who's That Girl," 1987.

"Causing a Commotion," 1987.

"Like a Prayer," 1989.

"Express Yourself," 1989.

"Cherish," 1989.

"Oh, Father," 1989.

"Keep It Together," 1990.

"Vogue," 1990.

"Hanky Panky," 1990.

"Justify My Love," 1990.

"Rescue Me," 1991.

"This Used to Be My Playground," 1992.

Stray Tracks

"Ain't No Big Deal" on *Revenge of the Killer B's* (various artists). Warner Bros., 1984.

"Gambler" from *VisionQuest*. Geffen, 1985.

"The Look of Love" and "Can't Stop" on *Who's That Girl* (various artists). Sire, 1987.

"Santa Baby" on *A Very Special Christmas* (various artists). A&M, 1987.

"Supernatural" ["Cherish" B side].

Cover Versions

"Sidewalk Talk" (Jellybean) on *Wotupski!?!* EMI America, 1984.

"Like a Surgeon" (Weird Al Yancovic). Scotti Bros., 1985.

"Into the Groove(y)" / "Burnin' Up" (Ciccone Youth). Blast First, 1986.

"Each Time You Break My Heart" (Nick Kamen) on *Nick Kamen*. Sire, 1987.

"Like a Prayer" (John Wesley Harding) on *God Made Me Do It—The Christmas EP.* Sire/Reprise, 1989.

▶ Movies

A Certain Sacrifice (Stephen Jon Lewicki, dir.). Commtron, 1980.

VisionQuest (Harold Becker, dir.). Warner, 1985.

Desperately Seeking Susan (Susan Seidelman, dir.). HBO, 1985.

Shanghai Surprise (Jim Goddard, dir.). Vestron, 1986.

Who's That Girl (James Foley, dir.). Warner, 1987.

Bloodhounds of Broadway (Howard Brookner, dir.). RCA/Columbia, 1989.

Dick Tracy (Warren Beatty, dir.). Touchstone, 1990.

Truth or Dare (Alek Keshishian, dir.). Live Home, Video, 1991.

Shadows and Fog (Woody Allen, dir.). Orion, 1992.

A League of Their Own (Penny Marshall, dir.). Columbia, 1992.

▶ Theater

Goose and Tom-Tom (by David Rabe). Lincoln Center Theater workshop, 1987.

Speed-the-Plow (by David Mamet). Produced by the Lincoln Center Theater at the Royale Theater, 1988.

Magnificat —

Mad —
hv to start ?
posthumous angle ———
WAVE of discourse
bio te
——————————————

find list of descriptive
phrases (a postmodernist
paragon - type
descrps)
——————————————

ED, not "fam"
——————————————

find Boorstin q.